Indian Mounds

of the

Middle Ohio Valley

A Guide to Mounds and Earthworks of the Adena,
Hopewell, Cole, and Fort Ancient People

Susan L. Woodward

and

Jerry N. McDonald

The McDonald & Woodward Publishing Company
Blacksburg, Virginia
2002

Indian Mounds of the Middle Ohio Valley: A Guide to Mounds and Earthworks of the Adena, Hopewell, Cole, and Fort Ancient People

A McDonald & Woodward Guide to the American Landscape

© 2001 by The McDonald & Woodward Publishing Company

All rights reserved
Printed in the United States of America
by McNaughton & Gunn, Inc., Saline, Michigan
Distributed by The University of Nebraska Press

10 09 08 07 06 05 04 03 02   10 9 8 7 6 5 4 3 2 1
First Printing February 2002

Library of Congress Cataloging-in-Publication Data

Woodward, Susan L., 1944 Jan. 20-
  Indian mounds of the middle Ohio Valley : a guide to mounds and earthworks of the Adena, Hopewell, Cole, and Fort Ancient people / Susan L. Woodward and Jerry N. McDonald.—2nd ed.
      p. cm.—(Guides to the American landscape)
  Includes bibliographical references and index.
      ISBN 0-939923-72-6 (alk. paper)
      1. Indians of North America—Ohio—Antiquities. 2. Mounds—Ohio. 3. Adena culture—Ohio. 4. Hopewell culture—Ohio. 5. Fort Ancient culture—Ohio. 6. Ohio—Antiquities. I. Woodward, Susan L., 1944 Jan. 20- II. McDonald, Jerry N. III. Title. IV. McDonald & Woodward guide to the American landscape.
E78.03 W67 2001
977.1—dc21

                                                        2001044861

Indian Mounds
of the Middle Ohio Valley

Contents

Preface

Indian Mounds of the Middle Ohio Valley is a guide to the extant, publicly accessible mounds and earthworks built by Native Americans who lived in the middle Ohio Valley. The book is divided into three sections. Section I provides an outline of the chronology, geography, and culture of the people who built these mounds and earthworks, and reviews the ways in which these structures have been perceived, studied, and managed by Americans during the last two centuries. Section II identifies and describes the extant, publicly accessible mounds, earthworks, and affiliated sites of the region. Section III provides sources of additional information about the mound-building Indians of the middle Ohio Valley. The first edition of this book was published in 1986 and identified forty-one publicly accessible sites in Indiana, Kentucky, Ohio, and West Virginia. This edition, the second, identifies seventy-three sites in those same states.

The primary purpose of this book is to facilitate public access to information about the mound-building Indians in the middle Ohio Valley, and especially to help our readers become aware of, visit, experience, and learn more about mounds, earthworks, affiliated sites, and the people who built them. We see this as a versatile book, being of use to various groups of people with differing, but focused, interests in the archeological heritage of eastern North America — travelers, educators, students, archeologists, naturalists, recreation leaders, librarians, planners, and anybody else with a curious mind and an interest in seeing, understanding, and preserving the remaining record of North American prehistory.

We hope this book will help increase public awareness of the significance of prehistoric cultural resources and the record of human experience they represent, the continuing loss of these resources, present management strategies and patterns, and their future prospects. Those who visit the sites identified in this book, for example, will see most of the remaining mounds and mound-like features that are accessible to the public today in the middle Ohio Valley — a mere handful of sites representing the thousands that once existed. Visitors to these sites will also see much regional variation in the number of publicly accessible sites, the condition of these sites, the management programs that envelope them, and the level of interpretation provided. Some sites reveal state-of-the-art visions, management policies, practices, and interpretation goals, whereas others afford room for improvement.

Since the appearance of the first edition, *Indian Mounds of the Middle Ohio Valley* has been in consistent and heartening demand as a source of information about the publicly accessible prehistoric mounds and earthworks of the middle Ohio Valley. Much, however, has happened since 1986 — new information has been acquired about the archeology of the mounds and their builders, new strategies and practices have appeared for the management of mounds and other archeological sites, more sites have become accessible to the public, and new information about the general subject of mounds and their builders has become available.

Possibly the most important new development within North American archeology during the past decade has been the increasing acceptance of the fact that humans have occupied the Western Hemisphere for more than the past eleven or twelve thousand years. In 1986, the Clovis culture was widely considered by North American archeologists to represent the earliest human presence in the Americas. Now, due especially to work at Monte Verde in southern Chile and Meadowcroft Rockshelter in western Pennsylvania, and bolstered by information from such other sites as Cactus Hill and Saltville in Virginia, Page/Ladson in Florida, and Topper in South Carolina, humans are known to have been in the Americas for at least sixteen thousand years and, perhaps, twice that long.

In 1986, artificial burial mounds dating from and after the middle Archaic period were known to exist in widely scattered localities along the Atlantic Coast and Mississippi Valley. Recent investigations, however, have demonstrated that early mound building, especially in the southeastern United States, was considerably more extensive, and intensive, than was previously recognized.

Directly pertinent to the focus of this book, archeological investigations in the middle Ohio Valley since 1986 have provided new insights into the domestic and corporate life of the people who built the mounds; the chronology, methods, and purposes of mound and earthwork construction; and the cultural affiliation of some of the previously problematic mound and earthwork sites. And, as always happens with new information and interpretations, new questions about the mounds and their builders have been raised and new frontiers of research have been defined.

While our understanding of the mounds and earthworks of the region expands, many of these features continue to be altered and destroyed by the intensifying demands of land use striving to accommodate and provide for an ever-increasing human population as well as by long-entrenched attitudes of indifference, disrespect, selfishness, and simple lack of awareness. Simultaneously, new strategies, revised policies, more stringent enforcement of existing statutes, and the rise of native voices have reduced the destruction and enhanced the appreciation of these unique and irreplaceable cultural resources. Among the strategies employed to preserve remaining mounds and earthworks are increased emphasis on the interpretation of these resources for the public, the voluntary and legally mandated mitigation of resource-threatening land uses, and the placement of sensitive lands in the ownership or trust of protective public agencies, such as the National Park Service, or private entities, such as The Archaeological Conservancy. Still, even with these informative and protective measures, the tangible resources of the prehistoric landscape are being lost, and they can never be replaced.

In this second edition of *Indian Mounds of the Middle Ohio Valley* we have tried to incorporate the major changes that have occurred in each of the foregoing areas and bring the guide into line with current concepts and information. This edition also describes thirty-two publicly accessible sites that were not included in the first edition. Significant parts of the revision of this book are based on comments that we have received from readers of the first edition. Continuing that tradition, we would very much appreciate hearing from readers who have used this book — what did you like about it, and what didn't you like about it? What improvements would you recommend? Have we overlooked sites that could have been included? Comments sent to the publisher at *mwpubco@mwpubco.com* will be forwarded to us.

Many people and institutions have helped us assemble and evaluate information used in this book, and we sincerely appreciate and thank each of them for their contributions. In particular, we would like to acknowledge the following people who were notably helpful in providing us with detailed information or otherwise facilitating our work: Serpell Adkins (Serpent Mound State Memorial), Dean K. Alexander (Hopewell Culture National Historical Park), Keith Bengtson (Fort Hill

State Memorial), Jack Blosser (Fort Ancient State Memorial), Don Bogosian (Cincinnati, OH), Penny Borgman (Hamilton County Park District), Arnold F. Brauer (River View Cemetery Association), John Briley (Campus Martius), Rick Burdin (William S. Webb Museum of Anthropology), Jim Burkhardt (Dearborn County Sheriff's Department), Charles Clark (East Fork State Park), Donald R. Cochran (Ball State University), Robert P. Connolly (Poverty Point State Historic Site), Elizabeth Cooperrider (Glenford, OH), Lewis W. Coppel (Chillicothe, OH), Frank L. Cowan (BHE Environmental, Inc.), Jeffrey B. Davis (West Virginia State Historic Preservation Office), Robert N. Drake (Reese, Pyle, Drake & Meyer), Penelope B. Drooker (New York State Museum), Ann DuFresne (Cleveland Museum of Natural History), Pat Ellis (Adams County Travel and Visitors Bureau), James P. Fenton (Wilbur Smith Associates), Jan Ferguson (Wright-Patterson Air Force Base), David Fey (Fairfield County Historical Parks Commission), Paul S. Gardner (The Archaeological Conservancy), Robert A. Genheimer (Cincinnati Museum Center), N'omi B. Greber (Cleveland Museum of Natural History), Thomas C. Grubb (Mount Vernon, OH), Nancy Hamblin (Newark Earthworks State Memorial), Nancy Hammerslough (Pictures of Record), John Hancock (CERHAS), Peg Hanley (Metropolitan Park District of Columbus and Franklin County), Jody Heaston (Mounds State Park), David Helgeson (Indian Lake State Park), A. Gwynn Henderson (Kentucky Archaeological Survey), Hilary Lambert Hopper (University of Kentucky), Richard W. Jefferies (University of Kentucky), Stephen Kelley (Adams County Historical Society), Duryea Kemp (Ohio Historical Society), Jim Kingery (Newark Earthworks State Memorial), Thomas Law (Pangea Productions Ltd.), Bradley T. Lepper (Ohio Historical Society), Joni L. Manson (Ohio Historical Preservation Office), Robert F. Maslowski (US Army Corps of Engineers), Michael J. Muska (MetroParks of Butler County), Richard E. Niccum, Jr. (Licking Park District), Nancy O'Malley

(Kentucky Office of State Archaeology), Martha Potter Otto (Ohio Historical Society), Robert V. Riordan (Wright State University), Franco Ruffini (Ohio Historical Preservation Office), Bonnie Seegmueller (MetroParks of Butler County), Janet E. Setchell (Mariemont Preservation Foundation), Lynn Simonelli (Boonshoft Museum of Discovery), Tom Stoffregen (University of Cincinnati), Tim Taylor (Battelle-Darby Creek Metro Park), John Watts (Metropolitan Park District of Columbus and Franklin County), Jennifer West (Cincinnati, OH), Bob Whyte (Glen Helen Ecology Institute), Joanna L. Wilson (West Virginia State Historic Preservation Office), and Dee Anne Wymer (Bloomsburg University). The maps were prepared by Ellen Compton-Gooding. Joe E. Murray, Richard W. Pirko (Rudinec and Associates), Robert V. Riordan, the Ohio Historical Society, and the William S. Webb Museum of Anthropology kindly extended permission to use photographs reproduced in this book.

The outline of the mound building cultures of the middle Ohio Valley presented in Section I is based on many sources, most of which are cited in the Bibliography. We would, however, like to acknowledge the particular debt we owe to the following scholars whose work of the past thirty years contributed significantly to the outline of the mound building cultures given below: R. Berle Clay, Robert P. Connolly, Frank L. Cowan, William S. Dancey, Penelope B. Drooker, N'omi B. Greber, A. Gwynn Henderson, Bradley T. Lepper, Robert C. Mainfort, Jr., Martha P. Otto, Paul J. Pacheco, David Pollack, Robert V. Riordan, and Mark F. Seeman.

We especially thank Carol Boone, N'omi Greber, Gwynn Henderson, Brad Lepper, and Judy Moore for reading and providing extensive critical comments about earlier drafts of part or all of the manuscript for this book. We, however, are solely responsible for the information presented here.

Indian Mounds
of the Middle Ohio Valley

Mounds as Landscape Features

Mounds, earthworks, and shell middens constitute the most conspicuous record of prehistoric Native American culture to be found on the landscape of eastern North America (Figure 1). They are the visible, tangible imprints of people who transformed their environment as they organized their resources and expressed their beliefs according to the needs, technological skills, and symbolic vocabulary of their cultures. As such, these artificial earthen, stone, and shell features provide both silent testimony of and appreciable insight into ways of life that are at once gone but also, inescapably, are parts of the cultural legacy of the region. At one time tens of thousands of these raised features occurred in diverse forms, sizes, levels of

Figure 1. The great Miamisburg Mound as it might have appeared during the 1840s. (From Squier and Davis, 1848)

1

complexity, and concentrations between the Atlantic seaboard and the Great Plains and between southeastern Canada and the Gulf of Mexico. Most of these features that were present five centuries ago when the European colonization of the Americas commenced have been destroyed as a result of the transformation of eastern North America into agricultural, urban, and transportation landscapes. Fortunately, however, a small number of mounds, earthworks, and middens has survived to the present, remnants not only of other people of other times, but also of people of our place, and they enhance the depth and texture of the modern cultural landscape while affording observers the opportunity to experience some of the physical expressions of cultural values and lifeways now vanished (Plate 1).

Study of these prehistoric architectural landmarks, especially the mounds and earthworks, over the last two hundred years has shown that they were built by several different groups of Native Americans at different times, in different ways, and for different purposes. Burial mounds are probably the most numerous, widespread, and familiar category of mounds. Ceremonial earthworks, hilltop enclosures, effigy mounds, platform mounds, and shell middens are also numerous and widespread — even though the reasons for their existence might not always be understood. Less common and more enigmatic, however, are the isolated earthen embankments and stone walls, piles of rock, mounds without discernable purpose, and other raised features of earth, stone, and shell that occur throughout much of eastern North America.

Shell middens and shell mounds, primarily accumulations of marine or freshwater mollusk shells that include a host of other debris as well, started taking form when humans first reached the continent and began to harvest mollusks and other aquatic food resources along coasts and inland waterways. The deliberate construction of earthen mounds in North America apparently had begun by about 7,500 years ago, and by 5,000 years ago both simple mounds and complex earthworks were being built at multiple locations in the southeastern quarter of the continent. The most intensive and widespread period of mound and earthwork construction began in eastern North America about 3,000 to 2,500 years ago and continued until around three hundred years ago. The first center of intensive mound building during this period developed in the middle Ohio Valley (Figure 2) about 2,500 years ago and continued for a millennium. Subsequently, several centers of active mound building arose to the south and west of the middle Ohio Valley, from Florida, Georgia, and the Carolinas in the east to Texas, Oklahoma, Iowa, and Minnesota in the west. Mounds were still being built by some native groups when the European colonization of North America began, but the practice essentially came to an end during the eighteenth century.

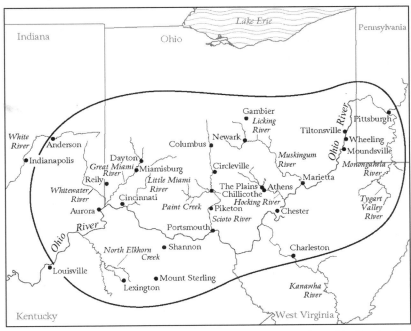

Figure 2. The middle Ohio Valley, with place names mentioned in Section I.

The Adena and Ohio Hopewell were the premier builders of distinctive and sometimes truly impressive mounds, geometric earthworks, and hilltop enclosures within the middle Ohio Valley. The later Fort Ancient people and some of their contemporaries, too, built mounds, although typically these were lower, less complex, and less numerous than those of the Adena and Hopewell. Recent investigations have shown that Ohio's two unequivocal zoomorphic effigy mounds probably were built by the Fort Ancient people. Taken as a whole, the prehistoric mounds and earthworks of the middle Ohio Valley are masterpieces; their number, size, precision, and grace, and the magnitude of the organizational and managerial effort that was marshaled to build them, require that these architectural monuments be ranked among the important prehistoric engineering — and artistic — accomplishments of mankind. They are important elements of the North American cultural landscape, and the purpose of the pages that follow is to open windows onto these elements so that they may be better understood, appreciated, and valued for their contribution to our collective cultural heritage.

Section I

*Mounds and Earthworks in
Archeological and Historical Context*

An Outline of the Prehistory of the Middle Ohio Valley

The human prehistory of North America has been divided into various units of time and culture by archeologists. In this book we refer to broad units of time as *periods* and broad units of culture as *traditions*. Each *period* represents a span of time during which, theoretically, certain general cultural characteristics were well established and widely distributed among populations of Native Americans. The sets of general cultural characteristics shared by widely dispersed populations of native peoples are called *traditions*. Within *traditions*, we identify distinct groups by their cultural names.

Generally, four periods and traditions are recognized in the prehistory of that part of eastern North America that includes the middle Ohio Valley; these are the Paleo-Indian, Archaic, Woodland, and Late Prehistoric periods and traditions (Figure 3). Another period and tradition, the Protohistoric, includes the transition from prehistory to history. Periods are typically bounded by specific dates or a relatively narrow range of time, but this practice, a necessity in order to establish any kind of working organization, is in fact an over-simplification of the process of long-term cultural change. Cultural change usually did not occur as rapid shifts, at least not with the rapidity implied by sharp breaks in periods and traditions, and did not occur throughout the conti-

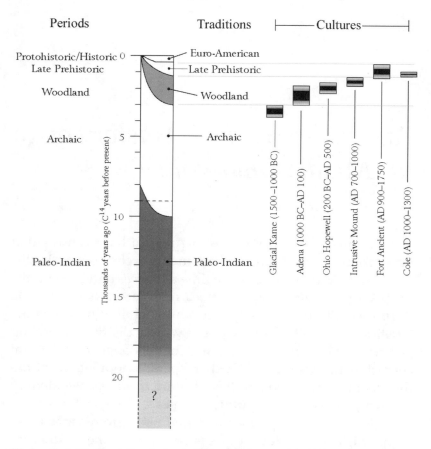

Figure 3. A timeline of periods, traditions, and mound-building cultures in the prehistory of the middle Ohio Valley.

nent, or even regionally, as in the middle Ohio Valley, at the same rate or in the same way. Since the details of culture change are not equally known for all groups or all places, this lack of directly comparable information adds yet more uncertainty to cultural chronologies. As a result, the bounding dates for periods are arbitrary and represent only a best approximation of the time at which most of the native populations had undergone sufficient cultural change to distinguish them from the preceding tradition.

The oldest native tradition in the Americas, the Paleo-Indian, is considered here to encompass the first people who inhabited the region and those who continued that lifestyle until it was substantially modified. The earliest humans to reach the Western Hemisphere are now known to have arrived no later than about 16,000 years ago, and perhaps were present 30,000 or more years ago. These early colonists arrived during the later part of the Wisconsinan glaciation, the most recent glacial phase of the current Ice Age. Traditionally, these early human populations were considered to have entered North America by migrating across the Bering Land Bridge from Siberia. Recently acquired evidence, however, is suggesting that, in addition to movement across the land bridge, colonists of perhaps several ethnic origins might have entered the Americas by sea, most likely by skirting intercontinental coastlines created by lowered sea levels and the formation of ice sheets. Once thought to be specialized nomadic hunters of large game animals such as mammoths, mastodons, horses, caribou, and bison — many of which are now extinct — Paleo-Indians appear to have followed many different subsistence strategies and exploited diverse plant and animal resources. As a group, Paleo-Indians probably were more mobile than any other Native American prehistoric tradition, and should be considered opportunistic generalist hunters, gatherers, fishers, and collectors, although it is likely that each group or groups within different ecological arenas narrowed the spectrum of possible subsistence strategies to the few that worked most effectively in their home ranges. The Paleo-Indian period ended between about 10,000 and 8,000 years ago when environmental change — especially the extinction of so many species of large mammals and the increased productivity of the plant and animal communities that developed in response to climatic warming — created both the necessity and the opportunity for America's human populations to make the modest but discernable shifts in subsistence activities that mark the beginning of the next period, the Archaic.

Like Paleo-Indians, early Archaic people were probably nomadic or semi-nomadic hunters, gatherers, fishers, and collectors who relied upon a great variety of plant and animal resources which they obtained by exploiting relatively large territories. As time passed, however, later Archaic populations came to occupy smaller group territories which they exploited ever more intensively; sedentism increased, populations grew, social interactions became more complex, home ranges developed, and mechanisms for forming and maintaining intragroup and intergroup relations evolved. One indication of these changes in eastern North America was the appearance of *artificial* mounds, some of which were burial monuments, and, at the very end of the period, complex earthworks — both signaling the development of group, or *corporate*, hereditary claims to territories and the evolution of increasingly elaborate ceremonies, especially, or perhaps most clearly, those associated with mortuary rituals. Some ceremonies appear to have been relatively widespread and widely understood, to have affected entire populations, and to have persisted for centuries, and therefore appear to have become *institutionalized*. Also appearing at this time were the increasing reliance on a narrow range of certain native plants for food and perhaps other uses in several parts of the region; the interregional exchange of select goods such as copper, galena, and marine shells, among others; and, in the southeast, the manufacture and use of simple fiber-tempered pottery.

The Archaic period was followed in the eastern United States by the Woodland period, which generally began about 3,000 years ago and, in the middle Ohio Valley, continued until about 1,000 years ago. The Woodland tradition is characterized by a continuing dependence on hunting, gathering, fishing, and collecting with increased reliance on the controlled production of indigenous plant foods, the widespread use of grit-tempered ceramic pottery, the development of extensive and active interregional exchange networks, and burial of the dead away from habitation sites — most notably, but certainly not always, beneath or in earthen or stone mounds. The native population continued to grow during the Woodland period and economic, social, and political complexity increased, at least in some parts of the region. Habitation sites probably were used for longer periods of time, some perhaps were even used permanently over a period of several years, but most continued to be small and probably accommodated only one or a few extended families. In some selected localities, and perhaps on a greater scale throughout the eastern woodlands in ways that are still transparent, significant and sometimes very sophisticated specialization took place in resource production, manufacture, and distribution; social and political organization; institutional planning; architectural planning and design; and geometry. It was during the Woodland period that most mounds and earthworks were constructed in the middle Ohio Valley.

Traditionally, the Woodland period is subdivided into three parts — early, middle, and late. It was during the early and middle parts of the period that what have long been considered the two great mound-building groups of the middle Ohio Valley, the Adena and the Ohio, or Classic, Hopewell, flourished (figures 3 and 4). Adena is the primary group associated with early Woodland times, and Hopewell is the primary group associated with middle Woodland times. No mound-building groups built more mounds or more complex earthworks than the Adena and Hopewell, and very few ever built larger mounds. Several more localized groups occurred on the periphery of the Adena and Hopewell homelands during early and middle Woodland times, and after the demise of Hopewell such localized groups characterized the region during late Woodland times.

About 1,000 years ago, the Late Prehistoric tradition developed in parts of eastern North America, including the middle Ohio Valley. Reliance upon hunting, gathering, fish-

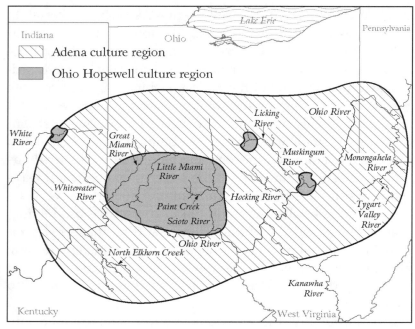

Figure 4. The homelands of the Adena and Ohio Hopewell cultures.

ing, and collecting remained important, but horticulture became a discernibly important source of food for many inhabitants of the region. Maize *(Zea mays)* and beans *(Phaseolus
vulgaris)* became significant crops, and squash *(Cucurbita pepo)*
and a few other domesticated species contributed to the subsistence effort. Villages, nucleated clusters of people that were
occupied for several years at a time, became the typical form
of settlement during the Late Prehistoric period. Sometimes
these villages were surrounded with a stockade or protected
by a combination of natural topographic features and artificial earthen walls, ditches, and stockades. Social and political
organization within the Late Prehistoric tradition became more
complex as the size of village populations increased and, perhaps, external pressures imposed the need for greater planning and cooperation within groups. Still, there was no insti-

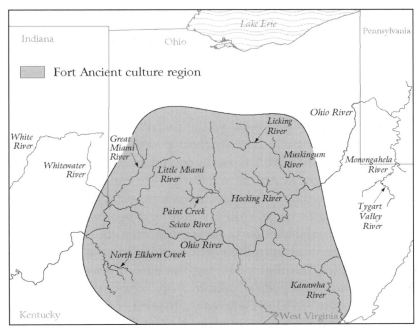

Figure 5. The homeland of the Fort Ancient culture in the middle Ohio Valley.

tutionalized political hierarchy within Late Prehistoric cultures so leadership had to be earned.

Throughout much of the middle Ohio Valley, the Late Prehistoric period was represented by the Fort Ancient culture (Figure 5), although, at times, some of the more geographically restricted and less-well-known cultures, such as Cole, were also present over parts of the region. Fort Ancient developed out of one or more late Woodland traditions after AD 900 and persisted until or about the time that Euro-American exploration of the region began. Cole also developed out of one or more late Woodland traditions, but endured for only two or three centuries as a distinct culture.

The Protohistoric period encompassed that brief span of time from the first arrival of Europeans in the earliest part of the sixteenth century until relatively constant contact between

Europeans and native people became established. The duration of this period varied considerably from place to place, and depended on the rate of spread of European people, the diffusion of their material culture and influence, and the specific history of contact between the Europeans and Indians. The influence of Spanish, French, and British presence on the Atlantic seaboard had reached the middle Ohio Valley by the seventeenth century. Fort Ancient people might have been among the native groups encountered in the region by the French, British, and Americans during the eighteenth century. The Shawnee, part of whom had a long-established affinity with the middle Ohio Valley when Europeans first entered the region, are the historic Indians most often considered likely to have descended from the Fort Ancient. Other native groups who occupied the region during the early part of the eighteenth century had been displaced from other locations. These groups included the Delaware, Miami, Mingo, Ottawa, Wyandot, and their contemporaries. The Protohistoric period for the middle Ohio Valley essentially ended by the middle of the eighteenth century when, following the French and Indian War, British and American efforts to occupy the region intensified.

Mound-Building Cultures in the Middle Ohio Valley

Mounds and earthworks were built throughout the middle Ohio Valley by most of the Woodland and Late Prehistoric groups who inhabited the region. The mound-building efforts of the Adena and Ohio Hopewell, however, far exceeded those of the other cultures, and it is the mounds and earthworks of these two groups that have made such a distinctive and lasting contribution to the prehistoric cultural landscape of the region. Less conspicuous but nonetheless important are the mounds built by the Fort Ancient people and the earthen embankments built by the Cole and their contemporaries.

The Woodland and Late Prehistoric people of the middle Ohio Valley were, of course, influenced by the environment in which they lived and operated. Population size and density, social organization, economy, and territorial control all have environmental dimensions, and the distribution, lifeways, and material culture of the mound-building groups of the middle Ohio Valley were all influenced by the environment of the region. The distribution of each culture corresponded in one way or another with some general physiographic, or landform, region, and the location, construction, and uses of mounds and earthworks were influenced significantly by the region's natural environment.

15

The Middle Ohio Valley

The middle Ohio Valley, for our purposes, is the area that is drained by the Ohio River between Pittsburgh, Pennsylvania, and Louisville, Kentucky. Extending from southwestern Pennsylvania to southeastern Indiana, and from central Ohio to central Kentucky and West Virginia, this area roughly corresponds to the Adena homeland (Figure 4). The Adena homeland, in turn, incorporates all of the core territory of Ohio Hopewell and most of the territory occupied by the Fort Ancient and Cole.

The middle Ohio Valley includes parts of three major physiographic provinces: the Appalachian Plateau, the Interior Low Plateau, and the Central Lowland (Figure 6). The three provinces differed in several ways, including the nature of the surface and subsurface of the land itself, the size and gradient of streams, the quality of soil, and the kinds of plants and animals that were to be found. As a result, each of the provinces provided different opportunities for and limitations upon its human inhabitants.

The heavily dissected Appalachian Plateau is characterized by numerous small tracts of level upland, rolling hills, and narrow ridges. Resistant rocks, especially sandstones, have been eroded into steep-sided valleys whose walls occasionally contain rock shelters. Most flood plains along streams are relatively narrow, if present at all. Consequently, large expanses of level land are scarce in this province, particularly in the eastern part. The sandstone-capped western edge of the Appalachian Plateau, especially from the vicinity of Circleville, Ohio, to northern Kentucky, is abrupt and scarp-like and, in many places, is dissected to the extent that steep-sided promontories and isolated buttes have formed.

The Interior Low Plateau in northern and central Kentucky and a small part of southcentral Ohio consists primarily of limestones. The surface here is more gently rounded than that of the Appalachian Plateau but it has more relief than

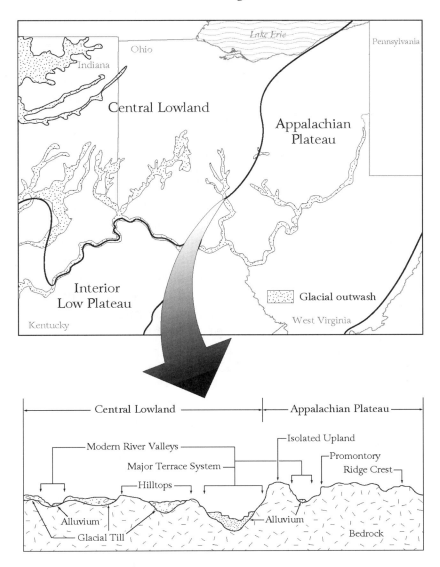

Figure 6. Parts of three physiographic provinces extend into the middle Ohio Valley and each offers a different combination of resources and environmental constraints. A schematic transect across the Central Lowland and Appalachian Plateau illustrates many of the physiographic features mentioned in the text as being correlated with the occurrence of prehistoric mounds and earthworks.

that of the Central Lowland. As in the Appalachian Plateau, streams in the Interior Low Plateau typically do not have wide flood plains blanketed with alluvium.

The Central Lowland in southern Ohio and Indiana has relatively level or gently rolling terrain with little relief as a result of having been scoured by glacial ice and coated with till on one or more occasions during the Quaternary period (the last 1.8 million years) — most recently between about 20,000 and 12,000 years ago. The spread of glaciers across this and adjacent areas also caused changes in the regional drainage patterns. In particular, the Ohio River drainage was enlarged considerably. Prior to glaciation, the headwaters of the Ohio River had been in the vicinity of Louisville, Kentucky. After glaciation, the Ohio River headwaters arose along a divide extending from southern New York to northwestern North Carolina. In addition to changing the length of the river and direction of flow in what is now the middle and upper Ohio Valley, glaciation changed the character of the river's north bank tributaries in other ways. Vast amounts of meltwater flowing toward the Ohio River first enlarged the valleys. Then, as the volume of meltwater decreased, great quantities of sediment from the glacier front were deposited in the valleys, creating wide alluvial flood plains. Subsequent downcutting by streams carved the flood plains into a series of terraces — tiers of flat land at different elevations above stream level (Figure 6).

The climate, vegetation, and animal life in the middle Ohio Valley during the Woodland and Late Prehistoric periods were generally similar to those of today. The average annual temperatures actually might have been slightly warmer during the Woodland period than now. The vegetation of the region was dominated by the Central Hardwood Forest, a forest that contained many species of trees, shrubs, vines, and non-woody plants, including such useful species as blackberries, elderberries, paw-paws, oaks, hickories, and walnuts. A great variety of economically important animals — such as turkey, box turtles, cottontails, black bear, raccoons, whitetail deer, and others — also was associated with this forest. The favorable climate and great plant and animal diversity provided a productive environment in which the Woodland and Late Prehistoric people could function with comparative security as hunters, gatherers, fishers, and collectors.

The Adena and Hopewell practiced horticulture on a small scale throughout their homelands, but the environmental conditions best suited for this activity probably occurred in the Central Lowland, where there was the most favorable combination of level land, alluvial soil, and long growing season. The Central Lowland also offered the best environmental conditions for farming by the Fort Ancient. The native peoples who lived in the middle Ohio Valley from the late Archaic to the Late Prehistoric periods participated in an important plant domestication process that gave rise to a suite of crops now known as the Eastern Agricultural Complex.

Where different physiographic provinces meet or where alluvial valleys interface with uplands, the varied local environments supported a greater variety of plant and animal resources than would have occurred in less diverse environments. These geologically diverse areas also would have provided a greater variety of microclimates, rock types, minerals, and soils than would have been available in less diverse regions. Such conditions might have existed along all or parts of the Great Miami, Little Miami, Scioto, Licking, Muskingum, and Kanawha rivers — where the best conditions for horticulture, travel, and trade probably also occurred. The convergence of such favorable circumstances could have allowed the growth of larger populations; the accumulation of greater wealth and influence; the development of more centralized class-oriented social, religious, and political organization; and the creation of more elaborate mound and earthwork complexes.

The correspondence between the landforms of these three

physiographic provinces and the types and locations of mounds and earthworks is significant. Adena mounds are the most widespread and are found in the greatest variety of sites; they occur on benches, ridge crests, promontories, and terraces overlooking and bordering major tributaries of the Ohio River and the main river itself. Flood plains, especially, provided relatively large areas of level land and great quantities of the clay, sand, gravel, and larger rocks used in the construction of the mounds. Adena earthworks (primarily circles), however, were usually built on more extensive level land and thus were less common in the Appalachian Plateau than in the Interior Low Plateau or Central Lowland — although important works were constructed on alluvial surfaces near Charleston and at Moundsville, West Virginia, and at Wolfes Plains and Marietta, Ohio. Hopewell geometric earthworks and mounds were almost always located on the second or higher terraces of major river valleys, most notably those of the Scioto River and its tributary Paint Creek, the Great and Little Miami rivers, the upper Licking and White rivers, and the lower Muskingum River. These terraces provided relatively large expanses of flat land above normal flood levels and an abundance of readily available sediments for use in mound and earthwork construction. They were also near navigable streams. Hopewell hilltop enclosures, however, were typically located atop isolated or semi-isolated erosional remnants, as Calvary Cemetery Enclosure, Fort Hill, Fort Ancient, or Pollock Works so clearly demonstrate.

The Archaic Tradition

The Glacial Kame Culture (before 1500 BC to about 1000 BC)

The mortuary traditions of burying some members of the population in *natural* mound-like landforms away from settlement sites, placing grave goods with the interred, and employing such other rituals as staining the skeleton of the deceased with ochre and sometimes defleshing or cremating the deceased appeared in western Ohio during the late Archaic period, most conspicuously among the Glacial Kame people. The Glacial Kame people lived from the southern end of Lake Michigan across southern Michigan to northcentral Ohio and south to the Ohio River. They were primarily hunters, gatherers, and collectors who also selectively utilized some plants that either already were, or soon were to become, domesticated (Table 1). They probably had seasonally shifting occupation sites within relatively well established home ranges. These people also participated in interregional exchange networks that resulted in exotic materials coming into, and passing through, their territories.

Glacial Kame people buried some of their dead in graves, sometimes quite deep graves, in glacial kames — naturally

Table 1. Food Plants Selectively Propogated during Woodland and Late Prehistoric Times in the Middle Ohio Valley

The Eastern Agricultural Complex[a]
Goosefoot *(Chenopodium* spp.*)*
Knotweed *(Polygonum erectum)*
Little Barley *(Hordeum pusillum)*
Maygrass *(Phalaris caroliniana)*
Sumpweed *(Iva annua)*
Sunflower *(Helianthus annuus)*

Other Plants
Beans *(Phaseolus vulgaris)*
Maize *(Zea mays)*
Squash/gourds *(Cucurbita pepo)*
Tobacco *(Nicotiana rustica)*

[a] The Eastern Agricultural Complex included other species, but they are not known to have been utilized in the middle Ohio Valley.

Notes: Not all crops listed in this table were propogated at the same time or by all cultures. Fort Ancient, Newark Earthworks, and SunWatch Village have gardens that contain many of the plants listed in this table.

occurring mounds or low hills formed of sand or gravel that was deposited beneath glaciers. Kame burials were most often flexed, but sometimes they consisted of extended burials, bundled burials, or cremated remains (Figure 7). Some Glacial Kame burial grounds were quite large and contained the remains of several hundred people. Red ochre, an iron oxide derived from ore such as hematite, was often placed on the interred remains. Ornaments such as sandal gorgets, polished birdstones, and tubular pipes were often included with the burials as grave goods. The repeated use of the same site for burials indicates that the group had established a lengthy in-

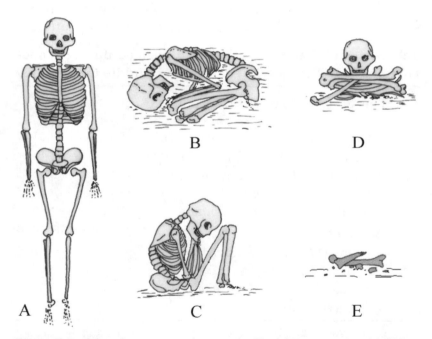

Figure 7. Burial modes represented among the Glacial Kame or mound-building cultures of the middle Ohio Valley: (A) Extended burial. (B) Flexed burial placed on side. (C) Flexed burial in sitting position. (D) Bundled burial. (E) Cremated remains. (From McDonald and Woodward, 1987)

vestment in the area, and the presence of grave goods and symbolic staining indicates the existence of strongly developed mortuary rituals.

Kames containing burials are known to exist, or to have existed, in the middle Ohio Valley in southeastern Indiana and southwestern Ohio, but none is presently in a publicly accessible location.

The Woodland Tradition

The Adena Culture (about 1000 BC to AD 100)

The Adena homeland, at its maximum extent, included the area from southeastern Indiana to southwestern Pennsylvania and from central Ohio to central Kentucky and West Virginia (Figure 4). As mentioned previously, this culture region closely corresponds with the watershed of the Ohio River between Louisville, Kentucky, and Pittsburgh, Pennsylvania. Although the Adena people surely moved overland and occupied even the highest places within their homeland, the importance of the Ohio River and its tributaries in integrating the cultural region must be recognized. These waterways might have been paralleled by foot trails, or, perhaps, they themselves carried people, material goods, and information that moved within, into, and out of the Adena homeland. It was, almost certainly, the integrating effect of the waterways that allowed the diagnostic traits of Adena culture to spread throughout the region and be maintained. The basic elements of Adena culture — hunting and gathering increasingly supplemented by the propogation of native seed crops, small and transient settlements, interregional exchange and the accumulation of exotic materials, and a mortuary complex that included ritualistic interments in mounds — were in place during the late Archaic period.

The Adena culture has been considered representative of all or part of the early Woodland tradition and, by some, the early part of the middle Woodland tradition, in the middle Ohio Valley, during the period from about 1000 BC to AD 100. However, Adena might not have appeared until several centuries after 1000 BC and might have endured until as late as AD 300 or 400, particularly in the Appalachian Plateau and Interior Low Plateau where the pronounced expression of Ohio Hopewell culture never materialized. The differences in these dates of appearance and disappearance are results of both different ideas about what evidence is diagnostic of Adena and when that diagnostic evidence appears in, or disappears from, different regions. Adena did not suddenly appear full-blown throughout the middle Ohio Valley, it did not remain static during its existence, and it did not disappear at the same time from all parts of this region. Indeed, the distinction between Adena and the later Hopewell culture *in areas outside the Ohio Hopewell homeland* (Figure 4) is blurred; it might be that the people who inhabited the Adena homeland changed very little from the early to the middle Woodland period.

The Adena complex included a relatively uniform tradition of building conical mounds of earth and stone (Figure 8). This tradition was adopted by a number of localized groups who were spread throughout the middle Ohio Valley and who differed in many of the details of their lifeways, yet were sufficiently alike to interact regularly and in mutually beneficial ways. Aside from the construction of distinctive conical mounds, the Adena lifestyle differed relatively little from that of its late Archaic predecessors. Most Adena people apparently lived in small, widely scattered, and probably seasonally occupied sites which were ephemeral and thus are not well represented in the archeological record. The typical dwelling most likely was a simple and expendable wood-framed structure perhaps formed of bent or upright saplings covered with woven branches, hides, or herb mats. Structures inhabited during the winter appear to have been more substantial. There is good evidence that the Adena periodically occupied rock shelters and caves, features that are relatively numerous in the Appalachian Plateau and Interior Low Plateau.

The Adena people were primarily hunters, gatherers, and collectors, although they do appear to have cultivated, or se-

Figure 8. Adena mounds typically were conical in shape. Representative examples of Adena mounds include (top) Adena Mound in Chillicothe, Ohio, the type site for the culture, and (bottom) Gaitskill Mound in Mount Sterling, Kentucky, one of the many Adena mounds that once existed in the Mount Sterling area. Both Adena and Gaitskill are burial mounds. (Photograph of Adena Mound courtesy of Ohio Historical Society)

lectively encouraged the propagation of, some native plants (Table 1). Some of the earliest plants to have been domesticated in eastern North America were known to the Adena, some as early domesticates and others probably as wild foodstuffs worthy of selective attention; among these were goosefoot *(Chenopodium)*, knotweed *(Polygonum)*, little barley *(Hordeum)*, maygrass *(Phalaris)*, sumpweed *(Iva)*, sunflower *(Helianthus)*, and squash *(Cucurbita)*. Maize *(Zea mays)* was once thought to have been a part of the late Adena food inventory, but this view is no longer accepted.

Within the basic hunter, gatherer, collector economy and the transient to semi-permanent habitation cycle of Adena were some notable exceptions that resulted from Adena's increasing participation in interregional exchange, occasional specialization in craftsmanship, investment in extended-term habitation sites, the development of modest and probably fluid social stratification, and long-term territorial affinity. The development of these cultural characteristics is strongly implied by the monumental mounds and earthworks that came to exist, especially during late Adena time, at places along North Elkhorn Creek and the White, Licking, Hocking, Kanawha, Scioto, and Ohio rivers.

Peter Village, north of Lexington, Kentucky, and a part of the Mount Horeb Earthworks complex, is an unusual Adena occupation site with several important special qualities. Peter Village was a palisaded enclosure with an exterior ditch bordering the wall. A small part of the site has been excavated and surface surveys of the site have been conducted following cultivation. The evidence suggests that this place was used at least periodically for both habitation and specialized reduction of minerals that were commodities within the interregional exchange system. The fact that the site was walled suggests that its occupants intended to use it for an extended period, although perhaps intermittently, and that some level of controlled access or egress was considered necessary. Occupied between about 310 and 190 BC, Peter Village might be the earliest known example of an earthen enclosure in the middle Ohio Valley. It is a rare example of an Adena enclosure.

Even though most aspects of Adena culture were broadly similar to those of the late Archaic cultures that had occupied the region, the Adena custom of creating *artificial* earthen mounds (Plate 2) represented one distinct innovation that set them apart from their Archaic predecessors. Many Adena mounds served as burial monuments and, as such, those mounds were important parts of Adena mortuary ceremonialism. The Adena retained some burial practices of the Glacial Kame and other late Archaic cultures, including the application of red ochre on bones and grave goods of the deceased, the placing of artifacts with burials, and the practice of cremation. The creation of artificial mounds as burial monuments represents one step in the Adena elaboration of the regional late Archaic mortuary complex. Other aspects of Adena burial ceremonialism that were probably innovations include the use of special wooden structures in the mortuary ritual, the use of charnel houses to prepare the dead for burial, the conversion of established ceremonial sites to mortuary functions, the use of specially prepared burial chambers, the placement of multiple and sometimes elaborately arranged burials in the same grave, and an increase in the quantity and variety of grave goods included with burials. The expression of these elaborations changed through time; expectedly, they were least well developed in early Adena time (about 1000 to 500 BC) and most well developed in late Adena time (about 200 BC to AD 100 and later).

The practice of building mounds also reflected, subtly and indirectly, important changes that might have been occurring in the lifestyle of the Adena people, especially in the social and political realm. Although mounds are typically thought of as burial monuments, not all were built for that purpose. Some mounds cover the remains of structures or prepared surfaces but contain no graves, and others seem to be independent of any preexisting activity. Burial mounds, however, were repositories for the dead, but they were also monuments to the dead whose bodies they covered and enveloped. The fact that the burial mounds required special effort to construct indicates that the deceased were sufficiently respected by their group to warrant the investment of time and labor required to erect the memorial. However, the burial mound also served the living, for it provided a visible and permanent statement of a group's commitment to its own lineage, to any clan or other social entity of which it was a part, and to its ancestral claim to the territory it considered to be its own. Beyond the self interest of the group, mounds, whether built for burial or other purposes, also served as territorial and perhaps diplomatic markers — statements of the vested interests of one group, or closely allied groups, in a given territory or to each other. The appearance and elaboration of mound construction among the Adena, therefore, reflected the ongoing intensification of resource exploitation, the tendency toward greater sedentism and home range affinity, and the need to more securely and clearly demarcate territories and declare and affirm alliances and reciprocal responsibilities within and among groups — all sufficiently important reasons to invest corporate resources in mound construction (plates 3 and 4).

Each of the individual, intragroup, and intergroup considerations just mentioned, and perhaps others as well, entered into the selection of sites at which mounds would be located. Whatever the reason or reasons underlying the decision about where to place a mound, topographic prominence seems to have been an important objective. While it is impossible to determine today what the visual opportunities for any given site might have been at the time that it was selected because we do not know the status of vegetation or land use by native peoples at the time, it appears to have been important that the mound could be seen easily. Consequently, Adena mounds in upland locations were typically placed on ridge crests, hilltops, bluff lines, and the tips of promontories such that they could be seen easily. Mounds in lowland locations were usually placed on higher terraces of flood plains, sites that would allow them to be visible from the waterways or the adjacent uplands, yet secure from all but the largest floods. The fact that clusters of mounds often developed in these lowland situations further suggests that intragroup identity and symbolism was an important dimension of the evolution of the local monumental landscape.

Adena burial mounds were normally conical in shape. Numerous small stone mounds were built, especially in upland locations in the Appalachian and Interior Low plateaus. Many of these were burial mounds, but all were not, and as a group the stone mounds are not well understood. Better known are the earthen mounds, especially the burial mounds, that occurred in both upland and lowland locations. In simplest outline, that part of the Adena mortuary ritual that involved the initial building of burial mound monuments consisted of four steps: a special surface or floor would be prepared according to prevailing ritual; the deceased person or persons to be interred beneath a mound would be ritually prepared for the burial; the deceased would be interred in an appropriate chamber beneath or on the surface, usually with some modest array of grave goods; and finally a mound, primarily if not entirely of earth, would be built over and around the grave. Additional interments frequently were placed within the original mound as it took shape. In practice, Adena mound burials incorporated great variability within each step of the funerary process.

Throughout Adena time, the natural surface at what would become a burial site covered by an earthen mound was ritually modified by clearing the surface vegetation or soil layer, adding sand or clay or other sediments, building a circular or rectangular wooden enclosure, or some combination of these or other modifications. The remains of circular wooden structures that often occur beneath burial mounds were once thought to represent Adena houses, and their frequent association with burial mounds led to the interpretation that the deceased had been buried in his or her home, the structure had then been taken down or burned, and the mound had been erected over the site. Now, the belief is that these circular structures were more likely related to some ceremonial use, perhaps — but not necessarily — the mortuary ritual, and were never intended for habitation, although their actual use is not known (Figure 9). Early Adena circular wooden structures, according to the current interpretation, had single-post walls while later ones had paired-post walls (figures 9, 10). Both large and small versions of these buildings are known; the more common smaller ones, less than about sixty feet in diameter, might have been roofed, and they often occupied space over which mounds, burial and non-burial, were built. The larger structures, greater than ninety-five feet in diam-

Figure 9. Postmolds of a paired-post circular structure exposed on the submound surface beneath the Crigler Mound in Boone County, Kentucky. (Photograph courtesy of William S. Webb Museum of Anthropology)

eter, probably had ritual functions that were different from, but perhaps related to, those activities that took place in the smaller structures. The Story Mound in Chillicothe, Ohio, was the first site at which the Adena circular submound wooden structure was recognized.

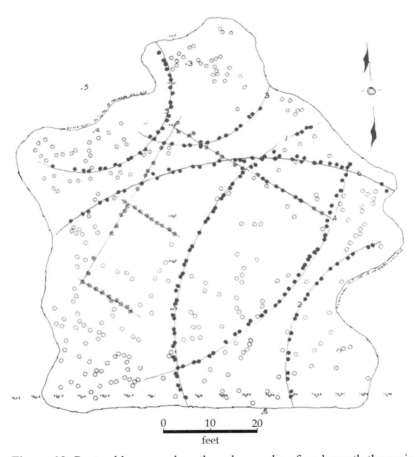

Figure 10. Postmolds exposed on the submound surface beneath the main mound of the Wright Group in Montgomery County north of Mount Sterling, Kentucky. Most of the wooden structures with paired postmolds (dark circles) represented here were circular, with at least three different diameters represented. One structure was rectangular. Open circles in this diagram represent scattered postmolds. (From Webb, 1940)

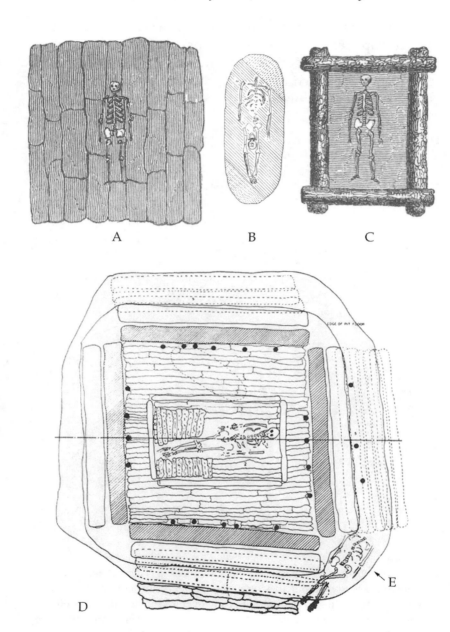

In early Adena time, a deceased person, once properly prepared for burial, usually would have been placed on a prepared surface or in a subsurface chamber and covered with bark, clay, or other appropriate materials (Figure 11). The body could have been placed in the grave in the flesh, it could have been defleshed and the bones bundled or reassembled in a more-or-less anatomically correct pattern, or it could have been cremated. If a cremation was done at the site, the crematory device, after being ritually cleaned, could have been left at the site. If a circular structure had existed at the site, it would have been burned or taken down before the mound was built over the site.

By late Adena time, the ritual had become more complex. Tombs, typically made of logs but sometimes partly or entirely of stones, had come into use as receptacles for the dead; these tombs appear to have afforded their managers substantial flexibility in the handling of the deceased (Figure 11). The general pattern of interment was that the tomb would rest either on the surface or be partly or entirely sunk into the ground. In simplest practice, the deceased would have been placed in the tomb, the tomb would have been sealed, and the container would have been covered with an earthen mound. Some tombs, however, might have been used over extended periods of time for all or parts of the burial phase for multiple corpses; some tombs were sealed containing multiple skeletons,

Figure 11 (opposite page). Representative methods of inhumation by the Adena included (A) surface burial on a layer of bark without additional preparation of a grave, (B) burial in a prepared pit grave without a tomb, (C) burial in a simple log tomb, (D) burial in an elaborate log and bark tomb, and (E) burial with negligible preparation of gravesite. All burials here represent extended primary inhumations. Note that the skeletons in burials B and E were decapitated. Burials A and C are from mounds in or near what is today Chillicothe, Ohio. Burials B, D, and E are from the main Wright Mound in Montgomery County, Kentucky; burial D was the initial interment at the site. (Figures A and C from Squier and Davis, 1848; figures B and D-E from Webb, 1940)

others might have held skeletons only temporarily before they were removed and interred elsewhere.

Additions were often made to primary mounds. One model of mound enlargement consisted of a larger cone-shaped mound being built over the primary mound as exemplified by Adena Mound (Figure 12). In such a case, one or more interments could be made on or in the ground adjacent to the primary mound and additional interments placed higher up in the mound fill of the secondary mound as it took shape. Another model consisted of building one or more primary mounds adjacent to each other. At some future time, additional burials and earth could be added above these primary mounds, after which only a single, larger mound existed, as exemplified by the Cresap Mound (Figure 13). Whatever the history of a specific mound, it is clear that the Adena mortuary ritual called for conical or near-conical monuments to mark the graves of the deceased who, for whatever reasons and by whatever processes, were determined worthy of burial and commemoration in this fashion.

Adena mortuary rituals included the practice of placing limited quantities of grave goods — tools or ornaments — near the deceased. Typical items placed in graves might include

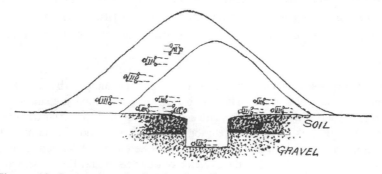

Figure 12. One geometrically simple method of enlarging an Adena mound involved building a larger cone over the primary mound. This method was represented by Adena Mound that once existed in Chillicothe, Ohio. (From Mills, 1902)

chert blades and projectile points, tubular pipes, exotic minerals, stone gorgets, copper jewelry, mica crescents, plain and engraved tablets, and objects of worked bone and shell (Table 2). In addition to grave goods in the narrow sense, other objects might have been placed in the mound for reasons that are unclear.

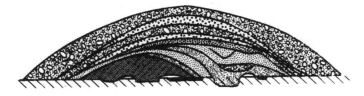

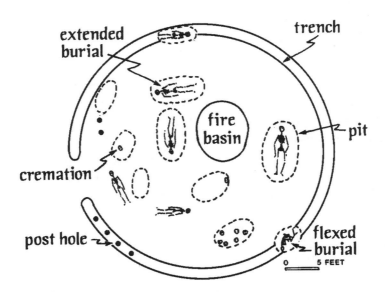

Figure 13. Multiple mounds sometimes were built on the natural surface and then the entire cluster was covered to produce a finished single cone. This pattern occurred at the Cresap Mound in Marshall County, West Virginia, where multiple burials were made in and on the original surface. Other burials were made in the mound as the upper levels of sediment were put in place. (From Woodward and McDonald, 1986, after Dragoo, 1963)

Table 2. Representative Adena and Hopewell Artifacts[1]

Adena
    Tubular pipes
    Rolled copper bracelets and beads
    Slate gorgets
    Stemmed and leaf-shaped projectile points
    Engraved stone and clay tablets
    Mica crescents

Hopewell
    Flint (chert) bladelets
    Obsidian
    Cymbal-shaped copper ear spools
    Grizzly bear teeth
    Platform pipes
    Copper gorgets and effigies
    Pearl beads
    Mica cutouts

[1] The artifacts listed here constitute a very short list of those that sometimes are considered most readily diagnostic of Adena or Hopewell culture. For considerably expanded lists and descriptions of artifacts from mounds, see publications listed in the bibliography by Greber and Ruhl, 1989; Seeman, 1979; Shetrone, 1926; Squier and Davis, 1848; Webb and Baby, 1957; and Webb and Snow, 1945. Also, see the list of graphic resources identified on page 285.

Adena tubular pipes were usually, but not always, made of pipestone, a mineral that occurred in large deposits in southern Ohio, especially east of the Scioto River. Early Adena pipes were cigar-shaped or cylindrical tubes, often with one end blocked. What are presumed to be late Adena effigy pipes are known, but these are rare; the most famous individual specimen is the unique human-like effigy found in Adena Mound itself (Plate 5).

THE ADENA PIPE

Near the left hand was found an effigy pipe. . . .
(Mills, 1902, p. 475)

During the excavation of the Adena Mound in 1901, William C. Mills discovered one of the most unusual Adena artifacts known, an eight-inch tubular pipe of Ohio pipestone carved in the likeness of a human being and ritually stained with red ochre (Plate 5). This object, unique among Adena pipes in that it represents a human subject, is often described as portraying a dwarf. Actually, the inspiration for the design is not clear — does it represent an actual human dwarf, a mythological or spiritual being, artistic norms of the time, or solely its maker's fantasy? The relatively large head and shortened lower limbs are the bases for interpreting it as an achondroplastic human dwarf. Although nude except for a loincloth tied into a bustle in the back, a headdress, and two ear spools, the image on the pipe has been seen as a source of information about costume styles of the Adena.

Among the details of the Adena pipe, however, are some that suggest affinity with the Hopewell culture. Most conspicuous are the cymbal-shaped ear spools, body ornaments typical of the Hopewell, but the subtle engraving on the loincloth also has been interpreted by some observers as a zoomorphic design similar to the bird-of-prey motif that is common among Hopewell. And, the pipe is carved as an effigy, a practice that was widespread among the Hopewell.

The Adena pipe clearly came from a late Adena mound. It is not Hopewell in origin or in all details, but it does serve as a metaphor of the obvious, yet provocatively elusive, relationship between these two Woodland cultures.

Copper ornaments were made of rolled native copper probably obtained through trade from the Great Lakes region and mica cutouts, especially crescent-shaped ones, were made from mica that probably originated in the southern Appalachian Mountains. Both of these materials reached the Adena through their participation in an extensive exchange network; outbound products included Adena pipes of Ohio pipestone and projectile points of Vanport flint that have since been found in sites well beyond the Adena homeland — places as far distant as the Chesapeake Bay area, Vermont, and New Brunswick.

Gorgets were thin ornaments worn around the neck. Early types were rectangular with two holes drilled at the center through which a cord could pass. These highly polished stones were concave on all four edges. In later gorgets the concavities were exaggerated, making the gorget reel-shaped. What have been identified as expanded-center bar "gorgets" found in late Adena burials, however, might have been atlatl weights and not ornaments at all.

Among the rarest of objects from Adena mounds are engraved tablets (Figure 14). These objects were small, thin, usually rectangular slabs of fine-grained stone or clay which contained geometric, curvilinear, or stylized zoomorphic (animal) designs on one side. Generally, these designs were smooth-surfaced patterns that were either incised or raised in *bas relief* created by removing the intervening background. The decorated side of the tablet was possibly a device for printing on textiles or hide, or for marking the skin — either temporarily or in preparation for tattooing. The reverse side of some tablets contain either a circular depression or grooves resulting from abrasion. The circular grinding on the reverse could be a consequence of powdering hematite to make red paint pigment, and the grooves may be from sharpening bone awls or needles.

In addition to burial mounds, the Adena developed a circular earthwork that appeared throughout much of their

Figure 14. The stone tablet from Gaitskill Mound in Mount Sterling, Kentucky. This artifact is about 4 inches high and 3 inches wide, and has been carved in *bas relief*. A second tablet, this one of clay, was also found in the Gaitskill Mound. (Photograph courtesy of William S. Webb Museum of Anthropology)

homeland in late Adena time (Figure 15). This class of earthwork carried over, in modified form, into Hopewell time and frequently was part of Hopewell earthwork complexes. The typical pattern of these simple but beautiful structures was a circular embankment bordered on the inside by a ditch

Figure 15. Biggs Mound in Greenup County, Kentucky, is an example of the circle-and-ditch earthworks that are usually considered to be late Adena in origin. The inset shows this same site as represented by Squier and Davis in *Ancient Monuments of the Mississippi Valley.* (Photograph courtesy William S. Webb Museum of Anthropology; inset from Squier and Davis, 1848)

surrounding a circular platform formed, usually, by the relatively unaltered natural surface of the land. A small passageway, or causeway, typically was left through the embankment and over the ditch to provide access to the inner platform from the outside. Although both smaller and larger examples are known, most of these circles varied from about fifty feet to 250 feet in diameter. A circular wooden structure, similar in design to those upon which burial mounds were built, was sometimes constructed inside Adena circles, near the edge of the interior platform. Occasionally, a burial mound was placed on the inner platform. Other variations in the basic pattern exist.

These circular earthworks, which have been referred to by such names as *sacred circles, ceremonial circles,* and *perfect circles,* were clearly important elements of both late Adena and Hopewell landscapes, but their specific ritual functions and meaning are not known. Adena circle-and-ditch earthworks can be seen at Mount Horeb Earthworks near Lexington, Kentucky, and Mounds State Park in Anderson, Indiana. Great Mound at Mounds State Park once contained a low burial mound on its central platform but this has since been removed by excavation. Conus, in Mound Cemetery, Marietta, Ohio, appears to be the sole surviving example in publicly accessible space of a perfect circle with ditch and interior mound intact. The Grave Creek Mound in Moundsville, West Virginia, once had a ditch around the central mound but there is no evidence that an encircling embankment was ever built.

The name Adena comes from Ohio Governor Thomas Worthington's Adena Estate, located northwest of Chillicothe, Ohio. In 1901, William C. Mills of the Ohio Archaeological and Historical Society excavated Adena Mound and, with the information obtained, provided what is considered the first systematic description of the Adena burial complex. Major concentrations of Adena mounds and earthworks were located in the central Scioto Valley near Chillicothe, Ohio; in the Kanawha Valley near Charleston, West Virginia; in the central Hocking Valley near Athens, Ohio; and along the upper Ohio Valley at Moundsville, West Virginia. Other significant clusters occurred at Anderson, Indiana; at Mount Sterling, Kentucky; near Lexington, Kentucky; along the Great and Little Miami rivers in southwestern Ohio; in the Licking Valley near Newark, Ohio; in Vinton County, Ohio; and at several other locations along the Ohio River in Kentucky, Ohio, and West Virginia.

The Ohio Hopewell Culture (about 200 BC to AD 500)

During the middle Woodland period, people occupying much of the eastern part of the United States, especially the valleys of the Mississippi, Ohio, and lower Missouri rivers, came under the loosely unifying influence of a set of cultural phenomena involving mortuary customs and commodity exchange. As with Adena, there was distinct variation among the many local populations of these people, but there was nonetheless sufficient interaction and sharing of a common world view to allow the composite population to interact regularly, effectively, and constructively. These people are now called Hopewell, their distinguishing unifying traits are called Hopewellian, and the social region they occupied is called the Hopewell Interaction Sphere (Figure 16). The basic elements of Hopewell culture appear to have originated, fused, or effloresced in two nuclei, one in Illinois and the other in southern Ohio. The former, perhaps slightly the older, sometimes is referred to as Illinois Hopewell, whereas the latter is called Ohio, or Classical, Hopewell. Both occupied geographically strategic locations; the Illinois Hopewell homeland lay astride the Mississippi River and was well positioned to take advantage of communication and the movement of information and commodities on the converging Mississippi, Missouri, and Ohio rivers, while the Ohio Hopewell was positioned to take advantage of movement on the Ohio River and between the Ohio River and the lower Great Lakes, the Atlantic Seaboard, and the Southeast.

The Ohio Hopewell homeland included most of southwestern Ohio, especially the valleys of the Scioto, Great Miami, and Little Miami rivers. Important outliers occurred to the west, near Anderson and New Castle, Indiana; upstream on the Ohio River at Marietta, Ohio; and to the northeast at Newark, Ohio. The Hopewell presence at the mouth of the Scioto River extended ever so slightly into Kentucky. A discernable but diluted Ohio Hopewell presence is also known

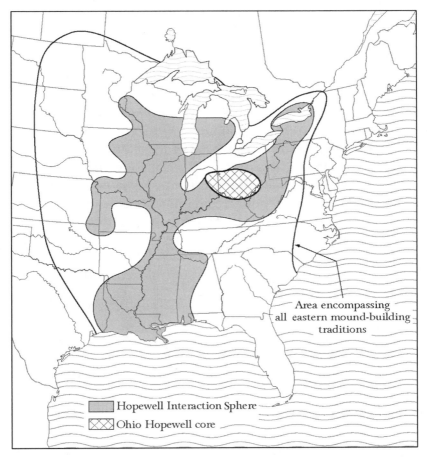

Figure 16. The Hopewell Interaction Sphere, that part of eastern North America throughout which Hopewellian cultural traits were most pronounced. The map shows the place of the Ohio Hopewell core within the overall interaction sphere, and the interaction sphere within the area that encompassed most of the eastern mound-building traditions. (After Coe *et al.*, 1986)

beyond this homeland in northern Ohio, in central and western Kentucky, and especially near Charleston and Moundsville, West Virginia. With few exceptions, the nuclear Ohio Hopewell homeland, the region in which the culture reached its most elaborate expression, consisted of that part of the Adena

THE HOPEWELL EARTHWORKS

Frederick Ward Putnam, curator of ethnology and archaeology at Harvard University's Peabody Museum, was a luminary of the infant discipline of anthropology during the latter decades of the nineteenth century. Ohio contained some of the most spectacular and well known archeological sites in the country, especially mounds and earthworks of the "Mound Builders." Putnam and Ohio's mounds came together in the 1880s when Putnam led a crusade to save Serpent Mound in Adams County from impending destruction. Interest in Ohio's past continued to hold Putnam, and when he was appointed director of the Department of Ethnology and Archaeology of the World's Columbian Exposition that was to be held in Chicago in 1893, he

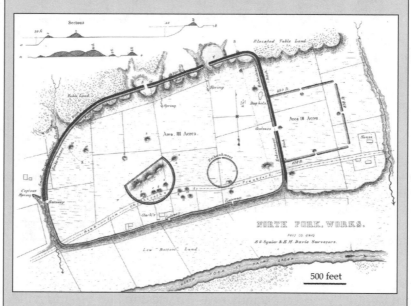

Figure 17. The Hopewell Earthworks along the North Fork of Paint Creek west of Chillicothe in Ross County, Ohio, as represented in Squier and Davis's *Ancient Monuments of the Mississippi Valley.*

set about to see that artifacts of Ohio's mound-building Indians were represented. Putnam hired Warren K. Moorehead to excavate some Ohio sites in search of materials for the exhibit. Failing to find sufficiently spectacular artifacts at Fort Ancient, Moorehead moved his search to a site on the North Fork of Paint Creek in Ross County, Ohio, where, from September 1891 to January 1892, his crew excavated parts of several mounds in a large earthworks complex on the farm of Mordecai C. Hopewell. His efforts were not wasted, and the fine work of the Hopewell craftsmen was well represented at the great celebration in Chicago.

Ephraim G. Squier and Edwin H. Davis, authors of the nineteenth-century classic study in archeology *Ancient Monuments of the Mississippi Valley*, had surveyed and excavated at this same site in the 1840s; they had called it both Clark's Work, after the W. C. Clark family who owned the land at that time, and North Fork Works, after its location on the North Fork of Paint Creek. Moorehead, however, called the site Hopewell in honor of the cooperative landowner with whom he worked.

The Hopewell Earthworks, home of the Hopewell Group of mounds, contained the largest of all the Hopewell geometric enclosures (111 acres; Table 3) and the largest of all Hopewell burial mounds (Hopewell Mound 25: thirty-four feet high, five hundred feet long) (Figure 17). This site also has produced one of the largest, most unusual, and most significant collections of artifacts representing the artistic expression and material wealth known for Hopewell culture. Although not typical of Hopewell sites, it is ironically appropriate that this place of so many superlatives should also become the type site for Ohio Hopewell culture, itself one of America's prehistoric cultural superlatives.

Table 3. Approximate Dimensions of Selected Adena and Hopewell Earthworks

ENCLOSURE	ESTIMATED AREA	DIAMETER

Geometric Enclosures

Cedar Bank	32 acres	
High Banks Circle	20 acres	
High Banks Octagon	18 acres	
Hopeton Circle	20 acres	
Hopeton Square	20 acres	
Hopewell Large Polygon	111 acres	
Hopewell Annex	18 acres	
Liberty Large Polygon	40 acres	
Liberty Square	27 acres	
Marietta Larger Square	50 acres	
Marietta Smaller Square	27 acres	
Mound City	16 acres[a]	
Newark Great Circle	30 acres	
Newark Observatory Circle	20 acres	
Newark Octagon	50 acres	
Newark Square (obliterated)	20 acres	
Peter Village Enclosure	23 acres	
Portsmouth Old Fort	15 acres	
Seip Square	27 acres	
Stubbs combined	85 acres[b]	

continued on page 47

homeland that was within the glaciated Central Lowland — rolling hills broken by oversized valleys filled with glacial alluvium. The valleys provided extensive tracts of productive level land, much of which was on terraces situated above normal flood levels to permit reasonably long-term, secure occu-

Table 3, continued

ENCLOSURE	ESTIMATED AREA	DIAMETER

Hilltop Enclosures

Calvary Cemetery Enclosure	24 acres	
Fort Ancient	125 acres[c]	
Fort Hill	48 acres	
Glenford Fort	27 acres[d]	
Miami Fort	12 acres	
Pollock Works	12 acres	
Spruce Hill	140 acres	

Circular Earthworks (inside diameters)

Anderson Great Mound Circle		250 feet[e]
High Bank Earthworks Circle		1050 feet
Hopeton Earthworks Circle		1050 feet
Liberty Large Polygon		1790 feet
Marietta Conus Circle		220 feet
Mount Horeb Circle		195 feet[f]
Newark Great Circle		1200 feet
Seip Large Polygon		1600 feet

Sources: All measurements given in this table are from Squier and Davis, 1848, except as follows: [a] Alexander *in litt.*, 2002; [b] Cowan *et al.*, 1998; [c] Connolly, 1998; [d] Thomas, 1894; [e] Lilly 1937; [f] Webb, 1941.

pation of sites, yet within easy reach of rivers that could be used as avenues of movement for people, commodities, and ideas.

Much of Ohio Hopewell culture came from the Adena. Certainly, Hopewell culture represents the further elaboration of trajectories that had been underway in the eastern wood-lands for millennia: population continued to increase, interregional exchange intensified, mortuary customs became increasingly elaborate, reliance on horticulture increased, and social organization and intergroup relationships became more complex. Some of these trajectories, however, changed more than others and in unique ways, and it was *the exaggerated expression of some cultural elements* that gave highly visible distinction to the Ohio Hopewell in the archeological record, setting it apart not only from Adena but even from other Hopewellian groups within the Hopewell Interaction Sphere.

The domestic life of most Hopewell probably differed little from that of the Adena, a circumstance which supports the belief by some archeologists that Adena might have survived well into the middle Woodland period in some, or even much, of the territory the Adena occupied during the early Woodland period. Although still not well known, Hopewell habitations appear to have been small, dispersed, and probably temporary or intermittent-use phenomena. Dwellings probably were wood-framed buildings covered with plant matter or hides and intended for short-term use by one or two families. Perhaps dwellings of one or a few extended families clustered together at times (Figure 18). Hunting, gathering, and collecting were probably the mainstays of their economy, but a reliance on the controlled production of food plants of the Eastern Agricultural Complex and squash (Table 1) became increasingly important. Maize was known to the Hopewell of Ohio, but it was not a significant food crop and possibly was used only in a ceremonial context. It is not known to what extent the domestic economy was affected by the production and modification of raw materials that entered the corporate and interregional exchange systems, but much of the extraction, initial preparation, and transportation of these materials would not have required the skills of artisans or other accomplished individuals. Whatever the role of citizen Hopewell in

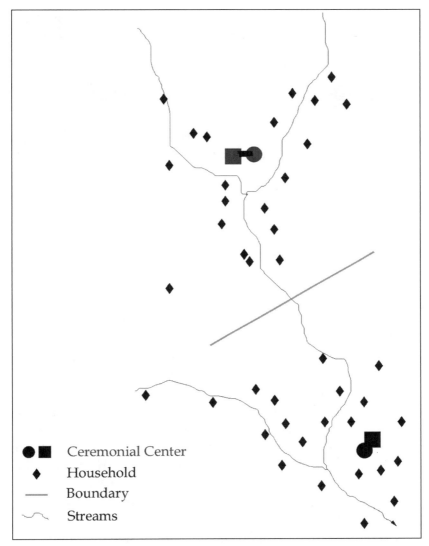

Figure 18. A schematic representation of the settlement patterns that might have characterized the use of river valleys by domestic and corporate elements of Hopewell society. According to this model, each settlement cluster consisted of a corporate center with monumental architecture and specialized activity areas surrounded by individual households or small groups of households. (Adapted from Dancey and Pacheco, 1997)

49

Figure 19. The finely sculpted pipes of the Ohio Hopewell were typically carved from Ohio pipestone, the most important sources of which were located east of the Scioto River upstream from Portsmouth. The pipes shown here, carved in effigies of birds, are among the many beautiful effigy and non-effigy platform pipes collected from the mounds of southern Ohio in the 1840s by Squier and Davis. Most Hopewell platform pipes were from 3 to 3.5 inches in length. (From Squier and Davis, 1848)

the extraction of raw materials for use within the Ohio Hopewell ceremonial sphere or for export, it is interesting to note that the two largest and most complex geometric earthworks of the Hopewell world, Newark and Portsmouth, were located near the source of two minerals that were extensively utilized by the Hopewell — Vanport flint (plates 6 and 7) and Ohio pipestone (Figure 19), respectively.

The corporate life of the Hopewell, however, was very different from any predecessor in the eastern woodlands and represents the most extreme development of institutionalized architecture and associated ceremonialism ever realized in the middle Ohio Valley. Mortuary ritual is one of the most conspicuous elements of Hopewell corporate ceremonialism available to us. Certainly, funerary practices seem to have been one anchor at many Hopewell sites around which monumental mound and earthwork complexes often developed. Less well known are the ceremonial reasons that led to the construction of the large and small enclosures, parallel walls, graded ways, and mounds that were not used for mortuary purposes — or the wooden architecture that predated or accompanied many of these earthworks. The idea of marking places of importance to a group with earthen monuments, and the implications of such demarcation, certainly had been implemented before Hopewell time. But whether it was mortuary practices or other important ceremonial functions that identified places as special, some and perhaps all of the lowland sites that developed earthwork complexes fulfilled multiple corporate functions and probably, with time and the development of tradition, assumed expanded symbolic importance. At the same time, it is difficult if not impossible to separate completely domestic and corporate values, behavior, and materials. While ceremonies unfolded at the major Hopewell sites, so too did such domestic endeavors as eating, sleeping, and bathing; hunting, gathering, and collecting; materials maintenance and, perhaps, crafting; and interpersonal socializing, including gossip, formal information and commodity exchange, and courtship.

Mounds and geometric enclosures at lowland sites probably developed over an extended period of time during which the population experienced relative stability. One model of development of a site with geometric enclosures includes the following possibilities. A site might have been occupied initially by an extended family of three or four households. This family cluster, a small population representing a single lineage, as necessary, attended to domestic matters that could have included ritually fulfilling mortuary expectations by disposing of the dead beneath inconspicuous mounds. As the population increased and multiple lineages vested in the site, corporate architecture appeared in the form of a rectangular multi-chambered wooden structure or cluster of contiguous structures, the *big house* or *great house*, which might have contained a charnel house or charnel chamber; specialized work areas; meeting chambers for men, women, and clans; and possibly other rooms as well. In the charnel chamber, the dead were prepared for burial by processes that sometimes included cremation. Burials, whether in the flesh, of reburied skeletons, or of cremated remains, usually were interred in the floor of one or more rooms of the structure. After the structure had been used over an extended period of time it was either dismantled or burned, its floor was covered with appropriate sediment, and the area in turn was covered with clean earth sufficient to form an initial mound over the site. If different rooms were used at different times, or were used by different social factions, each floor area could have been transformed separately from a dynamic use-space to a submound status. Under some circumstances, perhaps if the building were small, a single primary mound could have been built over the site of the former structure and the graves it contained. Under other circumstances, multiple primary mounds could have been built over the sites of different parts of the multi-roomed structure — some covering the sites of former rooms with burials while others covered non-funerary spaces. Thereafter, additional debris, including household and corporate waste and assorted other material, was added to enlarge the mound. At some point, and probably well into the occupation of the site, the construction of the geometric enclosure commenced; apparently the enclosure was built, unit by unit, over a period of multiple generations. Construction of the enclosure represented a new level of group investment in the site, including the elaboration and definition of ceremonial functions as envisioned by the group. Domestic activities appear to have been excluded from taking place inside many of the enclosures once they were in place. Then, at some point, the site was abandoned.

The mounds and earthworks that existed at the time that a site was abandoned — or, at least, at the time that construction was halted — represented the stage of development of the complex upon abandonment, not necessarily the completion of a grand plan that had been envisioned when the site was initially occupied by the original Hopewell settlers decades or centuries earlier. That said, the environmental and architectural similarities among the Ohio Hopewell sites indicate that ideals of form and scale — and meaning — were shared, not only by contemporaries but also by subsequent generations who continued to allow these ideals to be expressed as the multiple sites grew over time.

So, while monumental earthen architecture might have begun with the erection of low mounds by a small population, corporate architecture appeared on special sites of the Hopewell in the form of wooden buildings, typically with rectangular outlines though occasionally with circular or irregular floor plans. Other wooden structures, such as palisade walls, wind breaks, sun screens, or calendric devices corresponding to certain astronomic cycles, also could have been represented at these sites. As long as a site, or a part of a site, was in use, wooden architecture probably dominated the landscape (Figure 20). The great house, if one were present, would have been a major building within the complex (Figure 21). Other structures likely provided for specialized rituals, storage, raw materials reduction, crafts production, and other non-domestic uses. In addition to providing a center for mortuary functions, these special sites also could have been the central place where a region's calendric lore was maintained and monitored, where its geometric traditions were kept, where the spiritual basis of its world view was kept, where courts were conducted, where domestic unions were facilitated and perhaps formalized, where reciprocity played out, where standards of art were established or maintained, where exotic goods or services were exchanged, where alliances were created or formalized, where group and intergroup strategies were discussed, where tribute was paid, and so on.

As the use of a site continued, its architectural landscape changed. When the useful life of wooden structures came to an end, they often were dismantled or burned, and sometimes the site was covered ritually with earth, gravel, and stone —

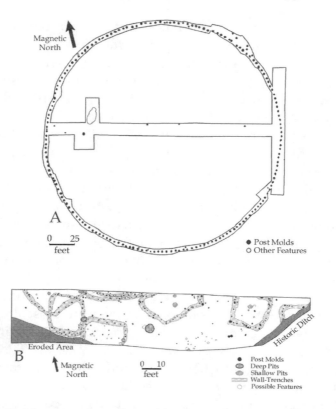

Figure 20. Monumental wooden architecture probably dominated Hopewell corporate centers while those places were in active use, and evidence of such wooden structures has been found at many such sites. Traces of at least twenty-one wooden structures were documented at Stubbs Earthworks in Warren County, Ohio, during excavations in 1998 and 1999, examples of which are illustrated here. (A) Evidence of the Great Post Circle was found beneath a circular earthen embankment located south of the main Stubbs enclosure. The wall of this wooden structure was nearly 240 feet in diameter and consisted of 172 upright posts, each the diameter and possibly the height of a telephone pole. Following use, the posts were removed and the remaining holes were refilled with earth, and the circle was covered with a low embankment. (B) Traces of eight house-like structures were identified in this transect of the Stubbs site; all were rectangular with rounded corners and were built using wall-trench foundations. These structures were probably not used as living quarters for extended periods, if at all. Note the difference in scale for figures A and B. (Figures from Cowan *et al.,* 2000)

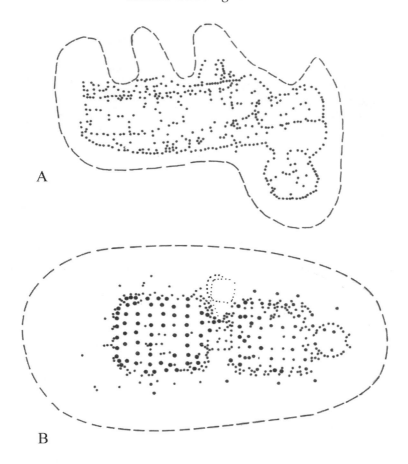

Figure 21. Postmolds of great houses from (A) Tremper Mound in Scioto County, Ohio, and (B) Edwin Harness Mound at the Liberty Earthworks south of Chillicothe, Ohio. The great house at Tremper was about 200 feet long, while that at Edwin Harness was about 165 feet long. Great houses were multichambered wooden-framed structures that probably comprised a number of distinct special-use areas. When their usefulness had been fulfilled, these structures were usually burned or dismantled and separate but conjoined mounds were built over the site of each of the chambers. The process of mound construction could have stopped at the stage of the conjoined mounds, as at Tremper, or continued with the erection of a larger elongate mound that covered all of the conjoined mounds, as happened at Edwin Harness. (Tremper figure after Mills, 1916; Harness figure after Greber, 1983)

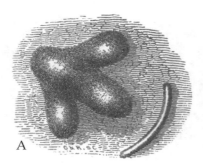

Figure 22. Hopewell conjoined mounds typically covered multiple-use areas, each mound covering a discrete use surface. (A) The four conjoined mounds that form the "eagle effigy" in the center of the Great Circle in Newark, Ohio, cover the site of a Hopewell great house. (B) Mound 25 and associated mounds within the large semicircular enclosure at the Hopewell site, Ross County, Ohio. Mound 25 is represented in this figure by the three largest conjoined mounds, although in reality its central mound was more uniformly elongate than is shown here. Mound 25, the largest known Hopewell mound, covers several conjoined primary mounds, each of which covered a different part of the floor of a Hopewell great house. (From Squier and Davis, 1848)

as local resources, tastes, and tradition directed. Great houses, after their function had been fulfilled and they had been leveled and the site properly prepared, were often covered with mounds, sometimes with symmetrical elongate mounds as at Seip and Liberty and sometimes with irregular amorphous mounds as at Newark Great Circle, Tremper, and Stubbs — although these amorphous mounds could represent intermediate stages in the conversion of a great house site to a finished elongate or conical mound (Figure 22). The geometric enclosures grew with the site, and they stopped growing either when the enclosure was considered complete or the site was abandoned. Once a mound or component of an earthwork complex was completed, what once had been ceremonial architecture became commemorative architecture. And commemorative architecture, too, held cultural significance to its builders and their descendants.

Several types of earthen architecture occurred at Hopewell lowland sites (Figure 23). Burial and other mounds are one; these are usually conical but can be subconical, elliptical, or amorphous, especially the larger ones built over the site of a great house. Geometric enclosures, earthen embankments surrounding sometimes very large areas and executed at times with truly amazing geometric and engineering precision, occur in several standard shapes — especially large and small circles, squares and other rectangles, and octagons (Table 3). Sometimes these enclosures stand apart from other associated features; at other times they are conjoined, or fused, with one or more enclosures. Normally, several gates occur in the walls or at the corners of the rectangles and octagons, and these gates are usually accompanied by conical or elliptical mounds (Plate 8). Circles, however, typically have only a single gate, sometimes with and sometimes without one or more associated mounds inside or outside the circle. Parallel-walled corridors sometimes lead to or from an enclosure, or appear to connect enclosures. Typically, parallel walls extended for relatively short distances between, or in the vicinity of, enclosures, but those that were parts of the Newark and Portsmouth earthworks extended for miles. Graded surfaces usually existed between these parallel embankments; often, the *graded way* would lead from an earthwork to a neighboring waterway. Rare at Hopewell sites, but known nonetheless, are platform mounds — flat-topped mounds, sometimes with ascending ramps, which are similar to the platform mounds that were known from the middle Woodland Pinson Mounds site in Tennessee. Lastly, the entire suite of typical Adena mounds and earthworks are known from some Hopewell earthwork complexes, such as at Marietta and Portsmouth, and it is assumed that in at least some cases these structures were integral parts of the overall complex.

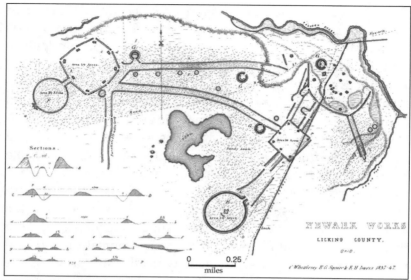

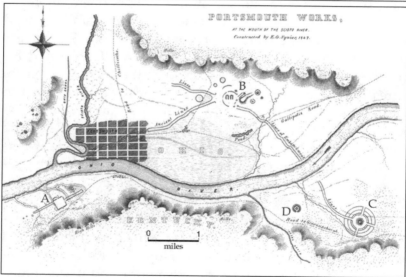

Figure 23. The two most extensive and complex lowland geometric earthworks built by the Ohio Hopewell are the (top) Newark Earthworks and (bottom) Portsmouth Earthworks. The letters A, B, C, and D that appeared on the original figure of the Portsmouth Works have been enlarged here for reference in the site description that appears later in this book. (From Squier and Davis, 1848)

The Great Hopewell Road

The Newark Earthworks (Figure 23) was one of two Hopewell earthworks complexes that contained inordinate lengths of parallel walls bordering, and bounding, broad avenues. Most of the avenues at the Newark Earthworks led from one geometric feature to another, but one deviated from this pattern. Extending south, then southwest from the octagon, this one walled avenue led away from the earthworks complex for several miles . . . . But for how *many* miles, and to what, if any, destination?

Early maps of Newark Earthworks showed the part of this avenue near the octagon, but they seldom continued it far, a cartographic convenience that created the impression that the path might have been merely one more short segment of parallel earthen embankments. Ephraim G. Squier and Edwin H. Davis, in their famous treatise on the western antiquities that was published in 1848, annotated this segment of parallel walls on the map of Newark Earthworks, their Plate XXV (our Figure 23, top), with the words "Parallels 2½ miles long," and went on to explain on page 70 of the text that the walls "finally lose themselves in the plain." Later, the brothers James and Charles Salisbury prepared a more detailed map of the earthworks to correct what they claimed had been inadequate representation of the features up to that time. The Salisbury map was completed in 1862 and was intended for publication by the American Antiquarian Society, but funding problems during the Civil War prevented publication of the map and it ended up in the society's archives. More than a century later, Bradley Lepper of the Ohio Historical Society located the Salisbury map and accompanying manuscript, and immediately recognized the importance of the documents that were before him.

Among other new information, the Salisbury map showed the southwesterly trending avenue to have extended more than eight miles, most of it straight as though heading directly toward some destination. Recalling the importance of long and straight roads to many prehistoric and traditional societies, and especially the religious significance of straight roads to such Native American cultures as the Maya and the Chaco Anasazi, Lepper wondered if the Hopewell, too, might not have had a monumental straight road connecting two of their important ceremonial centers. Lepper suspected that an extension of the straight section of road on the Salisbury map might lead to one of the large Hopewell earthworks near Chillicothe. In fact, the extension led directly to Chillicothe, arguably the cultural center of Ohio Hopewell.

Lepper combined his archival and library research with aerial surveys and field testing to explore the hypothesis that a Great Hopewell Road connected the Newark and Chillicothe centers. His results, while encouraging, were not conclusive, but the possibility of locating additional evidence of the road still exists.

Recently, Lepper, who clearly believes in the existence of a Great Hopewell Road, has suggested that it likely functioned as a route of pilgrimage, with the Hopewell centers of Chillicothe and Newark being destinations for Hopewell pilgrims. Lepper goes further to suggest that, in addition to the unknown and unknowable spiritual context of such a pilgrimage, the process might have entailed the exchange of valued material objects. Flint Ridge (or Vanport) flint, he notes, was one of the most highly valued raw materials produced in and used throughout the Ohio Hopewell homeland, so it might be reasonable to think that pilgrims to Newark might have taken away quantities of the colorful stone that the Licking Valley Hopewell exploited so intensively. In return, the pilgrims might have left objects of value at Newark, or Chillicothe, or other centers of spiritual significance, objects from their homelands or ones they had acquired in exchange — gifts, or spiritual tribute, of marine shells, mica, copper, obsidian, bear teeth, and the like.

But if the Great Hopewell Road did exist, did it connect only Newark and Chillicothe? Could it, or another road like it, not also have connected Chillicothe with the Portsmouth complex? Newark and Chillicothe are in different watersheds — the Licking and Scioto, respectively, so the pragmatic value of a road connecting the two is immediately more obvious than is the need for a road connecting the Chillicothe and Portsmouth works, since both of those centers lay on the Scioto River. But, as Lepper argues well, the purpose of the Great Hopewell Road might have been greater than its value as a work of civil engineering. Just as Newark lies near the single most important source of flint for the entire Ohio Hopewell culture, so does Portsmouth lie near the main source of Ohio pipestone, the most important stone used in the manufacture of platform pipes which, too, were conspicuously important to the Ohio Hopewell. Both Flint Ridge flint and Ohio pipestone assuredly had spiritual and symbolic value beyond their purely functional merits, so if a pilgrimage to the source of one was an important goal in the lives of many Hopewell, a pilgrimage to the

The Great
Hopewell Road

Newark

Chillicothe

? Piketon

Portsmouth

source of the other also might have been important.

The factual evidence for a road that might have connected Chillicothe and Portsmouth lay on the ground in this region during the early years of American settlement. Squier and Davis described the parallel embankments at Portsmouth, the most lengthy set of parallel walls documented for any Hopewell site, as collectively representing a remarkable aspect of the complex (Figure 23). Two of the three avenues led from the central site on a terrace on the north side of the Ohio River toward large satellite sites on the south side of the river. The walls picked up on the south side and continued to the respective sites. As at Newark, major geometric elements of the overall site were connected by walled avenues. Squier and Davis, in describing the Portsmouth earthworks, went on:

A third line runs north-west for a considerable distance, and loses itself in the broken grounds towards the Scioto. It may have communicated with other works in that direction, which have been obliterated by time, or, which is most likely, were destroyed in the manifest changes which the plain in that direction has undergone within a few centuries (p. 78).

As at Newark, there was one walled avenue that appeared to lead away from the Portsmouth complex toward Chillicothe and become lost in the distance. In the case of the Portsmouth avenue, disturbances to the land beyond the northwestern end of the avenue were obvious to Squier and Davis. A review of the maps of other sites in the Scioto Valley in Squier and Davis's book will also show that erosion due to both floods from below and runoff from above had destroyed parts of those sites. But, a review of these same sites also reveals that a well preserved segment of a walled avenue did still exist, in the 1840s, just south of Piketon. This segment of walled avenue was oriented north-south, paralleling the river. Another interesting aspect of the Piketon avenue is that only portions of it were walled, suggesting that, perhaps, not all parts of Hopewell roads, even important pilgrimage routes, if they in fact existed, would necessarily have been paralleled by embankments.

A special category of Hopewell upland earthworks is the hilltop enclosure (Figure 24, Plate 9). These enclosures are formed of embankments that typically are located on top of, and extend around all or part of the perimeter of, isolated or semi-isolated high points. Several of these enclosures occupy isolated mesa-like outliers on the edge of the Appalachian Plateau (Figure 6), while others occupy high ground left by advancing glaciers or, as they retreated, eroded by their vigorously flowing meltwater. From the time that these enclosures became known to American observers, they have been considered by many to have been defensive structures, but that belief has never been without its dissenters. Like the lowland enclosures, the hilltop enclosures probably served multiple functions simply because it is difficult if not impossible to separate elements of a functioning society and an integrated world view. That does not mean that the hilltop structures did not have a central reason for being built. Some hilltop enclosures have produced evidence of having been built in multiple stages and it is reasonable to suspect that most if not all had similar histories.

Opinions among archeologists differ as to the status of those Hopewell who were buried beneath mounds. One opinion is that burials later covered by mounds were reserved for people of status rather than being available to all of the population, while the contrasting belief is that such burials were probably available to a broad range of people regardless of

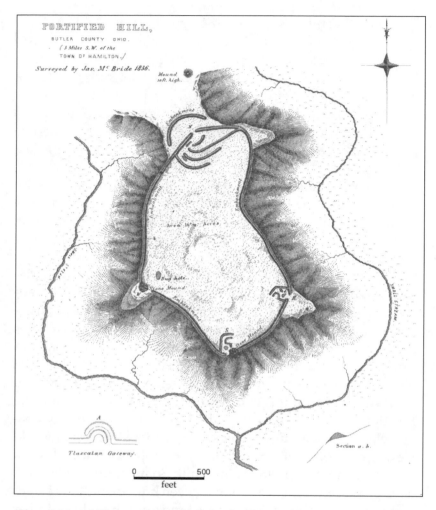

Figure 24. A hilltop enclosure built by the Hopewell on an upland promontory in what is today Butler County, Ohio. Basic elements of Hopewell hilltop enclosures included (a) a relatively flat and isolated upland surface, (b) embankments of earth and stone that closely followed the edge of the level upland surface, and (c) multiple and sometimes elaborately configured "gates." (From Squier and Davis, 1848)

status. Only a relatively small percentage of the Hopewell population was ever buried in or beneath mounds, and some process of selection had to be operating to determine who would be so interred. Burials were made in the flesh, as defleshed skeletons in both bundled and extended arrangements, and after cremation. Some burials were in crypts; usually, multiple bodies would be placed into the crypt over an extended period of time. Other burials took place in great houses, or charnel houses. Most burials in charnel houses were the remains of individuals who had been cremated in special basins often located on the floor of the house (Figure 25), but some bodies, perhaps those with higher status, were buried in

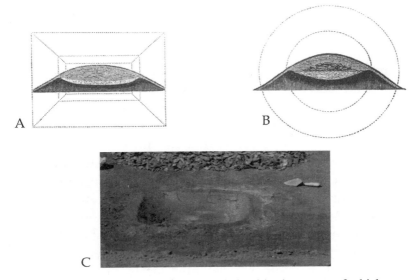

Figure 25. Three examples of Hopewell ritual basins, most of which were made of clay. Hopewell ritual basins have often been called crematory basins, but they probably were used for more than cremations and their symbolic function probably extended beyond the act of cremation itself. (A) The rectangular basin beneath Mound 9 at Mound City near Chillicothe, Ohio, was about 10 feet long and 8 feet wide. (B) The circular basin beneath Mound 1 at Mound City was about 9 feet in diameter. (C) A small rectangular basin beneath Mound 25 at Hopewell was about 3 feet long and 2 feet wide. (A and B from Squier and Davis, 1848; C courtesy of Ohio Historical Society)

the flesh and often were accompanied by grave goods. At some point, both the open crypts and the charnel house floor were covered by mounds.

Unlike the typical Adena burial mound, the Hopewell mound usually would be built in one or two phases with no additional burials placed in the mound once it was completed. Consequently, many Hopewell burial mounds were relatively small. The highest Hopewell mound, the central mound of Mound 25 of the Hopewell Group, which was never reconstructed after it was excavated, was thirty-four feet high, and very few other Hopewell burial mounds came near that height. The largest standing Hopewell burial mound is the reconstructed Seip-Pricer Mound, thirty feet high; other unusually large examples were Edwin Harness Mound at the Liberty site and Carriage Factory Mound, both near Chillicothe. The most extreme expression of Hopewell mortuary practice, in terms of the degree to which a site was devoted to the preparation and placement of the dead, is Mound City at Chillicothe, Ohio.

Artifacts from Hopewell mounds contain some of the finest examples of Hopewell craftsmanship known, and these goods are sometimes represented in extraordinary quantities that must have represented truly substantial prestige and accumulations of wealth by the deceased or those who grieved their loss. Many objects that were placed in mounds, sometimes accompanying burials and sometimes apart from graves, were made of materials that had been imported from great distances, whereas others originated locally. These goods included fresh-water pearls, hammered and embossed copper and gold, galena, mica, conch shells, grizzly bear teeth, fossil shark teeth, and obsidian, among others. Copper from Isle Royale in Lake Superior was hammered into jewelry, tools, and decorative ornaments (Plate 10). Mica from the southern Appalachians was used in many ways — as jewelry, geometric and effigy cutouts, and to cover or line working and cer-

Figure 26. Silhouettes of representative mica cutouts from Hopewell mounds.

emonial surfaces, among others (Figure 26). Large deposits of obsidian and flint objects have been found in some mounds, and caches of well crafted effigy platform pipes have been found in others; Mound of the Pipes in the Mound City Group and Tremper Mound are two structures that yielded noteworthy numbers of these effigy pipes (Figure 19). Fresh-water pearls, collected from mussels living in the streams of the region and beyond and fashioned into beads and strung in chains or sewn onto clothing provide an excellent example of the opulence that was part of Hopewell culture. More than 100,000 pearls were recovered from the Hopewell Group of mounds, 35,000 were found in a single cache at the Turner site in Hamilton County, Ohio, and 15,000 or so were found covering a multiple burial in Seip-Pricer Mound.

Although the quintessential corporate ceremonial world of the Ohio Hopewell did not extend beyond southern Ohio and its immediate environs, Hopewell influence did extend beyond the cultural core into southern Indiana, central and western Kentucky, northern and eastern Ohio, and western West Virginia. For the most part, however, the enduring cultural landscape of the Ohio Hopewell was never strongly imprinted on the Appalachian Plateau or the Interior Low Plateau, and it is not known to what extent the native people living in those regions participated in the cultural dynamics that focused on the lowland ceremonial centers.

By around AD 500, much of the Hopewell Interaction Sphere had disintegrated and the Ohio Hopewell had disappeared as a distinct regional culture. The reason for the demise is not known but various possibilities have been suggested, among which are assimilation of the Hopewell by some other culture, drought or cooling sufficient to disrupt their gardening, epidemic disease, and warfare. Another possibility is the collapse of their exchange network due to social instability in non-Hopewell regions and the consequent loss of access to a disproportionate amount of the continent's wealth by the Hopewell elite. Yet another opinion is that local populations could have become increasingly self-sufficient and thus had less reason to maintain long distance exchange networks to obtain both essential resources and non-essential luxury goods. It may well be that, as Hopewell culture aged and came to invest more and more corporate energy in increasingly opulent ceremonies and ceremonial architecture, the point was reached at which regional populations found it more to their long-term advantage to restructure their overall organizational model in ways that would render the essential elements of Hopewell ceremonialism unnecessary. According to this model, late Woodland people shifted from dispersed shifting habitations to concentrated permanent settlements and thereby eliminated the need for the ceremonial rituals that probably took place at the geometric earthwork locales.

The great Hopewell earthworks were most numerous in southwestern Ohio. Today, the best preserved sites open to the public are Fort Ancient, Fort Hill, Miami Fort, Mound City, and the Newark Earthworks.

The Intrusive Mound Culture (about AD 700 to 1000)

The poorly known Intrusive Mound culture occupied southern Ohio, especially the Scioto River Valley, and nearby parts of Kentucky, Pennsylvania, and West Virginia from some time after the disintegration of Ohio Hopewell until the ascent of Fort Ancient culture. These late Woodland hunting, gathering, and collecting people possessed some cultural traits that were similar to Hopewell, such as the production and use of finely crafted platform pipes, participation in interregional exchange, and funerary ritual that included the use of burial mounds. In other respects, the Intrusive Mound people more strongly resembled cultures to their north and east.

William C. Mills named and described the Intrusive Mound culture after excavating burials at Mound City near Chillicothe. The name Intrusive Mound comes from the practice of sometimes burying the dead in graves dug into the surface of mounds built by earlier people (Figure 27). The Intrusive Mound people did, however, also build low burial mounds, and they were not the only people to bury some of their dead in pre-existing mounds.

Mound City is the only publicly accessible site that contains mounds that were used by the Intrusive Mound people.

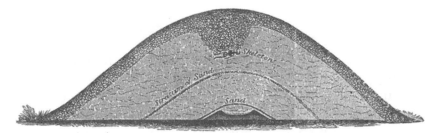

Figure 27. An intrusive burial in Mound 2 at Mound City. The grave in the upper part of the mound pictured here contained two skeletons and associated grave goods, and was known to be intrusive because the pit in which the skeletons were placed was opened by digging through the upper layers of the mound. (From Squier and Davis, 1848)

The Late Prehistoric Tradition

The Fort Ancient Culture (about AD 900 to AD 1750)

Sometime after about AD 900, the late Woodland people living in the western part of the middle Ohio Valley started to adopt a way of life that depended significantly on the production of domesticated plant foods. Although hunting, gathering, and collecting continued to be important, a large-scale dependence upon maize, supplemented strongly by beans, along with squash, sunflowers, and chenopods, developed in the region for the first time. These earliest farmers in the Ohio Valley, known as the Fort Ancient people, were distributed from extreme southeastern Indiana to the Muskingum Valley in eastern Ohio, and from central Ohio to central and eastern Kentucky and western West Virginia (Figure 5). During the seventeenth century, however, the cumulative influences of internal changes and, especially, external forces — largely those set in motion by Europeans a century earlier — resulted in the depopulation or abandonment of large parts of the Fort Ancient homeland. Although the actual fate of the Fort Ancient people is not known, some researchers believe that they might have been the ancestors of the Shawnee or one or more of the other Algonquian groups.

The Fort Ancient culture has been divided into three units — early (about AD 1000 to 1200), middle (about AD 1200 to 1400), and late (about AD 1400 to 1750). Little change in the basic economy of the Fort Ancient occurred throughout their history, but there were changes in such other cultural characteristics as the size, plan, and duration of settlements; the size and diversity of houses and other wooden structures; mortuary practices; domestic wares; and perhaps in regional unity and social complexity.

Generally, Fort Ancient society was egalitarian. The leadership of groups was an achieved and tenuous role rather than an inherited and institutionalized one. The very fact that larger populations lived together for longer periods of time, how-ever, required that cooperation and planning within, and on behalf of, the groups take place.

Settlements were located on terraces of alluvial valleys, on bluffs overlooking valleys, and in upland settings, and they appear to have been occupied over periods of several years, and perhaps, in some cases, for one or more decades. Houses and other roofed buildings were built of rectangular or circu-lar sapling frames covered, probably, with mats, bark, or hides. During early Fort Ancient time, settlements consisted of only a few households, probably extended families. These settle-ments probably were not occupied for extended periods. The houses usually were small, although some relatively large struc-tures are known to have existed. By middle Fort Ancient time, settlements had become larger and typically were occupied for extended periods. The preferred plan of many villages was circular (Figure 28). In villages that followed this organiza-tional plan, houses and other structures were arranged in a circle on the outside of the settlement site, storage and waste debris were located inside the ring of houses, and a burial area was located inside the storage and midden ring either adja-cent to or sharing a plaza that was located at the center of the village. The adoption of a plaza suggests the growing impor-tance of group ceremonialism, a sharing of accumulated knowledge and tradition, and a reinforcement of community bonds and focus. Some villages were surrounded by a stock-ade, and the fields of maize and other food crops typically were located outside, but near, the compound. Village plans other than the one just described, however, also were used.

Throughout early and middle Fort Ancient time, local differences existed among settlements in material culture and, by implication, other aspects of culture. After AD 1400, how-ever, Fort Ancient material culture became more uniform, the Fort Ancient culture area contracted, and villages tended to be concentrated on or near the Ohio River.

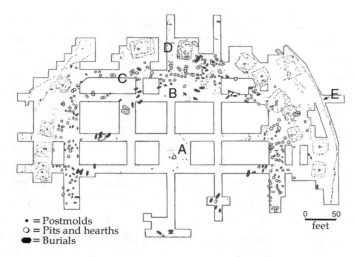

• = Postmolds
○ = Pits and hearths
● = Burials

Figure 28. A map of the Incinerator Site in Dayton, Ohio, showing excavations through 1978. This map illustrates well that form of Fort Ancient village plan that consisted of distinct use areas arranged concentrically around a central plaza. The arrangement that occurred at this site consisted of (A) a central plaza surrounded by (B) a burial ground, (C) storage pits and cooking hearths, (D) residential and other structures, and (E) a wooden stockade. The Incinerator Site is now known as the SunWatch Site. (Adapted from Heilman *et al.*, 1988)

Burial, effigy, and platform mounds were part of the Fort Ancient landscape. Subconical burial mounds were built at Fort Ancient sites until about AD 1300 or 1400. These low mounds were usually located near the central plaza or immediately outside the residential zone of villages. Typically, burial mounds contained multiple interments.

The Fort Ancient people also appear to have constructed effigy mounds. Recently, both of the unequivocal zoomorphic effigy mounds located in Ohio —Alligator Mound and Serpent Mound — have provided radiocarbon dates that place them in early Fort Ancient time, not Adena or Hopewell time. Fort Ancient village sites are located near both of these mounds.

At least one platform mound is known from a Fort Ancient site — the Baum site near Bourneville, Ross County, Ohio.

The name Fort Ancient was applied to this culture because the earliest recognition of its distinctiveness came from sites that were excavated by Warren K. Moorehead and others at the Fort Ancient hilltop enclosure. These sites were located both within the south compound of the earthwork and below the enclosure on the flood plain of the Little Miami River. Moorehead assumed that the occupants of these sites had built the Fort Ancient enclosure, a position shared by William C. Mills of the Ohio Archaeological and Historical Society when, in 1906, he proposed that the name Fort Ancient be adopted for the culture then known from several sites in southwestern Ohio.

Today, the premier site managed for public visitation that interprets Fort Ancient culture is SunWatch Village in Dayton, Ohio, a middle Fort Ancient village that has, in part, been reconstructed in order to more clearly demonstrate Fort Ancient village design and architecture. Fort Ancient culture is, however, represented by other publicly accessible sites such as Fort Ancient, Alligator Mound, Edgington Mound, Serpent Mound, and Voss Mound.

The Cole Culture (about AD 1000 to 1300)

Relatively little is known of the Late Prehistoric Cole people who occupied central Ohio, north of the emerging Fort Ancient culture area, in the upper Scioto and Muskingum drainages around and after AD 1000. The Cole people, like many of their Late Prehistoric contemporaries in and beyond the middle Ohio Valley, did build earthworks — embankments with exterior ditches — at some of their village locations, presumably as protective features. These embankments were utilitarian and adapted to local topography, not geometrically controlled or artistically inspired, and they were sometimes — perhaps always — reinforced with a stockade.

The only publicly accessible site in the middle Ohio Valley attributed to the Cole culture is the Highbanks Park Works at Highbanks Metro Park, a short distance north of Columbus, Ohio.

Institutionalized mound building in the middle Ohio Valley essentially came to an end around AD 1400, during the middle part of the Late Prehistoric period. The reasons for this are unclear, and no explanation is attempted here. The mound-building tradition did continue after AD 1400 among some groups near the middle Ohio Valley, most notably the Mississippian and Protohistoric traditions of the southeastern United States and, to a considerably lesser extent, the Late Prehistoric and Protohistoric traditions of western New York and environs. Protohistoric and Historic Indians did, however, bury some of their dead in Woodland and Late Prehistoric mounds as intrusive interments. Interestingly, this same practice was adopted by some American settlers in the middle Ohio Valley, one consequence of which was the occasional establishment of historic cemeteries near mounds.

Mounds during the Historic Period

The earliest explorers, missionaries, and settlers to enter the Ohio Valley from the European colonies along the Atlantic seaboard described the artificial mounds and earthworks they encountered in the forested land west of the Appalachian Mountains. Some of these mounds were known to be burial features, while the function of others was unknown. Many Indians living in the Ohio Valley at the time that American settlement began late in the eighteenth century had no knowledge of why, or when, the mounds had been built. Once the uninterrupted flow of American settlers into the Ohio Valley began shortly after the end of the Revolutionary War, however, more and more of the prehistoric earthworks became known — the wave of new settlers followed the same water routes and selected many of the same sites for their settlements as had the Adena and Hopewell nearly two millennia earlier.

As the number of American settlements increased and the valley forests were cleared, the number and variety of mounds and earthworks that were discovered expanded to levels that intrigued, perplexed, and amazed informed and curious people of the time. Continuing interest in the mounds led to continued and expanded descriptions, visitations, and explorations, and eventually fostered significant contributions to the development of archeology in North America. Simultaneously, agriculture, urban development, and the construction of reservoirs and transportation facilities obliterated or otherwise obscured much of the prehistoric cultural landscape of the region.

Early American Perception of the Mounds

Most of the early settlers in the Ohio Valley had little or no serious interest in the mounds and earthworks they encountered — but a few did take notice. One of the most enlightened reactions to the mounds and earthworks encountered by the newcomers took place at Marietta, Ohio. In 1788, leaders of the Ohio Company of Associates — just arrived from New England — formally acted to save a large part of the mound and earthworks complex they had found at the site of their new settlement where the Muskingum River joined the Ohio River. The two large rectangular enclosures, the great conical mound, and the graded way leading from the terrace earthworks to the Muskingum River were set aside as public parks. Some parts of the reserve have since given way to other uses but, nonetheless, much of this unusual complex still remains — including one of the best surviving examples of an Adena mound-and-circle, a Hopewell graded way, and two rare Hopewell platform mounds. It is intriguing that the Ohio Company, founders of the first organized American settlement in the Northwest Territory, set such an enlightened precedent in recognizing and valuing the prehistoric earthworks in whose midst they found themselves — and that such precedent was almost totally ignored at most subsequent settlements.

Even before the end of the eighteenth century, some mounds had become popular tourist attractions. Since many mounds and earthworks were located near the rivers, it was an easy matter for travelers to take in the local curiosity while the boat on which they were traveling was tied up at the wharf. Grave Creek Mound, near the Ohio River in what is today Moundsville, West Virginia, was perhaps the most famous of these early river-side attractions (Figure 28, Plate 3).

Figure 29. The Grave Creek Mound as it might have appeared around 1848. Grave Creek was possibly the first instance of a mound being developed as a significant tourist attraction. This figure shows the fence that surrounded the base of the mound, the entrance to the underground museum, the observatory atop the mound, the circular stairway that ascended the outside of the mound, and the general pastoral environment that typified the area during the middle of the nineteenth century. The inset shows the two tunnels and the shaft that were opened when and after the mound was excavated in 1838. (From Squier and Davis, 1848)

Nearly seventy feet high and located on a high terrace looking down on the Ohio River, Grave Creek Mound dominated an important Adena mound and earthwork complex. In 1805, Meriwether Lewis reported finding the initials of numerous travelers carved in trees that were growing on and near the mound. In 1838, in an effort to enhance this mound's appeal to tourists, it was partly excavated and a museum was set up inside the excavation shaft. An observation structure was placed on top later. The museum failed and the observatory was taken down, but the mound remained a center of local attention for any number of reasons until, near the end of the nineteenth century, it was acquired by the State of West Virginia.

Another early reaction of the American settlers to the mounds and earthworks they encountered was to name places after them. Circleville, Ohio, was established within an earthworks complex that contained two concentric circular embankments. Some of the streets of this community were laid out in circles and were given names such as Circle Street and Circle Alley. Moundsville, West Virginia, derived its name from the numerous mounds and earthworks located there. Mount Sterling, Kentucky, reflects the many prominent Adena burial mounds that occurred in and near the settlement. The tendency to name places after the mounds was widespread, was applied to many different elements of the cultural landscape, and continued through the years. Dozens of small towns and large cities in the middle Ohio Valley have a street named Mound or Moundview, Ridgecrest, Adena Drive, Indian Mound, Mound Circle, Mound Terrace, Hopewell, and others obviously derived from the mounds and their builders. There are many mound cemeteries, and among the public parks in the middle Ohio Valley are Mound Park, Indian Mound(s) Park, Mounds State Park, and Woodland Mound Park. Even businesses have adopted such names. The regal Miamisburg Mound overlooks what once was the Atomic Energy Commission's Mound Laboratory, while the telephone directory of Newark, Ohio (nicknamed "Mound City"), contains thirteen businesses using Indian Mound, Mound Builder(s), or Mound City as part of their name.

Even though the Ohio Valley mounds were in the western part of what was the settled frontier of the United States in the early nineteenth century, much of the fascination with these antiquities was among people living in the east. An important part of this interest was nationalistic. The Jeffersonian crusade to convince both Americans and Europeans that

America's natural history, and perhaps even parts of its cultural history, were the equal of Europe's dragged the mounds and earthworks into this campaign of national self-assertion and confidence-building. In these numerous, large, and sometimes complex earthen features was a prehistoric validation of advanced vision, organization, and enduring accomplishment. Daniel Webster, one of the nation's more eloquent senators, had a personal interest in the western antiquities. In 1833, he attended the commencement at Kenyon College in Gambier, Ohio, where he heard a youthful Edwin H. Davis give a graduation address titled "Antiquities of Ohio." Webster encouraged Davis to continue with his interest in this subject. Later, Webster would make a revolutionary proposal that the Newark Earthworks be acquired by the federal government as a national park, and Davis, who became a physician, would help underwrite and coauthor one of the most important pioneering studies in North American archeology.

Most citizens of the Ohio Valley, however, viewed the mounds and earthworks passively and assigned them relatively little importance. Occasionally, cemeteries were established around mounds — which provided a degree of protection because the primary land use presented little physical threat to them. Mounds that have survived because they were incorporated into cemeteries occur at such places as Aurora, Indiana; Shannon, Kentucky; Chester, Fairmount, Piketon, Reily, and Tiltonsville, Ohio; and South Charleston, West Virginia (Figure 30, Plate 11). Other settings that were often safe for mounds included institutional grounds, recreational areas, residential plots, and generally inaccessible sites.

Most of the thousands of mounds and earthworks that were in the Ohio Valley, however, were not protected by location or other serendipitous factors and either have been destroyed or altered to the extent that their identity is lost to all but the most perceptive or informed of observers. Agriculture, inundation by reservoirs, urban and industrial development,

Figure 30. Fairmount Mound, Licking County, Ohio, lies doubly protected adjacent to the Fairmount Cemetery and the Fairmount Presbyterian Church.

and the construction of transportation systems have been responsible for the destruction or degradation of most mounds and earthworks (Figure 31). Excavations by curiosity seekers, looters, and amateur and professional archeologists, too, have altered or destroyed many mounds, especially during the nineteenth century and early part of the twentieth century before modern research methods and objectives and legislative controls were implemented, and public awareness and concern were heightened. Natural and human-induced erosion has also taken its toll on mounds and earthworks.

The Search for the Mound Builders

While settlement spread through and increased in the Ohio Valley, and the antiquities of the region became better known, differing ideas about the origin of the mounds and their builders arose and were discussed, debated, and eventually investigated. Some of the earliest students of mounds, Thomas Jefferson among them, felt that the mounds found

Figure 31. Infirmary Mound, Licking County, Ohio, has been significantly leveled by decades of agriculture and is representative of the many, many mounds and earthworks in the middle Ohio Valley and elsewhere that were significantly altered or destroyed by cultivation and trampling by livestock. Today, this mound, located beneath the arrow in the photograph, is part of Infirmary Mound Park.

throughout the eastern United States were the work of American Indians. Among many Americans of the early nineteenth century, however, were those who perceived the historic Indians as being wild, nomadic, unorganized, and undisciplined. Such people, it was assumed, could never have built structures of the number, size, complexity, and precision that occurred in the Ohio Valley. Surely, if these antiquities had been built by Indians, those Indians must have been more numerous, settled, and organized — more civilized — than the Indians the Americans of the Atlantic Coast had come to know over the previous two centuries. In addition, there was romantic — perhaps nationalistic — appeal in the notion that a true civilization might have existed in America prior to its most recent discovery by the Europeans.

Although all observers did not share these beliefs, there

nonetheless arose widespread feelings during the nineteenth century that the mounds and earthworks had been built either by civilized Indians or by a Lost Race of civilized people of, no doubt, European or Southwest Asian origin. Advocates of the civilized Indian concept believed that the mound builders either must have emigrated voluntarily — perhaps to Mexico to become the Toltecs — or were displaced or destroyed by the ancestors of the historic American Indians. Advocates of the Lost Race idea suffered no shortage of candidates; Vikings, Greeks, Persians, Hindus, Phoenicians, emigrants from Atlantis, and, especially, the Lost Tribes of Israel were all put forth as people who could have brought their civilization to America.

The idea that the mounds owed their origin to a "civilized" people began to receive credible opposition near the middle of the nineteenth century with the combined emergence of critical thought and the collection, organization, and analysis of relevant scientific data. Prominent voices focusing on the problem, albeit for substantially different reasons, included such respected anthropologists and geographers as Albert Gallatin, Samuel G. Morton, Samuel F. Haven, George Perkins Marsh, Frederick Ward Putnam, and John Wesley Powell. The scientifically based death-blow to the idea of "civilized" mound builders, however, came from the investigations of mounds and their contents carried out by the Smithsonian Institution's Bureau of (American) Ethnology under the supervision of Cyrus Thomas between 1881 and 1894. The summary opinion of the archeologists involved with this work was that the widespread prehistoric earthworks had indeed been built by American Indians, and by a number of cultural groups who apparently differed very little from the historic Indians.

Major Studies of the Ohio Valley Mounds

The systematic investigations and descriptions of mounds and earthworks, and their contents, began to appear during the early part of the nineteenth century. These descriptions were important contributions to the growth of knowledge at the time they were prepared, and some are particularly important because they document artifacts that have since been destroyed. Three regional studies conducted during the nineteenth century were especially important in describing, calling attention to, and investigating the origin of the mounds and earthworks of the middle Ohio Valley. The publication of all three of these studies represented milestones in the literature of North American archeology and are recognized as classics in the field.

Caleb Atwater, the postmaster at Circleville, Ohio, was commissioned to prepare a description of the Ohio Valley earthworks by the newly formed American Antiquarian Society located in Worcester, Massachusetts. Atwater's report, published in 1820 under the title *Description of the Antiquities Discovered in the State of Ohio and Other Western States*, often is considered to be the first regional synthesis of an archeological study in the United States. At the time of its publication, Atwater's work was unparalleled in its scope and level of thoroughness in identifying and describing the mounds and earthworks of the middle Ohio Valley.

A quarter century later, Ephraim George Squier, editor of *The Chillicothe Gazette*, and Dr. Edwin H. Davis, a physician, also of Chillicothe, undertook another, more extensive and thorough survey of the mounds and their contents in the eastern part of the Mississippi Valley. Mostly in 1845 and 1846, these men investigated some 150 mounds and 100 earthworks as they gathered information intended for publication in the *Transactions of the American Ethnological Society*. James McBride, Constantine Rafinesque, Charles Whittlesey and other antiquarians of the day made the results of their work available to Squier and Davis for inclusion in the planned volume. Most of the earthworks, and some of the mounds, were surveyed and illustrated. The report grew to an unprecedented size, and in the process outgrew the American Ethnological Society's budget. Consequently, the work was published in 1848 by the Smithsonian Institution under the title *Ancient Monuments of the Mississippi Valley*; this was the first scientific publication of the new Smithsonian Institution.

Part of Squier and Davis's motivation for exploring the mounds was to expand their collection of artifacts and, eventually, to sell some or all of the material collected. After the field work had been completed and the manuscript for *Ancient Monuments of the Mississippi Valley* was being prepared for publication, however, Squier and Davis's friendship ruptured and never healed. Most of the artifacts that had been collected from the mounds stayed with Davis, and he tried for years, unsuccessfully, to sell the collection to an American institution, none of which had sufficient interest in the material, or the money, to purchase it. Finally, in 1864, Davis sold the collection to William Blackmore, an Englishman, who housed the collection in his newly built personal museum in Salisbury, England. In 1931, when Blackmore's museum closed, the collection was transferred to the British Museum, where it remains today.

The third major study of mounds conducted during the nineteenth century was that of the newly formed Bureau of Ethnology, created within the Smithsonian Institution in 1878 and placed under the direction of John Wesley Powell. In 1881, Powell put Cyrus Thomas in charge of the Bureau's archeology program and, using money appropriated by Congress specifically for the purpose, instructed him to investigate the nature of the mound builders in order to put to rest questions about their identity. Thomas sent several field teams into various parts of the eastern half of the United States to survey and excavate representative samples of mounds in the different regions. Several publications resulting from this work were issued during the course of the twelve-year investigation, and the summary report, *Report on the Mound Explorations of the*

Bureau of Ethnology, was issued in 1894. Thomas's report described many mounds and their contents but it also revised many opinions about the identity and relationships of the mound-building cultures and, in doing so, set the archeology of North American mound-building cultures on an entirely new course.

Studies of the mound-building cultures of the middle Ohio Valley during the last century have resulted in the recognition of several different mound-building groups. Most prominent of these are the Adena and Hopewell, but others are represented as well. Other investigations have focused on attempts to find chronological patterns within each of these groups, to document the lifeways of each group, and to determine the relationships among these groups and their antecedents, their contemporaries, and those who came later. Recent research has investigated myriad aspects of the culture, chronology, and relationships among the various mound-building people. Studies directly related to the mounds and earthworks have dealt with the chronology, patterns, and processes of their construction and the various uses to which the different sites were put (Figure 32, Plate 12). Although much progress has been made toward better defining and understanding the mound-building people of the region, much work still remains to be done on such basic questions as the domestic and corporate lifeways, interregional influences, and the origins and demise of the various cultures.

Some Significant Consequences of the Study of Mounds

Investigations of mounds and earthworks have produced some noteworthy impacts on the development of American archeology and the protection and management of American antiquities. The first scientific excavation of an archeological site in the United States is attributed to Thomas Jefferson, who systematically excavated a mound in Virginia in order to an-

Figure 32. The long-term study of Pollock Works by Robert Riordan of Wright State University has provided extended opportunities for students to gain valuable experience in archeological field work while yielding abundant data that can be acquired only over extended periods of research. Riordan's research is particularly focused on understanding the history of construction and use of the Pollock Works. (Photograph by Robert V. Riordan)

swer questions about the manner in which Indians were buried in mounds. General Rufus Putnam, a leader of the settlement at Marietta, Ohio, prepared one of the earliest maps of archeological features when he platted the Marietta Earthworks. When large trees were being removed from upon the mounds in Marietta, the Reverend Manasseh Cutler, another leader of the Marietta settlement, counted the growth rings of these trees in order to approximate the minimum number of years that had elapsed since the Marietta mounds were built. One tree yielded 463 rings, leading Cutler to conclude that the mounds could be no younger than the early fourteenth century. This represented possibly the first recorded attempt in what is now the United States to use tree ring dating to address an archeological problem.

Caleb Atwater's description of many of the major earthworks of Ohio was the first regional synthesis of an archeological problem in the United States, and his report was included in the first volume of the *Transactions and Collections of the American Antiquarian Society.* The Squier and Davis report in 1848 was the first scientific publication of the Smithsonian Institution, the principal institution supported by the United States government dealing with the study of natural history and anthropology, among other fields. This publication set the standard for future publications of the Smithsonian. The Mound Builder Survey directed by Cyrus Thomas was the first major systematic project undertaken by the Bureau of (American) Ethnology. This project, the scientific investigation of the mounds in order to determine who built them, had been selected as the most important question of the day in American archeology by the Bureau's Director, John Wesley Powell.

Largely through the efforts of Frederick Ward Putnam, curator of the Peabody Museum of Archaeology and Ethnology at Harvard University, Serpent Mound was saved from probable destruction. Eventually, this site was given to the Ohio State Archaeological and Historical Society by Harvard University to be used as a public park. The threat to Serpent Mound, made increasingly visible by Putnam's efforts, resulted in the Ohio Legislature passing, in 1888, the first antiquity law in the United States to protect archeological resources. When the ownership of Serpent Mound was transferred to the Ohio State Archaeological and Historical Society, it became one of the first archeological preserves in the United States to be managed for public visitation. This feature and adjacent mounds remain accessible to the public as a result of the society's long term preservation and management efforts. Ohio's antiquity legislation and the creation of Serpent Mound park played a significant role in arousing nationwide interest in passing antiquities legislation and in preserving archeological sites for the public's enjoyment and enlightenment.

Protecting Archeological Resources

Increasingly, archeological resources — sites and the material artifacts and other information they contain — are being viewed as public resources that should be protected and managed in the public interest. On one level, this is true because many people within our society enjoy seeing artifacts, visiting sites, and understanding how, why, and when these records of other cultures were produced. On another level is the opinion that all of society stands to benefit from a clearer, more complete understanding of the past. A more thorough understanding of what has gone before allows present conditions and future prospects to be more realistically appraised.

Much information about the prehistory of the United States has been extracted from the land already. This information has contributed greatly to our current understanding of the past and will certainly provide additional insight with further analysis and revision of thought. A great amount of data, however, is still in the ground in the numerous known and yet to be discovered prehistoric archeological sites. As has been happening for the past four hundred years, these archeological sites are being destroyed regularly — by reservoir construction, mechanization and intensification of agriculture, transportation systems development, and urban sprawl, as well as by natural processes — and with each loss passes information that never can be replaced. Clearly, there is a widespread opinion and sense of urgency that strong steps should be taken to protect as many sites as possible in the public interest.

Important tools for protecting archeological resources are federal and state legislation and local ordinances. Through law, the protection of governments is extended to archeological resources (sites, artifacts, and other associated information) located on lands owned by the respective governments and, with increasing frequency, on other lands that will be altered by the direct activities of, or activities receiving financial or administrative support from, those governments. Beyond protection, some federal legislation also provides extensive support for the identification, investigation, and preservation of archeological resources. Principal pieces of federal legislation that have protected, or supported inventory of, archeological resources are listed in Table 4. Most states now provide some form of legal protection for archeological resources on state-owned lands, and some states have provisions for extending protection to sites on county, municipal, and private lands as well.

At present, essentially all archeological resources on federal, state, and municipal lands are protected by one or more pieces of legislation, as are many sites on privately owned lands, by trespassing and vandalism laws if not otherwise. The typical provision of laws protecting antiquities on public lands is that excavations of protected sites can be conducted only with permits from the regulating agency and that all artifacts and other data from such sites are public property and must be deposited in specified repositories. Disturbing protected sites and possessing artifacts from those sites without the necessary permits are crimes and, increasingly, the various judicial systems are recognizing and supporting the laws that protect antiquities.

Legal protection is only one way of protecting archeological resources and the information they contain. The effectiveness of laws is minimal if the administering and enforcing agencies are underfunded, understaffed, or uncommitted to their mandate. Ultimately, effective protection must come from an informed and supportive public — the public that, reciprocally, is the final beneficiary of the protection provided.

Table 4. Major Federal Legislation Related to the Protection of Archeological Resources

---

1906   **Antiquities Act** – Protects federally-owned sites and provides for proper curation of artifacts and information from federally-owned sites.

1935   **Historic Sites and Buildings Act** – Declares national policy of preserving sites, structures, and objects of national significance.

1960   **Reservoir Salvage Act** – Authorizes salvage recovery of resources threatened with inundation by reservoirs.

1966   **National Historic Preservation Act** – Major legislation which, with amendments and supplements, expands and strengthens the identification, preservation, and management of sites, structures, and places of national, state, and local significance.

1974   **Archaeological and Historic Preservation Act** – Strengthens the salvage recovery of archeological data from sites being altered by land use or construction activities receiving federal support.

1979   **Archaeological Resources Protection Act** –Modernizes the protection and management of archeological resources on federal land.

1990   **Native American Graves Protection and Repatriation Act** – Provides for the possible repatriation of Native human remains and objects of cultural patrimony.

Many archeological sites have been deliberately protected over time by private landowners and stewards of public lands (Figure 33). Threats to the security of protected sites often come about when land ownership changes, when a change of administration of public lands takes place, or when competition for land use develops and choices must be made. Strategies for instituting or continuing the protection of sites that come under stressful conditions have been in operation for years. When the privately owned Grave Creek Mound, the largest Adena burial mound known, was threatened with destruction near the end of the nineteenth century, the citizens of Moundsville, West Virginia, rallied to protect it by obtaining an option to purchase the landmark and then set about raising funds to do so. Their effort failed, but it did delay the planned destruction of the mound until a change of ownership came about. Recent examples of mitigation between conflicting interests in order to preserve and protect mound and earthwork sites have involved Alligator Mound in Granville, Ohio; Stubbs Earthworks in Morrow, Ohio; and Octagon Earthworks in Newark, Ohio (Plate 8).

Figure 33. Reynolds Mound, near Saint Marys, West Virginia, is owned by The Archaeological Conservancy and is representative of those mounds that are deliberately protected while in private ownership.

Transfer of ownership is another way that mounds, earthworks, and other archeological sites have obtained extended protection. Recently, in Ohio, the National Park Service has acquired important sites in the middle part of the Scioto River Valley which it manages under the aegis of Hopewell Culture National Historical Park. The most visible and far-reaching private entity involved with the protection of archaeological sites is The Archaeological Conservancy, a nation-wide organization whose mission is to acquire and protect endangered prehistoric sites. Several sites described in this book are properties owned by The Archaeological Conservancy (Figure 33).

Section II

Publicly Accessible Mounds and Earthworks in the Middle Ohio Valley

Publicly Accessible Mounds and Earthworks in the Middle Ohio Valley

Section II identifies, describes, and provides access information to seventy-three archeological and historical sites in the middle Ohio Valley that are open to visitation or view by the public (Figure 34). Most of the sites included in this section feature mounds or earthworks, but we have also included one flint quarry (Flint Ridge), one reconstructed village (SunWatch), and the estate after which the Adena culture was named (Adena). For each site, we have attempted to describe briefly its history and cultural affiliation, what you can expect to find at the site today, directions for finding the site, and sources of additional information about the site.

With but few exceptions, the name we use for each site is the official site name, the name listed in the respective State Historical Preservation Office site file. When we have departed from this general rule it is either because the property upon which the site is located contains more than one named feature or there is such great disparity between the official name and the familiarity of a popular synonym that we have elected to use the synonym.

The sites included in this section are arranged alphabetically by state and county, and where more than one site occurs in any given county, those sites are arranged by proximity. The sites are mapped on Figure 34 and are listed in Table 5. Table 5 also identifies the page upon which the site description begins.

Many mounds included in this section have not been excavated and their cultural affiliation has not been confirmed. When this circumstance exists for a mound, we attempt to qualify any cultural assignment that we might provide. In the absence of confirming archeological evidence, it is even possible that some mounds might not be authentic prehistoric features. However, we have not knowingly included any mounds in this book that are not prehistoric. Also, many of the mounds identified in this section have experienced some alteration, sometimes significant alteration, during the prehistoric and historic periods. Burrowing rodents, denning foxes, and falling trees have blemished virtually every mound at some period. Erosion has modified others. And among the remaining mounds and earthworks, agricultural practices, urban development, and the construction of transportation facilities have often wrought extreme damage. Some mounds identified in this section show the scars of alteration, whereas others have been restored to what is presumed to be a former condition.

Certain considerations and courtesies are expected of visitors to the mounds and earthworks identified in this section. First and foremost, digging into the features or otherwise disturbing them and removing artifacts is strictly prohibited in all cases by one or more applicable laws. Many of the sites are on private property and, although they can be seen from public space, trespassing is strictly prohibited without permission from the landowner. Walking on the features, unless walkways or stairways are provided, is inconsiderate and should be avoided; mounds and earthworks are scarce and dwindling resources and walking encourages erosion. Lastly, the mounds and earthworks you might be visiting are products of different cultures, yet they are a part of our cumulative cultural landscape; different views might exist about the purpose and significance of these features, but all appreciative and insightful views, and the features themselves, deserve respect.

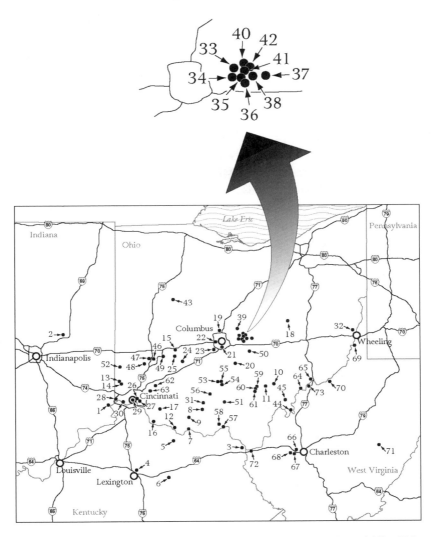

Figure 34. Publicly accessible mounds and earthworks in the middle Ohio Valley that are described in Section II of this book. The names and locations of these numbered sites are provided in Table 5.

Table 5. Publicly Accessible Mounds, Earthworks, and Related Sites in the Middle Ohio Valley

MAP NUMBER	SITE NAME	PAGE NUMBER FOR SITE ACCOUNT
1	River View Cemetery Mounds	101
2	Anderson Mounds	103
3	Ashland Central Park Mounds	107
4	Mount Horeb Earthworks	109
5	Shannon Mound	114
6	Gaitskill Mound	115
7	Island Creek Mound	117
8	Serpent Mound	118
9	Winchester Works Mound	123
10	Hartman Mound and the Wolfes Plains Group	124
11	Straight Mound	129
12	Roadside Mound	130
13	Enyart Mound	132
14	Reily Cemetery Mound	133
15	Enon Mound	134
16	Edgington Mound	136
17	Elk Lick Road Mound	137
18	Porteus Mound	138
19	Highbanks Park Earthworks	140
20	Tarlton Cross Mound	143
21	Indian Mound Park	146
22	Shrum Mound	147
23	Voss Mound	149
24	Indian Mound Reserve	150
25	Orators Mound	155
26	Mariemont Embankment	157
27	Odd Fellows Cemetery Mounds	159
28	Miami Fort	160
29	Norwood Mound	163

continued on page 99

Table 5, continued

MAP NUMBER	SITE NAME	PAGE NUMBER FOR SITE ACCOUNT
30	Shorts Woods Park Mound	165
31	Fort Hill	167
32	Tiltonsville Cemetery Mound	171
33	Alligator Mound	172
34	Infirmary Mound	177
35	Dawes Arboretum Mound	178
36	Fairmount Mound	179
37	Flint Ridge	180
38	Huffman Mound	184
39	Dixon Mound	185
40	Ferris Owen Mound	186
41	Newark Earthworks	187
42	Upham Mound	193
43	Dunns Pond Mound	193
44	Buffington Island Mound 1	195
45	Mound Cemetery Mound	196
46	Calvary Cemetery Enclosure	198
47	SunWatch Village	202
48	Miamisburg Mound	205
49	Wright Brothers Memorial Mound Group	207
50	Glenford Fort	209
51	Piketon Mounds	211
52	Hueston Woods Park Mound	214
53	Adena	216
54	Story Mound	220
55	Hopewell Culture National Historical Park	221
56	Seip Mound	226
57	Portsmouth Mound Park	230
58	Tremper Mound	234
59	Hope Furnace Mound	236
60	Ranger Station Mound	238

continued on page 100

Indian Mounds of the Middle Ohio Valley

Table 5, continued

Map Number	Site Name	Page Number for Site Account
61	Zaleski Methodist Church Mound	239
62	Fort Ancient	241
63	Stubbs Earthworks	246
64	Blennerhassett Island Overlook Mound	251
65	Marietta Earthworks	252
66	South Charleston Mound	258
67	Wilson Mound	261
68	Shawnee Reservation Mound	263
69	Grave Creek Mound	265
70	Reynolds Mound	271
71	Hyer Mound	273
72	Camden Park Mound	275
73	Boaz Mound	277

INDIANA - DEARBORN COUNTY

1. River View
Cemetery Mounds

Near the precipitous edge of the high third terrace, over-looking the junction of Laughery Creek and the Ohio River in southeasternmost Indiana, is a conical mound that, in the early 1930s, Glenn A. Black described as "quite large, 120 feet in diameter and at present 7 feet high. The building of a foun-tain on the apex of the mount undoubtedly removed part of the crest" (p. 205). Black also found evidence that there had been occupation sites in the area around this mound, but he did not conclude that the mound had been built by the people who lived at these sites. Today, this grass-covered and regu-larly mowed mound constitutes the highest point in the River View Cemetery. It is located in Section A.

A second mound is located at the base of the terrace, east of the Lochry Massacre Monument, below Section F of the cemetery. The monument memorializes the ambush and death, in 1781, of a band of Pennsylvania Volunteers enroute to join George Rogers Clark during his campaign against the British garrison at Detroit.

Neither mound appears to have been excavated, and the possibility exists that either or both could be Fort Ancient mounds. Several Fort Ancient sites containing mounds are known to have existed along or near this section of the Ohio River.

Signs direct visitors to interesting and historic sites within the cemetery, including the mounds.

DIRECTIONS: From the intersection of US 50 and SR 56 in Aurora, take SR 56 (becomes Water Street) east, then south, 2.25 miles, then take

East Laughery Creek Road west and immediately bear left to the cemetery entrance, then go west into the cemetery. The larger mound is on the crest of the ridge south of the chapel (Figure 35).

PUBLIC USE: Season and hours: May through October, 7 AM to 7 PM; November through April, 8 AM to 5 PM.

FOR ADDITIONAL INFORMATION: Contact: River View Cemetery Association, SR 56 at Laughery Creek Road, Aurora, IN 47001; 812-926-1496. **Read:** G. A. Black, 1934. "Archaeological survey of Dearborn and Ohio counties."

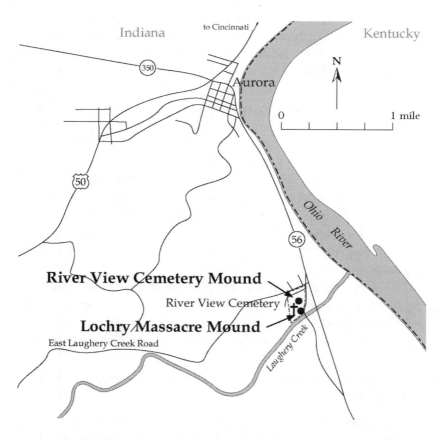

Figure 35. The location of River View Cemetery mounds.

2. Anderson Mounds

Mounds State Park contains an unusual array of mounds and earthworks known as the Anderson Mounds. On a terrace 50 to 60 feet above the White River are 10 structures representing 2 earthworks complexes, a southern group characterized by circular features and a northern group characterized by rectangular features. Some of the individual mounds and earthworks are well preserved and easily discernible; others are, at best, remarkably subtle.

The complex in the southern part of the park (Figure 36) contains the largest of the earthworks, Great Mound. Great Mound is a perfect circle about 300 feet in diameter. An embankment averaging 9 feet in height surrounds an inner ditch of about the same depth. The center of the enclosure is reached by an entranceway on the southeast side which passes through the embankment and across the ditch. A small mound about 45 feet in diameter and 4 feet in height once was located at the center of the inner platform. The park's unusual fiddle-shaped or panduriform earthwork can be seen immediately west of Great Mound. Two small circular enclosures to the southwest and southeast of Great Mound are the only other earthworks in this complex that are visible today. About 0.5 mile upstream in the northern part of the park is the complex of rectangular enclosures, represented today by Circle Mound, a well preserved subrectangular enclosure with an interior ditch. Of the two other rectangular enclosures in the northern complex, one has been destroyed and the other is difficult to see. Other earthworks, although shown on the park's trail guide, are difficult or impossible to locate on the ground.

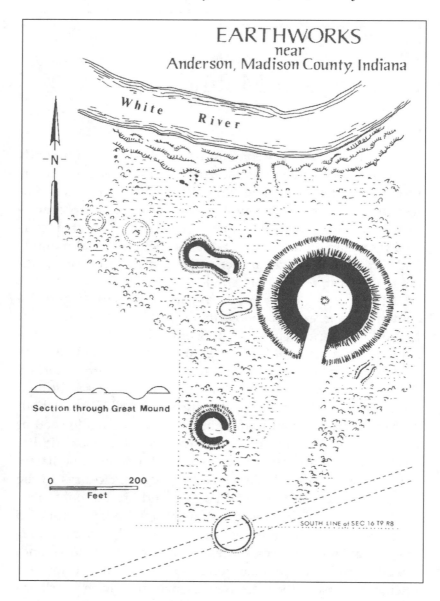

Figure 36. The southern group of the Anderson Mounds as represented in 1937. (From Woodward and McDonald, 1986, after Lilly, 1937)

Archeological investigations at Great Mound have shown that the site probably was occupied over a period of at least 300 years. Around 250 BC, a circular clay floor was created in the center of the platform of Great Mound and 18 upright posts were placed along the north, east, and west sides of this clay floor. These posts were later burned, and a second, and then a third, clay floor was placed over the first. Each of the three prepared floors was covered by a layer of white calcite powder. These superimposed clay floors were covered with a mantle of earth, producing the primary mound. At about AD 50, a log tomb was constructed alongside the primary mound and two interments were made inside — an extended primary burial and a redeposited cremation. The limited grave goods found in this tomb included a platform pipe of Middle Woodland age. Once the tomb was completed, both the tomb and the primary mound were covered with a final layer of earth.

At some time during the early use of this earthwork, more than 400 small posts were placed upright in the ground around the edge of the platform. About 160 BC, the Great Mound embankment was built by excavating a circular ditch and placing the earth outside the ditch. Soon after the construction of Great Mound was started, the panduriform enclosure was built a short distance west of Great Mound. At about the same time that the prepared floors at Great Mound were being used, the subrectangular earthworks to the north were being built.

The Anderson Mounds currently are considered to have begun to take shape during late Adena time, about 250 BC, and to have been in relatively continuous use into Hopewell time, at least to about AD 50. The mounds were used for ceremonial purposes throughout the period of occupation, but the details of use changed with time. The large upright posts that were in place around 250 BC appear to contain alignment markers for some astronomical events, such as the rising and setting points of some bright stars and the Pleiades in addition to serving as markers for the setting sun at the winter and summer solstices and the equinoxes. Confirmation of some of these alignments occur between earthworks in the southern complex while Circle Mound is laid out to record solar alignments. The presence of astronomical alignments supports the idea that the site was used, at least in part, for astronomically based calendric purposes, perhaps as a way to schedule major ritual activities at the site. The wall of posts surrounding the central platform has been considered evidence of a fence or screen that existed to separate the activities taking place within the circle from those on the outside. Not until AD 50 is there evidence of mortuary activity within either the northern or southern complex of Anderson Mounds.

A nature center located near the entrance to the park contains exhibits that include a scale model of the mounds and earthworks along with a timeline of the history of the park, dioramas featuring animals that can be found in the park, and a bird-viewing room. Great Mound and other earthworks of the southern complex are reached by a short walk along trails that begin at the park office. These trails are scenic, well maintained, and traverse relatively level terrain. Circle Mound lies a short distance west of the park road immediately north of the Woodland Shelter, and parking is available nearby. Alternatively, it can be reached by trail from the park office.

DIRECTIONS: Southbound, exit I 69 at Exit 34, go west on SR 32 to SR 232 (Mounds Road), then west on SR 232 to Mounds State Park on north side of road. Northbound, exit I 69 at Exit 26, go north on SR 9 (Scatterfield Road) to SR 232, then east on SR 232 to Mounds State Park (Figure 37).

PUBLIC USE: Season and hours: The park is open year round. **Fee area:** Admission. **Recreational facilities.**

FOR ADDITIONAL INFORMATION: Contact: Park Naturalist, Mounds State Park, 4306 Mounds Road, Anderson, IN 46017; 765-642-6627, *www.state.in.us/dnr*. **Read:** (1) K. D. Vickery, 1970. "Preliminary report on the excavation of the 'Great Mound' at Mounds State Park in

Madison County, Indiana." (2) B. K. Swartz, Jr., 1976. "Mounds State Park." (3) D. R. Cochran, 1992. "Adena and Hopewell cosmology: New evidence from eastcentral Indiana." (4) D. R. Cochran, 1996. "The Adena/Hopewell convergence in east central Indiana."

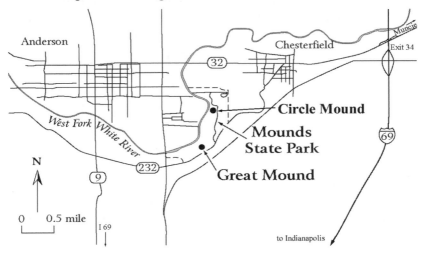

Figure 37. The location of the Anderson Mounds and Mounds State Park.

3. Ashland
Central Park Mounds

A string of six small mounds, each approximately 4 to 5 feet high, is located in the northwest part of Central Park in downtown Ashland. These mounds have not been excavated by archeologists and, consequently, their cultural affiliation is not known.

This cluster of mounds in Central Park contains but a few of the many individual and grouped mounds that once occurred in Ashland on the Ohio River flood plain a short distance downstream from where the Big Sandy River empties into the Ohio. The number, size, shape, and location of these mounds suggest that most or all are of Adena origin, but this part of Kentucky also was within both the Hopewell and the early and middle Fort Ancient culture region. It is not possible, with information now available, to determine which culture was responsible for the Ashland mounds. The Ashland mounds were one of the most extensive prehistoric earthworks along the Ohio River between Moundsville, West Virginia, and Portsmouth, Ohio.

DIRECTIONS: Follow US 60 (12th Street) south from US 23 (Winchester Avenue) in downtown Ashland for about 0.4 mile (5 blocks from Winchester Avenue) to Lexington Avenue, then go east on Lexington Av-

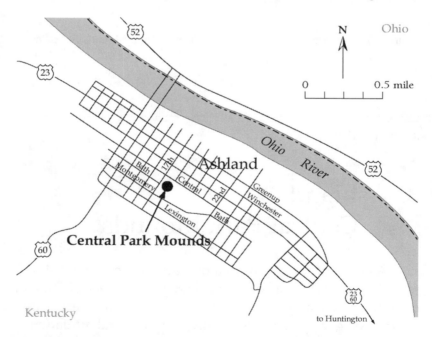

Figure 38. The location of the Ashland Central Park Mounds.

enue 0.5 mile to park entrance on north side of street. Parking is available in the park (Figure 38).

PUBLIC USE: Season and hours: The park is open daily throughout the year during daylight hours.

FOR ADDITIONAL INFORMATION: Contact: Parks and Recreation Department, City of Ashland, P. O. Box 1839, Ashland, KY 41105; 606-327-2046.

4. Mount Horeb Earthworks

The Mount Horeb Earthworks lie in the heart of the Kentucky Blue Grass region immediately south of North Elkhorn Creek. The complex includes two perfect circles, two mounds, and two enclosures — all attributed to the Adena (Figure 39). The larger perfect circle is the centerpiece of the University of Kentucky's Adena Park; the other earthworks are located on private property. Although these sites are combined here into a single complex, all were not necessarily in use at the same time.

The jewel of the group is Mount Horeb Site 1, a perfect circle situated on a bank 75 feet above North Elkhorn Creek in what is today Adena Park. This feature consists of a circular central platform, a surrounding ditch with an outside embankment, and an entrance that faces to the west. The central platform and the entrance causeway occupy the natural surface of the land. The platform is about 105 feet in diameter, the ditch about 45 feet wide, and the embankment 12 to 14 feet

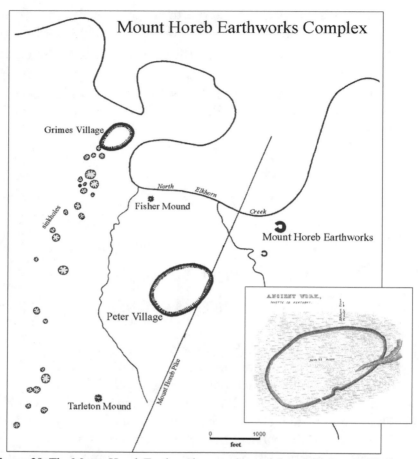

Figure 39. The Mount Horeb Earthworks complex and (inset) the Peter Village enclosure as portrayed by Rafinesque. (After Clay, 1985; inset from Squier and Davis, 1848)

across at the base. The entrance is 33 feet wide. No mound was built on the platform of this enclosure.

Excavation by the Works Progress Administration in 1939 revealed that a wooden structure once stood on the central platform. Paired post holes, with all holes aligned on a single arc rather than pairs arranged at right angles to the arc of the circle, formed a circle 97 feet in diameter. This circle lacked apparent passageways, and no evidence was found that the structure was roofed or that it contained benches or poles in the interior. William S. Webb, director of the excavation, felt that the discovery of the structure represented the most important result of the excavation. Webb was uncertain about the probable function of the structure, but he contemplated that it most likely represented the ceremonial or social center of one clan which, he presumed, lived near the site.

At least five other Adena sites lie close to the large Mount Horeb circle. These include Grimes Village, Peter Village, Tarleton Mound, Fisher Mound, and the smaller circle (Figure 39). Grimes Village and Peter Village were surrounded by earthen enclosures that were mapped by Constantine Rafinesque in 1820 and published in Squier and Davis as Plate XIV, figures 3 and 4.

Rafinesque described the Peter Village enclosure as being a 20-sided polygon (his term was "icosogonal") 3,767 feet in length. The embankment was bordered on the outside by a ditch about 15 feet wide and 4 to 8 feet deep. One narrow opening faced to the south. The enclosure occupied high ground between two tributaries of North Elkhorn Creek.

R. Berle Clay of the University of Kentucky excavated part of the ditch, bank, and interior space of Peter Village in 1983. He found remains of a stockade that had been built around 310 BC; subsequently this stockade decayed, and part of it burned. Afterwards, the earthen embankment had been built over the former location of the stockade. The site apparently was abandoned about 190 BC, after some 100 years of use. Clay considered the Peter Village enclosure to represent the earliest stage of Adena earthwork construction.

Relatively little evidence of cultural activity within the enclosure was found, and what was found suggested that the space was used temporarily and for specialized purposes only. Perhaps most noteworthy among the objects recovered was the proportionately high number of pieces of barite and galena. The barite was available locally, and both minerals were used to make several types of tools. Some of the pieces had been modified into forms suggestive of atlatl weights. The collective evidence found, along with the absence of certain other types of evidence, led Clay to interpret the site as one where specialized craftsmanship, focusing on the barite and galena, took place. From Peter Village, according to his interpretation, the minerals entered, or were returned to, the Adena exchange network.

References to the Mount Horeb Earthworks complex, and especially the larger perfect circle, had made their way into print as early as 1824, and the site continued to receive notice through the nineteenth century. By 1910, there was growing sentiment that the perfect circle should be acquired by either the state or local governments and set aside as a public park. Colonel Bennett H. Young advocated this position when he wrote:

> . . . *so that at least one of the great earthworks of Kentucky, constructed with such beautiful and symmetrical proportions, may be preserved for all time to come. Thickly set with bluegrass, with clay embankments and gate, it is an earthwork that may be preserved in its present state, with a slight degree of care, for thousands of years to come* (Webb, 1941: 144).

In 1936, the site, with 6 acres surrounding it, was purchased by private contributions and transferred to the Kentucky Archaeological Society. Today, the property is owned by the University of Kentucky and maintained for day use by the university's faculty, staff, and students and their families.

DIRECTIONS: Exit I 75 at exit 120 onto Iron Works Pike, go east on Iron Works Pike 2.7 miles to Mount Horeb Road, then north on Mount Horeb Road 2.2 miles to UK Adena Park on east side of road. Exit I 64/75 at exit 115, go north on SR 922 2.25 miles to Iron Works Pike, then east on Iron Works Pike 0.2 mile to Mount Horeb Road, then continue as above (Figure 40).

PUBLIC USE: Season and hours: Open year round, by reservation, to students and employees of the University of Kentucky. Persons not affiliated with the university should obtain permission to enter the park from the Campus Recreation Department. Park closes at 10 PM. **Fee area:** $10.00 deposit is required to obtain the gate key. **Restrictions:** Driving or parking on the earthworks, and trespassing on the park, is prohibited.

FOR ADDITIONAL INFORMATION: Contact: Campus Recreation Department, University of Kentucky, Seaton Building, Room 145, Lexington, KY 40506-0219; 859-257-2898. **Read:** (1) W. S. Webb, 1941. "Mt. Horeb Earthworks, site 1 and the Drake Mound, site 11, Fayette County, Kentucky." (2) R. B. Clay, 1985. "Peter Village 164 years later: 1983 excavations." (3) R. B. Clay, 1988. "Peter Village: An Adena enclosure."

Figure 40. The location of the Mount Horeb Earthworks.

5. Shannon Mound

Shannon Mound (Plate 11) is located on the ridge line, near the summit, of a promontory of the Interior Low Plateau drained by two branches of Shannon Creek. The mound is conical in profile and oval in outline; it is about 8 to 10 feet high and 100 feet in diameter along the greater axis of its base. The north end of the mound, perhaps an additional 15 to 20 feet of diameter, is missing. This feature is located on the west side of US 62 in the older part of Shannon Cemetery, immediately north of the Shannon Methodist Church, and about 1 mile southwest of the small community of Shannon. Historic burials have been made into the mound. The cultural affiliation of this mound has not been determined.

DIRECTIONS: From the intersection of US 62 and SR 596 in Shannon,

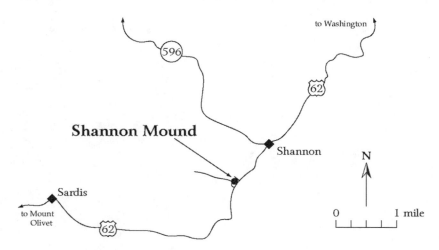

Figure 41. The location of Shannon Mound.

114

go south on US 62 for 1 mile to Shannon Cemetery. The mound is on the west side of the road, prominently visible in the cemetery (Figure 41).

PUBLIC USE: Season and hours: The mound may be viewed from US 62 at all times.

6. Gaitskill Mound

Gaitskill Mound, one of many Adena burial mounds that once occurred in and around Mount Sterling, is a broad, oblong mound measuring some 12 to 15 feet high (Figure 8). The diameter of its base varies from about 100 feet along the shorter axis to 150 feet along the longer axis. The eastern end of the feature has been truncated and converted to a parking lot, and the entire surface is irregular, possibly reflecting a history of exploration, uprooted trees, or other forms of disturbance without restoration of the surface contours. The mound is grass covered and regularly mowed.

This mound has been partly excavated. Among the artifacts recovered were two Adena engraved tablets, one made of clay and another of stone (Figure 14). Both tablets showed accumulations of red pigment in the engraved side, a circumstance that gave rise to the interpretation that the Adena might have used tablets to transfer graphic motifs onto clothing or skin, perhaps for tattooing.

DIRECTIONS: Exit I 64 north of Mount Sterling at exit 110, go south on US 460 / SR 11 0.15 mile to Indian Mound Drive, go west on Indian Mound Drive 0.15 mile to Kentucky Historical Society marker on south side of road. Gaitskill Mound lies immediately southwest of the high-way marker adjacent to the private business parking area (Figure 42).

PUBLIC USE: Season and hours: The mound may be viewed from public space at any time. **Restrictions:** The Gaitskill Mound is on private property and trespassing is strictly prohibited.

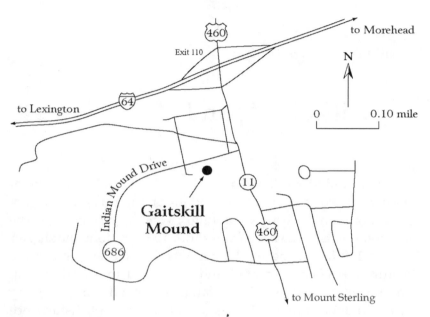

Figure 42. The location of Gaitskill Mound.

OHIO - ADAMS COUNTY

7. Island Creek Mound

Island Creek Mound is located south of US 52 a short distance east of Manchester on the second terrace of the Ohio River. The mound is about 5 feet high and presently is covered with trees and undergrowth.

Island Creek Mound has not been formally excavated and its cultural affiliation is unknown. At the time of initial American settlement in this region, an Adena circle reportedly existed near this mound, but a Fort Ancient village also is known to have existed in the vicinity.

DIRECTIONS: On US 52, go east from the Manchester High School 0.25 mile, then enter the boat launch grounds on the south side of US 52, then go to the east end of the parking area. The mound is at the northeast corner of the parking area (Figure 43).

PUBLIC USE: The mound may be viewed from the parking area at any time.

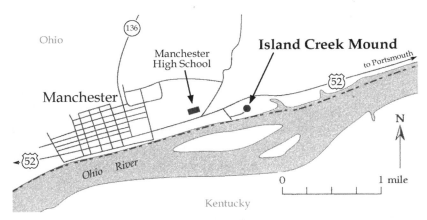

Figure 43. The location of Island Creek Mound.

117

OHIO - ADAMS COUNTY

8. Serpent Mound

Serpent Mound and three burial mounds are located on Serpent Mound State Memorial, a property of the Ohio Historical Society. Largest of all effigy mounds in North America, Serpent Mound is perhaps the best known example of the mound builders' work in the middle Ohio Valley. Writhing across a level ridge top more than 100 feet above Ohio Brush Creek on the very eastern margin of the Interior Low Plateau province, the total length of the serpent is around 1,348 feet — approximately one-quarter mile (Figure 44). The serpent was built by first laying out a pattern made of stones. Yellow clay then was placed over the stones and that, in turn, was covered with soil sufficient to bring the finished structure to a height of 4 to 5 feet. The greater part of the body has an average breadth of about 20 feet at the base. A short trail leads along the full length of the mound, and an observation tower 25 feet high provides a rewarding oblique view from about midway along the serpent's body.

Serpent mound has given rise to a rich, diverse, and dynamic body of folk and scientific lore — there is no shortage of thoughts about how the effigy came to exist or, perhaps more importantly, why. At one time this earthen serpent was considered by some people with Christian affinity to be a mark of God that indicated the location of the Garden of Eden and served as a reminder of His moral authority. Today, New Age pilgrims find power and enlightenment, traditional views revere unrevealed distant purpose and perspective, and others seek meaning in geometric relationships between mounds and astronomical concurrences. Does the viewer see the serpent

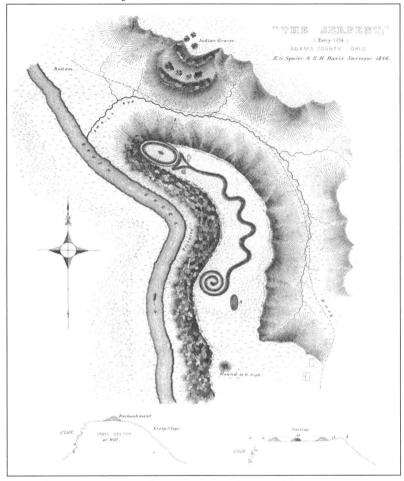

Figure 44. Serpent Mound. (From Squier and Davis, 1848)

from above, or from the side?

Mysterious and elusive meanings aside, literal interpretations of the effigy agree that the mound does indeed represent a serpent. There is no consensus, though, on the shape and intended meaning of the head. Some views hold that the serpent is carrying an egg or that it is about to catch a frog. Others see enough detail to make the serpent into a dragon, or a snake with its tongue extended. Perhaps the most prevalent contemporary opinion is that it represents an open-mouthed, striking snake — a venomous snake, given the relatively wide head — as seen from above. Visitors to Serpent Mound can gain a bird's-eye view of the effigy from atop the observation tower and personally explore the misty world of motivation and explanation. But, the visitor should also look at the mound from ground level, perhaps low and from behind, or low and from the front, to explore other perspectives that might have been part of the effect desired by the creators of this effigy.

Part of Serpent Mound was excavated from 1887 to 1889 by Frederick Ward Putnam, Curator of Archaeology and Ethnology at Harvard University's Peabody Museum. The mound became especially well known after Putnam's collections from the site were exhibited at the World's Columbian Exposition in 1893. Less well known is Putnam's successful campaign to preserve the serpent. When the mound was about to be sold and thus faced almost certain destruction, Putnam managed to raise $5,880 by private subscription in Boston. The mound was purchased with this money in 1887 and then given in trust to the Peabody Museum. In recognition of Putnam's efforts at preservation, the Ohio legislature, in 1888, passed the nation's first state law for the protection of archeological sites. Nationwide interest in the coiling snake effigy led to programs across the country for the preservation of archeological sites as state or national parks. In 1900, Harvard deeded the effigy to the State of Ohio, stipulating that it be preserved and always open to the public. It became one of Ohio's first state memorials.

For more than a century following Putnam's excavation, Serpent Mound was thought to have been built by the Adena because burial mounds attributed to the Adena were located near the effigy. In 1991, however, excavations adjacent to Putnam's work area located charcoal from below the mound that yielded a radiocarbon-based age of AD 1030 for the mound. This date, representing the earliest date that the mound could have been constructed, is much too late for the mound to be Adena, but it does fall within the range of time for both the Fort Ancient people and the effigy mound-building people of the northern Mississippi Valley. Given that serpents were an important part of the symbolism of early historic Algonquian people, and the belief by some ethnologists and archeologists that some Algonquian groups were descendents of Fort Ancient people, Serpent Mound is now tentatively considered to be a product of the Fort Ancient farmers — some of whom maintained a village immediately south of the mound. One of the nearby burial mounds, the one often referred to as the elliptical mound, is also considered to be Fort Ancient in origin. The other two burial mounds are considered to be Adena.

The area including and immediately surrounding Serpent Mound is of some geologic importance, for the serpent was constructed on an unusual cryptoexplosion structure. A nearly circular geologic feature with a diameter of 4.5 to 5 miles, the cryptoexplosion structure is extensively faulted as a result of one or more powerful underground explosions of gas that occurred some 200 million years ago. This explosion drove the plug of near-surface rocks upward at least 1,000 feet.

The site museum contains exhibits on the archeology of Serpent Mound as well as the unique geology of the area. A diorama of the construction of the Serpent and a model of an Adena burial mound are prominent among the exhibits.

DIRECTIONS: From Locust Grove follow SR 73 north 4 miles to park entrance on north side of highway. From Hillsboro, follow SR 73 south 18 miles to park entrance (Figure 45).

PUBLIC USE: Season and hours: *Grounds*: 9:30 AM to 8 PM daily, Memorial Day through Labor Day; 10 AM to 5 PM daily, remainder of the year; closed Thanksgiving, Christmas, and New Year's Day. *Museum:* 10 AM to 5 PM, April to end of May and Labor Day through end of October; 9:30 AM to 5 PM daily, Memorial Day through Labor Day;

closed November through Memorial Day. **Fee area:** Parking only. **Food service. Recreational facilities.**

FOR ADDITIONAL INFORMATION: Contact: Ohio Historical Society, 1982 Velma Avenue, Columbus, OH 43211; 1-800-686-1535, *www.ohiohistory.org*. **Read:** (1) F. W. Putnam, 1890. "The Serpent Mound of Ohio." (2) E. O. Randall, 1905. *The Serpent Mound, Adams County, Ohio.* (3) C. C. Willoughby, 1919. "The Serpent Mound of Adams County, Ohio." (4) R. C. Glotzhober and B. T. Lepper, 1994. *Serpent Mound: Ohio's Enigmatic Effigy Mound.* (5) R. V. Fletcher and others, 1996. "Serpent Mound: A Fort Ancient icon?" (6) M. C. Hansen, 1998. "The Serpent Mound disturbance." (7) B. T. Lepper, 1998. "Great Serpent." (8) W. F. Romain, 2000. *Mysteries of the Hopewell*, pp. 233-253. (9) B. T. Lepper, 2001. "Saving the Serpent."

Figure 45. The location of Serpent Mound.

OHIO - ADAMS COUNTY

9. Winchester Works Mound

Winchester Works Mound is located a short distance north of Winchester atop the crest of a broad ridge overlooking two tributaries of the West Fork of Ohio Brush Creek. The mound is covered with a dense growth of trees and brush at this time, a condition that provides the easiest method for identifying the structure but which prevents any realistic appreciation of its size. Three large, broadly U-shaped embankments were located to the south and west of this mound on the same upland surface, but these have been destroyed by cultivation and road construction. The cultural affiliation of this mound is not known.

DIRECTIONS: From Winchester, go north on SR 136; after crossing the railroad track on the north side of Winchester, go 1.2 miles to the mound (Figure 46).

PUBLIC USE: This mound may be viewed from SR 136 at any time. **Restrictions:** Winchester Works Mound is on private property and trespassing is prohibited.

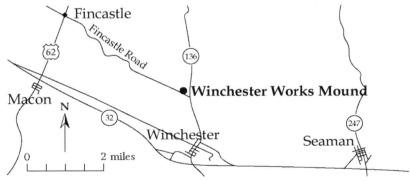

Figure 46. The location of Winchester Works Mound.

10. Hartman Mound and the Wolfes Plains Group

Within the hilly uplands of the western Appalachian Plateau, in the valley of the Hocking River, is an unusual level surface encompassing approximately 3 square miles. This place is known as Wolfes Plains, or The Plains, and it was formed by the deposition of glacial outwash sediments carried away from the ice front by meltwater during the Illinoian or Wisconsinan glaciations. Such broad expanses of level ground are rare in the unglaciated parts of Ohio.

Between about 300 BC and AD 200, Wolfes Plains was occupied by Adena Indians who built there one of the largest concentrations of their burial mounds and circles (Figure 47). Most mound and circle construction at this site is considered to have taken place during late Adena time. At least 2 dozen burial mounds and 8 circles are known to have existed on Wolfes Plains, but, as elsewhere, most of these features have been destroyed and the survivors are disappearing. Those that remain are in various stages of preservation and provide both a record of this important complex as well as — instructively — the processes that continue to destroy it. Six burial mounds and one sacred circle remain wholly or partially intact within the village of The Plains. At least 3 other mounds and 1 circle are known to exist in the surrounding areas.

The largest and best preserved of the Wolfes Plains Group is the Hartman Mound, also known as the George Connett Mound. This mound is 40 feet high and 140 feet in diameter at the base. It has never been excavated properly, although at least three unauthorized explorations are known to have taken place, the most recent in 1997. A smaller mound, about 6 feet

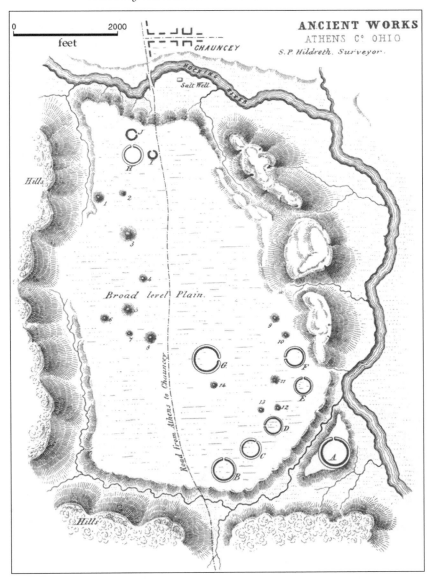

Figure 47. The mounds and circles of Wolfes Plains as portrayed by Squier and Davis, based on a sketch by S. P. Hildreth completed in 1836. Several problems exist with this map: some clusters were rotated relative to others, some structures were omitted, and some features were simply misplaced. (From Squier and Davis, 1848)

high, was once located near the Hartman Mound. It was excavated by E. B. Andrews, who in 1875 and 1876 supervised the first survey of archeological sites in the Hocking Valley. In this mound, Andrews discovered a log tomb with a skeleton surrounded by 500 rolled copper beads. There was also a copper tubular block-ended pipe in this smaller of the George Connett Mounds, the only such artifact of its type ever found in an Adena burial. The surviving Hartman Mound is situated on a small privately owned tract of land within the Adena Park housing development.

A second well preserved mound is the largest of what was a cluster of three mounds called the Woodruff Connett Mounds (Figure 48). This conical mound is 15 feet high and 90 feet in diameter at the base. The second largest of the group was 6 feet high and 40 feet in diameter; it is now discernible as a mere swell in the ground. The third has been destroyed completely. These mounds are owned by the Athens County Historical Society and Museum and are being maintained as open green space.

Figure 48. Woodruff Connett Mound, the one well-preserved mound of three that once constituted the Woodruff Connett Mounds, in the northern part of The Plains.

Dorr Mound 1, reported by Squier and Davis to have been 15 feet high, is presently cultivated as part of a cornfield, while Dorr Mound 2 (10 feet high according to Squier and Davis) is within a fenced chicken yard. Both of these mounds have been excavated, but no reports of findings exist.

Martin Mound 2 is a small, crescent-shaped mound from which a child's skeleton was excavated. This mound is discernible from West First Street. Martin Mound 1 was 18 feet high before most of it was leveled in 1875 to provide an elevated site for a schoolhouse. Excavation caused excitement among the village residents when a piece of buckskin clothing with copper beads was discovered. The dress was torn in pieces so everyone could have a sample. A residence whose base is slightly but noticeably higher than adjacent buildings now occupies the site of Martin Mound 1 on the west side of SR 682 between West First Street and Connett Road.

Armitage Mound was originally 7 feet high and 100 feet in diameter. It is reduced in size today as a result of long agricultural use.

Among the mounds of The Plains that have been destroyed was the large Beard (Baird, or Coon) Mound, whose excavation by Emerson F. Greenman resulted in one of the earlier treatises on Adena culture. This mound was 30 feet high and 114 feet in diameter at the base. The mound was subsequently destroyed by road building; its site is occupied, in part, by The Plains volunteer fire department.

DIRECTIONS: Exit US 33 at SR 682 (The Plains exit), go south on SR 682 about 0.25 mile into The Plains to Mound Street, then go west on Mound Street about 0.1 mile to Hartman Mound, located immediately north of Mound Street. Figure 49 shows the location of Hartman Mound and the other burial mounds and circles in The Plains.

PUBLIC USE: Season and hours: All of the extant mounds and circles can be viewed from public roads at any time. **Restrictions:** All of the extant mounds and circles are on private property, and trespassing is prohibited.

FOR ADDITIONAL INFORMATION: Contact: Athens County Historical Society and Museum, 65 North Court Street, Athens, OH 45701; 740-592-2280, *www.frognet.net/~achsm*. **Read:** (1) E. B. Andrews, 1877. "Report of exploration of mounds in southeastern Ohio." (2) E. F. Greenman, 1932. "Excavation of the Coon Mound and an analysis of the Adena Culture." (3) J. L. Murphy, 1989. *An Archeological History of the Hocking Valley.* (4) N. B. Greber, 1991. "A study of continuity and contrast between central Scioto Adena and Hopewell sites." (5) E. M. Abrams, 1992. "Archaeological investigations of the Armitage Mound (33At434), The Plains, Ohio." (6) E. M. Abrams, 1992. "Woodland settlement patterns in the southern Hocking River Valley, southeastern Ohio."

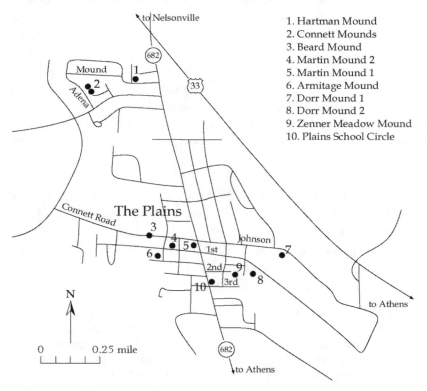

1. Hartman Mound
2. Connett Mounds
3. Beard Mound
4. Martin Mound 2
5. Martin Mound 1
6. Armitage Mound
7. Dorr Mound 1
8. Dorr Mound 2
9. Zenner Meadow Mound
10. Plains School Circle

Figure 49. The location of Hartman Mound and selected other mounds and circles in The Plains.

OHIO - ATHENS COUNTY

11. Straight Mound

Straight Mound, also known as New Marshfield Mound, Stright Mound, and Dunn Mound, is a conical Adena burial mound located in a commercial campground on the picturesque Appalachian Plateau of southeastern Ohio. The mound, now approximately 7 feet high and 60 feet in circumference, is situated near the top of a gently arching ridge that divides the headwaters of Coal Run and Mud Lick Run, both tributaries of Raccoon Creek. The surrounding field was cultivated for several years. The mound is now grass-covered and mowed, and its shape, somewhat flattened by tilling, is easily discernible. A level terrace that borders the mound to the northwest suggests that a smaller secondary mound might have been present at one time.

The mound was partly excavated in 1940 by sinking a vertical shaft from the top. A nearly complete skeleton of an adult male was encountered at a depth of about two feet; apparently this body had been interred in the flesh, extended, facing upward. A number of grave goods were found associated with this skeleton. Nineteen fossils exotic to the region, consisting of brachiopods and shark teeth, were found in a narrowly circumscribed area of the plow zone atop the level terrace northwest of the mound.

DIRECTIONS: Exit US 33 onto SR 682 either northwest of Athens (if southbound) or in southern Athens (if northbound). Take SR 682 to SR 56, go west on SR 56 to CR 6, then go south on CR 6 through the community of New Marshfield to CR 8, then go west on CR 8 for about 1.0 mile to Roundhouse Road, then go south on Roundhouse Road 0.1 mile to the campground entrance. The mound is immediately north of the campground road (Figure 50).

PUBLIC USE: Season and hours: The mound may be viewed from CR 8 at any time. Indian Mound Campground is open from April through November.

FOR ADDITIONAL INFORMATION: Contact: Indian Mound Campground, 7896 Roundhouse Road, New Marshfield, OH 45766; 740-664-8700, *www.indianmound.com*. **Read:** J. N. McDonald, 1989. "A collection of fossils from an Adena mound in Athens County, Ohio, and notes on the collecting and uses of fossils by Native Americans."

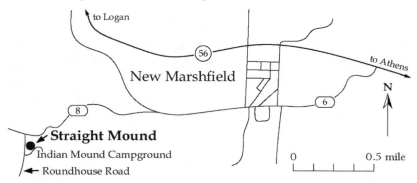

Figure 50. The location of Straight Mound.

OHIO - BROWN COUNTY

12. Roadside Mound

Roadside Mound, a subconical structure about 4 feet high and 40 feet in diameter at the base, is located in Stivers Memorial Park, between RULH Elementary School and Maplewood Cemetery, in the riverside village of Ripley. The mound is situated on an upper terrace about 0.25 mile east of the Ohio River. It is mostly covered with grass, which is regularly mowed. A spruce tree is growing on its summit. This mound is not known to have been excavated.

DIRECTIONS: From the intersection of US 62/68 and US 52 in Ripley, go east on US 52/62/68 0.3 mile to Stivers Memorial Park on the east side of the road (Figure 51).

PUBLIC USE: This mound is visible from US 52/62/68 at all times.

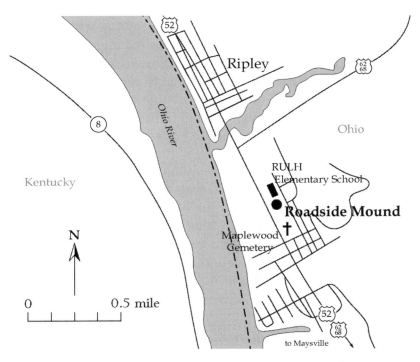

Figure 51. The location of Roadside Mound.

13. Enyart Mound

When J. P. MacLean conducted a survey of the archeological resources of Butler County in 1878 or 1879, he described a 6-foot-high mound situated on the highest point of a bluff overlooking Indian Creek and the town of Reily. MacLean estimated that cultivation had probably reduced the mound to half of its original height by the time that he recorded it. Cultivation continued, and by 1969, when it was recorded by the US Army Corps of Engineers, Enyart Mound was only 2.8 feet high.

Enyart Mound, also known as Enyarts Mound, is now a part of the 135-acre Indian Creek Preserve, a property of MetroParks of Butler County. In 1971, the mound was partly excavated but the evidence retrieved was not sufficient to determine the cultural affiliation of the feature. Miami University directed the reconstruction of the mound, in 1976, to a height of 6 feet. The mound occupies a cleared area in a regenerating forest, and it is mowed regularly.

DIRECTIONS: From SR 732 in Reily, go west on Stillwell Road / Springfield Road 0.6 mile to Indian Creek Preserve, enter the preserve and park at the picnic shelter, and walk about 0.25 mile to the mound as directed (Figure 52).

PUBLIC USE: Season and hours: The preserve is open daily, sunrise to 9 PM, or otherwise as posted. **Fee area:** Admission.

FOR ADDITIONAL INFORMATION: Contact: MetroParks of Butler County, 2200 Hancock Avenue, Hamilton, OH 45011; 1-877-727-5836.

14. Reily Cemetery Mound

The Reily Cemetery Mound is located in the southeast corner of Reily Cemetery, southwest of the village of Reily. There is no record that this mound has been excavated. It is presently covered with grass and mowed regularly. The mound is about 5 feet high.

DIRECTIONS: From SR 732 in Reily, go west on Stillwell Road 0.1 mile to Peoria-Reily Road, then go west on Peoria-Reily Road 0.3 mile to Reily Cemetery on the south side of the road (Figure 52).

PUBLIC USE: Reily Cemetery is open to the public daily from dawn to dusk.

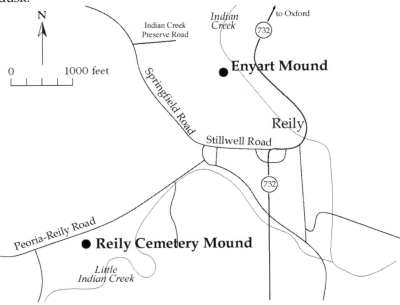

Figure 52. The location of Enyart and Reily Cemetery mounds.

15. Enon Mound

Enon Mound, also known as Knob Prairie Mound, Prairie Knob Mound, Engle Park Mound, and Adena Mound, is a large, well preserved, and conveniently displayed mound. Although presumed to be Adena based on size, shape, and location, the actual cultural affiliation of this mound appears to be undetermined. This mound has been reported to be as much as 49 feet high and some 180 feet in diameter at the base, but the dimensions given on its nomination for the National Register of Historic Places (1972) describe it as being 27.5 feet high and 110 feet in diameter. The mound is owned by the Village of Enon and it occupies a fenced tract of about 1 acre in the center of a residential district called Indian Mound Estates. In years past a horse racing track encircled the mound, but today automobiles drive around the structure on Mound Circle Drive.

It is not known for certain that this mound has been excavated, but local tradition maintains that it was explored late in the nineteenth century at which time a stone altar was found at some depth near the center of the mound. Another version of the event is that material was planted in the mound at about this same time. Yet one more story involving this structure holds that, in 1780, George Rogers Clark used the mound as an observation tower prior to his attack on the Shawnee village of Picawey about 2 miles to the north. Whatever the validity of these stories, collectively they represent a good example of the lore that has grown up around many mounds and earthworks during the past two centuries.

DIRECTIONS: Exit I 70 at Exit 48 (via SR 4 if eastbound) onto Enon Road, go south about 1 mile to Enon, then northeast on Main Street 0.3 mile, then southeast on Indian Drive 0.05 mile to the mound. Mound Circle is one-way to the right. Curbside parking is available on Mound Circle (Figure 53).

PUBLIC USE: Season and hours: Enon Mound is visible from Mound Circle at all times.

FOR ADDITIONAL INFORMATION: Contact: Village of Enon, 363 East Main Street, Enon, OH 45323; 937-864-7870.

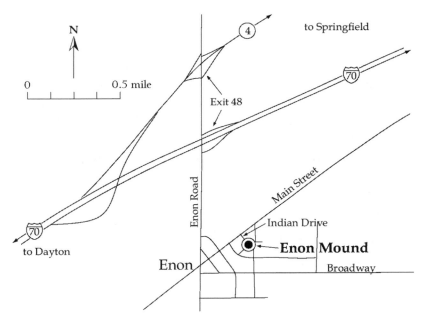

Figure 53. The location of Enon Mound.

16. Edgington Mound

Edgington Mound, also known as Adomeit Mound and the Neville Mound, is located 1 mile east of Neville, about 200 feet south of US 52, on the second terrace of the Ohio River. The mound is 16 feet high and 113 feet in diameter at the base. A commemorative plaque is located immediately west of the mound. The area around the plaque is mowed, but the remainder of the site has grown up in tall grasses and other herbs. The site is privately owned by The Archaeological Conservancy and is open to the public only with the written permission of the conservancy.

This mound has never been excavated, but its cultural affiliation is likely Fort Ancient. It is adjacent to a Fort Ancient village, and shell-tempered pottery has been found at groundhog burrows on its summit.

DIRECTIONS: This mound is located 1 mile east of downtown Neville, about 200 feet south of US 52, immediately east of Indian Mound Campground. The mound is not on campground property (Figure 54).

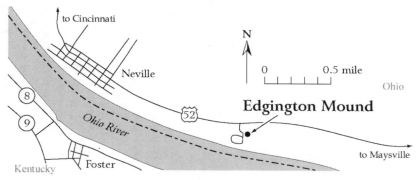

Figure 54. The location of Edgington Mound.

PUBLIC USE: Restrictions: This mound is located on private property. Trespassing is strictly prohibited.

FOR ADDITIONAL INFORMATION: Contact: The Archaeological Conservancy, 5301 Central Avenue, Suite 402, Albuquerque, NM 87108; 505-266-1540.

OHIO - CLERMONT COUNTY

17. Elk Lick Road Mound

Elk Lick Road Mound, also known as Evans Mound, is located in a fenced enclosure adjacent to the picnic grounds in the southern part of East Fork State Park. The small subconical mound is approximately 5 feet high and 50 feet in diameter. It is presently covered with brush and young trees.

This structure has never been excavated and its cultural affiliation is unknown.

DIRECTIONS: From SR 125 at Bantam, go north into East Fork State Park on Park Road 1 for 1 mile, then north on Park Road 2 for 0.25 mile, then go east into the picnic area. The mound is in the fenced tract west of the parking area (Figure 55).

PUBLIC USE: Season and hours: The park is open year round during daylight hours.

FOR ADDITIONAL INFORMATION: Contact: Division of Parks and Recreation, 1952 Belcher Drive, C-3, Columbus, OH 43224; 614-265-6561, *www.dnr.state.oh.us.*

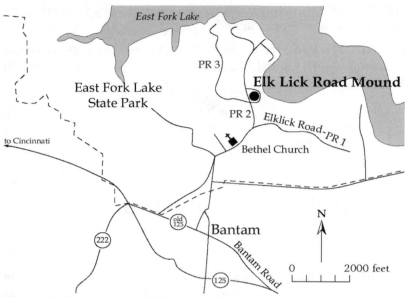

Figure 55. The location of Elk Lick Road Mound.

OHIO - COSHOCTON COUNTY

18. Porteus Mound

The Porteus Mound is located south of Coshocton on the second terrace of the Muskingum River and about 100 feet east of the precipitous edge of the terrace. County Road 271 passes between the mound and the bluff, and when the road was widened in the early 1980s a portion of the west side of the mound was removed. The area east of the mound and road is actively cultivated. This mound was 23 feet high and

120 feet at the base when it was described in 1897 by Warren K. Moorhead. The mound is a bit lower today. Except for the scar on the west side, it is covered with trees and brush. A commemorative plaque was placed at the base of the mound on the north side in 1982.

Although Porteus Mound has been considered to be Adena in origin based on its size, shape, and location, Moorehead's excavation failed to produce evidence that confirms this belief.

DIRECTIONS: From SR 16 south of Coshocton, go east on SR 83 0.3 mile to CR 271, then go south on CR 271 0.3 mile to the mound on the east side of the road (Figure 56).

PUBLIC USE: This mound may be viewed from CR 271 at any time.

FOR ADDITIONAL INFORMATION: Read: W. K. Moorhead, 1897. "Report of field work carried on in the Muskingum, Scioto and Ohio valleys during the season of 1896," pp. 192-195.

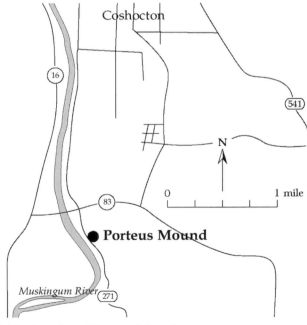

Figure 56. The location of Porteus Mound.

19. Highbanks Park Earthworks

Highbanks Metro Park is located north of Columbus in southernmost Delaware County, immediately east of the scenic Olentangy River. Most of the park consists of a gently rolling upland, but this gives way to an abrupt precipice along its western edge where it borders the river. Two subconical mounds and an earthen embankment occur in this park and are interpreted for the public. The mounds are presumed to have been built by the Adena and the embankment is considered to be Cole.

Highbanks Park Mound I, also known as Muma Mound, is located near the north edge of Highbanks Park about 300 feet south of Powell Road and 900 feet west of US 23. This mound, about 7 feet high and 54 feet in diameter, is located in an open field that formerly was farmed. Because of this farming, the mound had been reduced to a height of about 3 feet before Metro Parks acquired the property. The park reconfigured the mound to what is considered more nearly its prehistoric size and shape. A polished slate gorget reportedly was found in this mound while the property was in private ownership, but the feature has not been scientifically excavated. This mound is located on an unimproved trail leading from the nature center near the east entrance of the park, and it can be viewed from Powell Road.

Highbanks Park Mound II, previously known as Orchard Mound and Selvey Mound, is a small, subconical mound about 2.5 feet high and 45 feet in diameter. This mound, too, has been reduced in height by farming activities. Although unexcavated, the mound is presumed to be Adena because of its size, shape, and upland location. The mound is reached by taking a short spur of the Dripping Rock Trail which leads from the Oak Coves Picnic Area.

Highbanks Park Works, also known as Orange Township Works, is a semi-elliptical earthen embankment located at the top of a 100-foot cliff overlooking the Olentangy River to the west (Figure 57). The walls of the embankment are about 3 feet high, and they are bordered by a shallow ditch on the east and north. Three openings, probably gateways, occur in the embankment. This earthwork appears to have been a protective or defensive feature associated with a settlement of late Woodland or Late Prehistoric Indians, most likely those of the Cole tradition who, along with other late Woodland groups in central and northern Ohio, built protective earthen embankments with exterior ditches. The Highbanks Park Works, one of the longer Late Prehistoric earthen embankments known to exist in Ohio, was probably constructed between AD 800 and AD 1300. This structure is reached by the 2-mile-long Overlook Trail which begins at the Oak Coves Picnic Area.

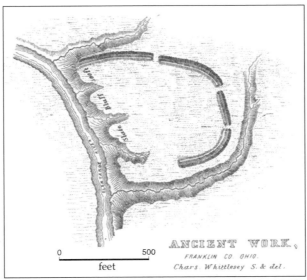

Figure 57. Highbanks Park Works. (From Squier and Davis, 1848)

Highbanks Park provides many miles of well maintained trails through a great variety of habitats ranging from open old fields to mature hardwood forests. Exhibits at the Nature Center interpret the natural and cultural history of the park and environs, including the Adena and Cole cultures that are represented by the mounds and earthworks in the park.

DIRECTIONS: Highbanks Metro Park is located at 9466 Columbus Pike (the northward continuation of North High Street) on the west side of US 23, about 3.5 miles north of the I 270/US 23 interchange north of Columbus. The park is on the west side of US 23 (Figure 58).

PUBLIC USE: Season and hours: *Grounds:* open daily 7 AM until dark, year round; *Nature Center:* open regularly, but the hours vary.

FOR ADDITIONAL INFORMATION: Contact: Metropolitan Park District of Columbus and Franklin County, P.O. Box 29169, Columbus, OH 43229; 614-891-0700, *www.metroparks.net.*

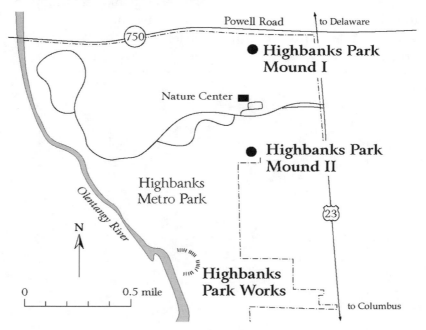

Figure 58. The location of Highbanks Metro Park and its mounds and earthworks.

OHIO - FAIRFIELD COUNTY

20. Tarlton Cross Mound

Tarlton Cross Mound (Figure 59) is a simple earthen cross-shaped mound composed of four identical arms, each about 20 to 25 feet in width, 3 feet high, and 45 feet in length, measured from the center of the feature. A circular depression about 20 feet in diameter and 20 inches deep occupied the center of the feature when Squier and Davis surveyed it in the 1840s, but it is not certain whether this was a part of the original native design of the mound or a result of later exploration by curiosity seekers. The arms of the cross are nearly aligned with the cardinal directions. A small circular mound of stones

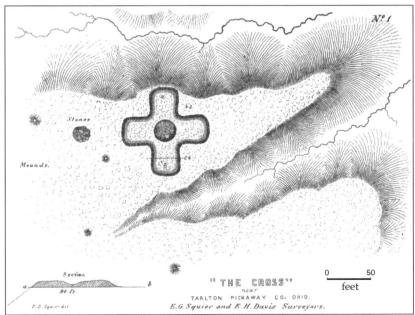

Figure 59. Tarlton Cross Mound. (From Squier and Davis, 1848)

143

was located a short distance from the cross; Squier and Davis called attention to the similarities between this mound of stone and one they had seen at the Alligator Mound in Granville, which they called an altar. Several other mounds, both small and large, occurred near the Tarlton Cross Mound when this site was surveyed by Squier and Davis.

The Tarlton Cross site occupies a small, relatively level upland spur that projects into the west side of Salt Creek Valley a short distance north of the village of Tarlton. This mound has been thought to be a Hopewell effigy mound, but other such structures are rare if not nonexistent, given the recently revised interpretations of the Alligator and Great Serpent effigy mounds. The Great Hopewell Road, if actually a part of the Hopewell landscape, would have been located a short distance to the west of Tarlton Cross Mound.

Tarlton Cross Mound is located within Cross Mound Park, a property of the Fairfield County Historical Parks Commission. The mound is reached by a primitive foot trail that

Figure 60. The location of Tarlton Cross Mound.

leads about one-third mile from the parking area. Part of this trail is uphill.

DIRECTIONS: From SR 159 in Tarlton, go north on CR 12 (Redding Road) 0.5 mile to Cross Mound Park on the west side of the road. From the parking area, cross the bridge and follow the trail signs to the mound (Figure 60).

PUBLIC USE: Cross Mound Park is open daily from dawn to dusk.

FOR ADDITIONAL INFORMATION: Contact: Fairfield County Historical Parks Commission, 407 East Main Street, Lancaster, OH 43130; 740-681-7249. **Read:** E. G. Squier and E. H. Davis, 1848. *Ancient Monuments of the Mississippi Valley*, p. 98.

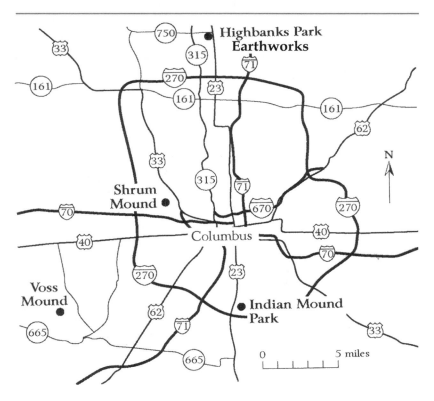

Figure 61. Publicly accessible mounds in and near Columbus, Ohio.

OHIO - FRANKLIN COUNTY

21. Indian Mound Park

A single mound is located in the northcentral part of Indian Mound Park in south Columbus (Figure 61). Immediately to the north, largely on private property, is another mound. Both mounds lie on a higher terrace of the Scioto River. Their shape has been extensively altered by farming activities to the extent that they are now low, gently sloping hillocks. In fact, the southeast edge of the mound in the park forms part of center field for the softball field. Neither of these mounds is a registered archeological site, and there is no information that either has been excavated.

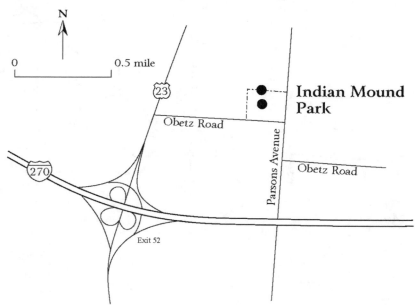

Figure 62. The location of Indian Mound Park.

DIRECTIONS: From the intersection of I 270 and US 23, go north on US 23 0.23 mile to Obetz Road, then east 0.7 mile on Obetz Road, then north 150 feet on Parsons Avenue to Indian Mound Park on west side of road (Figures 61, 62).

FOR ADDITIONAL INFORMATION: Contact: Department of Recreation and Parks, City of Columbus, 420 West Whittier Street, Columbus, OH 43215; 614-645-7410.

OHIO - FRANKLIN COUNTY

22. Shrum Mound

Shrum Mound, also known as Campbell Mound, a flat-topped conical feature measuring 20 feet high and 100 feet in diameter at the base, is one of the few remaining Adena burial mounds in Columbus. At the time it was originally built, the mound occupied a high bluff immediately west of the Scioto River. The mound is situated in the center of James E. Campbell Park, a small tract of land approximately 1 acre in size that is owned and maintained by the Ohio Historical Society as a public roadside park. The mound and park grounds contain several trees but, in general, they are grass-covered and regularly maintained. A stone wall extends along the front, or road, side of this park. A circular path leads to the top of the mound, from which an adjacent limestone quarry can be seen.

Campbell Park is small and undesignated; no signs direct you to the site or tell you that you have arrived. Vegetation along the road in this semi-developed area obscures the site until you are nearly upon it. Our suggestion is to drive slowly, traffic (which is sometimes heavy) permitting, and be prepared to pull off the pavement along side the stone wall when it comes into view. This wall extends along the edge of the site and is more easily seen from a moving car than is the mound itself.

DIRECTIONS: Exit I 70 at Exit 94 (Wilson Road), go north on Wilson Road about 1 mile to Trabue Road, then go east on Trabue Road about 1.6 miles to McKinley Avenue (at second set of traffic lights on Trabue Road — do not cross multiple railroad tracks), then go south on McKinley Avenue 0.5 mile to Campbell Mound on the west side of street. Roadside parking is on the west side of McKinley Avenue (Figures 61, 63).

PUBLIC USE: Season and hours: Campbell Park is open all year round during daylight hours.

FOR ADDITIONAL INFORMATION: Contact: Ohio Historical Society, 1982 Velma Avenue, Columbus, OH 43211; 800-686-1535, *www.ohiohistory.org*.

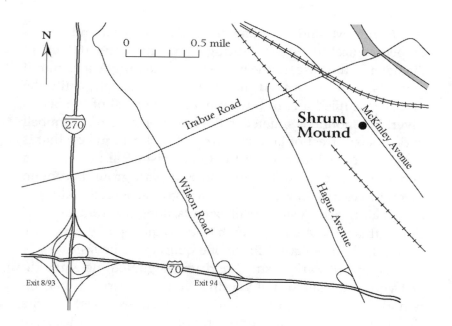

Figure 63. The location of Shrum Mound.

23. Voss Mound

Voss Mound is a subconical structure about 5 to 6 feet high and 50 feet in diameter located in Battelle-Darby Creek Metro Park southwest of Columbus. The mound is situated on a high terrace some 25 to 30 feet above Big Darby Creek, about 30 feet east of the bluff overlooking the lower terrace and flood plain. Excavation of this mound in 1962 revealed that it covered the remains of a circular structure that burned around AD 966. Following the excavation, the mound was restored. It is now interpreted as being Fort Ancient in origin.

The mound lies alongside the western arm of the 1.9-mile-long Ancient Trail loop which originates southwest of the Indian Ridge Picnic Area near the middle of the park. The feature lies in an open field now managed as prairie and wildlife habitat; it is covered with several years' growth of woody and herbaceous vegetation.

DIRECTIONS: From US 40, go south on Darby Creek Drive for about 3 miles to Indian Ridge Picnic Area entrance on the west side of the road (Figures 61, 64).

PUBLIC USE: Season and hours: Grounds are open daily, 7 AM until dark, year round.

FOR ADDITIONAL INFORMATION: Contact: Metropolitan Park District of Columbus and Franklin County, P. O. Box 29169, Columbus, OH 43229; 614-891-0700. **Read:** R. S. Baby, M. A. Potter, and A. Mays, Jr., 1966. "Exploration of the O. C. Voss Mound, Big Darby Reservoir area, Franklin County, Ohio."

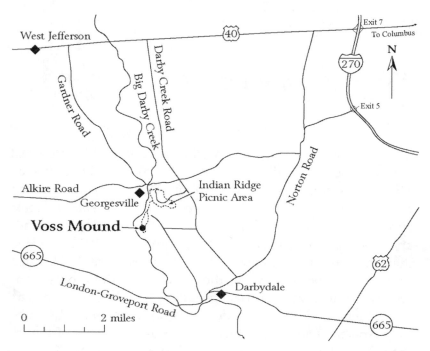

Figure 64. The location of Voss Mound.

OHIO - GREENE COUNTY

24. Indian Mound Reserve

Indian Mound Reserve, a property of the Greene County Park District, contains a delightful and noteworthy blend of significant natural and cultural landscape features. The dominant natural feature of the property is the Cedarcliffs Falls and Gorge section of Massies Creek, flowing water set against dramatic limestone cliffs within a beautiful hardwood forest. The prehistory of the area is well represented by two important Woodland sites, Williamson Mound and Pollock Works. An early nineteenth-century log building and remnants of the area's flour and paper mills add even more depth to a landscape rich with variety.

Williamson Mound, 28 feet high and 150 feet in diameter at the base, is one of the larger remaining mounds in Ohio (Plate 4). The size, shape, and location of this mound suggest that it was built by the Adena, but this affiliation has not been confirmed by excavation. Several amateur excavations probed this mound during the nineteenth century and, probably, the early twentieth century, but much of the original feature apparently remains intact. This mound is situated in an open field on the level upland surface of a ridge some 80 feet above Massies Creek. The approach side of the field is mowed which emphasizes the mound's height and makes it clearly visible and more dramatic in appearance. A stairway of 62 wooden steps leads to the top.

Pollock Works, Hopewell in origin, are located upon a limestone plateau that is nearly isolated from the adjoining land surface by steep slopes and precipitous cliffs that descend to the present and former channels of Massies Creek on the north, east, and south. The approach to the west side of the enclosure is more gradual. Squier and Davis provided a figure of the enclosure showing that it consisted of four horseshoe-shaped embankments, three small mounds, and a linear embankment broken by three gates (Figure 65). Only the linear embankment is visible today.

Robert Riordan of Wright State University has excavated portions of the Pollock site (Figure 32, Plate 12) over a period of several years and has been able to determine that the earthworks were constructed in at least five phases from around AD 50 to AD 225. Phase 1 consisted of building an earthen embankment about 300 feet in length and 5 feet high

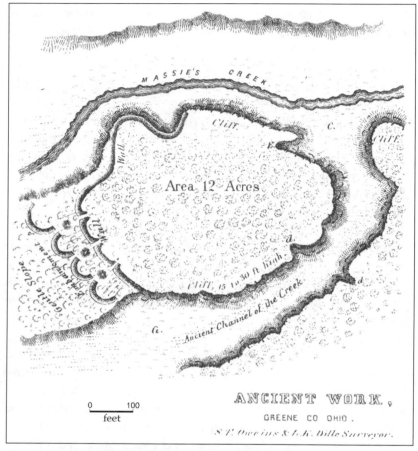

Figure 65. Pollock Works. (From Squier and Davis, 1848)

between the north cliff and the south cliff across the surface that gradually ascended the limestone plateau from the west. Phases 2 and 3 consisted of increasing the height of the embankment, leaving one or more breaks in the additions to form the entrances, and possibly adding the three external mounds and four external crescents. These alterations occurred over a period of perhaps 50 to 100 years. Phase 4 consisted of building a fence, about 5 feet high, upon and just inside the crest of the embankment and adding a mud-plastered wooden stockade, 13 to 16 feet high, along the creek bluff to extend the perimeter of the enclosure. The period of fence and stockade building took place at one time, quickly, sometime between about AD 130 and AD 228. The final phase of construction consisted of burning the stockade and covering its remains with an embankment of earth and stone 3 feet high and adding another 1 to 2 feet of height to the segments of the western embankment wall.

Williamson Mound is reached by a foot trail, about 0.75 mile in length, that leads north from the parking lot on US 42 down the paved road and across the bridge over Massies Creek, then into the forest. The trail is well maintained and well marked.

To see Pollock Works, follow another trail, about 0.3 mile in length, that leads east from the parking lot on US 42. The trail to the Pollock site is not as well maintained as the one to Williamson Mound, especially as it nears the site. Once the trail ascends the short slope and passes through a gate of the enclosure, it comes to a T with no signage. This is actually a circle loop, and it has some side trails which allow the visitor to get closer views of some of the remaining earthworks and the cliffs, and to more fully appreciate the use of local relief by the Hopewell architects. But, we advise that you keep one eye on the main trail!

DIRECTIONS: Follow US 42 west from the center of Cedarville about 1 mile to the Indian Mound Reserve parking area on the north side of US 42; a log cabin is located at the entrance of the appropriate parking area (Figure 66).

PUBLIC USE: Season and hours: The park is open year round during daylight hours. The terrain here is beautiful; the Greene County gorges are justifiably well known for their natural beauty.

FOR ADDITIONAL INFORMATION: Contact: Greene County Park District, 651 Dayton-Xenia Road, Xenia, OH 45385; 513-376-7441. **Read:** (1) R. V. Riordan, 1995. "A construction sequence for a middle Woodland hilltop enclosure." (2) R. V. Riordan, 1998. "Boundaries, resistance, and control: Enclosing the hilltops in middle Woodland Ohio."

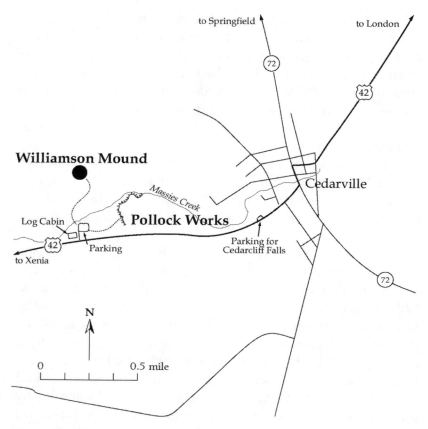

Figure 66. The location of Pollock Works and Williamson Mound in Indian Mound Reserve.

OHIO - GREENE COUNTY

25. Orators Mound

Orators Mound, so named because a pavilion from which speeches were given once crowned its summit, is a small subconical structure about 5 feet high and 45 feet in diameter at the base located on high ground midway between Birch Creek and Yellow Springs Creek, 1.4 miles north of their confluence with the Little Miami River. Yellow Springs, a perpetually flowing mineral spring and the inspiration for the name of the nearby town, rises to the surface 550 feet northwest of the mound.

Orators Mound has been excavated, in part, on at least two occasions and the evidence recovered relates it to the late Adena period. In 1953 and 1954, avocational archeologists from Wright-Patterson Air Force Base explored approximately one-fourth of the structure. The second excavation was carried out in 1971 by Wolfgang Marschall of Antioch College. Marschall's work recovered skeletal remains of several individuals, but the possibility existed that some of the bones disturbed by the 1953-1954 exploration had been reburied in the mound. Marschall reckoned that, at minimum, 4 individuals, and perhaps as many as 6, had been interred in the mound. Grave goods included mica crescents and Adena-style projectile points. Since some bones were out of sequence and misoriented, the skeletons could have been defleshed before interment. The nuclear mound was built primarily of limestone, and an earthen enlargement apparently was added later.

Orators Mound, also known as Glen Helen Mound, lies in Glen Helen — one of the beautiful forested glens and gorges of Greene County — a property of Antioch University that is

155

managed by the Glen Helen Ecology Institute. The Glen Helen Ecology Institute Trailside Museum, located next to the Corry Street parking lot, has exhibits interpreting the natural and cultural history of the Glen Helen region, and it maintains and interprets an intricate system of trails that lead through all parts of Glen Helen. The Inman Trail, a scenic self-guiding nature trail about 1 mile in length, leads past several significant features of the Glen, including Orators Mound, which is located about 20 feet south of the trail. The institute's Nature Shop, located in the Glen Helen Building at the north end of the Corry Street parking lot, offers educational materials for sale.

DIRECTIONS: From US 68 in Yellow Springs, follow SR 343 east about 750 feet, then go south on Old Stage Road 500 feet, then go south about 1,000 feet beyond where Old Stage Road departs to the southeast to reach a parking area. An alternate route is to follow Corry Street south from US 68 0.45 mile to Trailside Museum parking area on the east side of the road, then take the foot trail about 0.3 mile to the mound (Figure 67).

Figure 67. The location of Orators Mound.

PUBLIC USE: Season and hours: *Grounds:* Open year round during daylight hours. *Trailside Museum:* 9:30 AM to 4:30 PM, Wednesday through Saturday; 1 to 4:30 PM, Tuesday and Sunday. *Nature Shop:* 9:30 AM to 4:30 PM, Tuesday through Friday.

FOR ADDITIONAL INFORMATION: Contact: Glen Helen Ecology Institute, 405 Corry Street, P. O. Box 280, Yellow Springs, OH 45387; 937-767-7375. **Read:** W. Marschall, 1972. "Exploration of Glen Helen Mound."

OHIO - HAMILTON COUNTY

26. Mariemont Embankment

The Mariemont Embankment is an elongate earthen structure that extends along the southeast-facing edge of a glacial terrace that overlooks the lower reaches of the Little Miami River. This tree- and brush-covered embankment extends along the south side of much of the 0.8-mile length of Miami Bluff Drive, but it is most apparent toward its western end where it approaches a height of 4 to 5 feet.

The origin of the Mariemont Embankment is uncertain. The Fort Ancient Madisonville site, one of the largest and most important late Fort Ancient village sites, occupied much of the terrace to the west of the embankment, but there is no direct evidence that it was built by the Fort Ancient people who lived at Madisonville. Because of the proximity of the embankment to the village site, some observers have considered the wall to have been built by the Fort Ancient. Others see it as more typical of Hopewell. This feature has not been excavated so its actual cultural affiliation is unknown.

Parking near the embankment is available at the Mariemont Concourse on the south side of Miami Bluff Drive. A park, pavilion, and historical marker located a short distance west of the Mariemont Embankment, near the swim club, lie upon what was part of the Madisonville site. Artifacts from the site are on exhibit at the Mariemont Preservation Foundation Museum.

DIRECTIONS: From US 50 (Wooster Pike) in Mariemont, go south on Pleasant Street 0.1 mile to Mariemont, then go southwest on Mariemont 0.7 mile to Miami Bluff Drive, then go northeast on Miami Bluff Drive. The embankment is on the south side of Miami Bluff Drive (Figure 68).

PUBLIC USE: *Earthworks:* The Mariemont Embankment may be viewed from Miami Bluff Drive at any time. *Museum:* Mariemont Preservation Foundation hours are Saturday, 9 AM to noon, or by appointment.

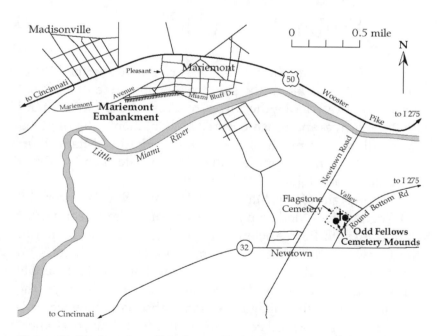

Figure 68. The location of Mariemont Embankment and Odd Fellows Cemetery Mounds.

FOR ADDITIONAL INFORMATION: Contact: Mariemont Preservation Foundation, 3919 Plainville Road, Mariemont, OH 45227; 513-272-1166. **Read:** (1) E. A. Hooton and C. C. Willoughby, 1920. "Indian village site and cemetery near Madisonville, Ohio." (2) S. F. Starr, 1960. "The archaeology of Hamilton County, Ohio." (3) P. B. Drooker, 1997. *The View from Madisonville: Protohistoric Western Fort Ancient Interaction Patterns.*

OHIO - HAMILTON COUNTY

27. Odd Fellows Cemetery Mounds

Two mounds of unknown cultural affiliation are located in Flagstone Cemetery, formerly Odd Fellows Cemetery, in Newtown, just east of Cincinnati. The site occupies part of the broad elevated terraces of the Little Miami River and lies about two-thirds of a mile south of the river.

The larger mound is located near the center of the cemetery. It is about 12 feet high and has diameters of 90 feet by 110 feet at the base. Grass grows over the entire mound, and trees are growing on part of the east side. The smaller mound is near the eastern edge of the cemetery; it is only about 2 feet high and 40 feet in diameter. Several historic graves have been placed on the smaller mound, and part of its north side has been removed.

DIRECTIONS: From SR 32 in Newtown, go north on Round Bottom Road 0.2 mile to main entrance to Flagstone Cemetery. The larger mound is straight ahead and the smaller mound is to the northeast (Figure 68).

PUBLIC USE: Flagstone Cemetery is open daily during daylight hours. The mounds may be viewed from Round Bottom Road at any time.

28. Miami Fort

The 1,156-acre Shawnee Lookout Park contains a rich and diverse array of burial mounds, earthworks, habitation sites, and other archeological features that collectively constitute the Shawnee Lookout Archaeological District and document more than 10,000 years of Indian occupation of the region. The most significant earthwork in this park is Miami Fort, a hilltop enclosure which occupies the relatively level summit of an elevated peninsula of land wedged between the Ohio and Great Miami rivers at their confluence (Figure 69).

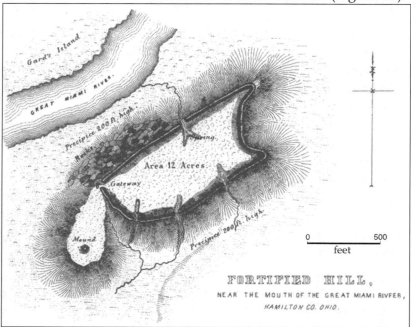

Figure 69. Miami Fort. (From Squier and Davis, 1848)

Lying 300 feet above the rivers, the walls of the enclosure, built on the side of the hill near its crest, varied from 1 to 12 feet in height and enclosed an area of about 12 acres. The wall was built, at least in part, of earth from within the enclosure laid upon a fire-hardened clay base and reinforced along the outer edge with low stone retaining walls. Wood also might have been used to build the walls. Several breaks or gateways separated segments of the walls. A radiocarbon dated sample of burned earth suggests that at least some part of the wall was being built around AD 270. Evidence of habitation within the enclosure suggests that some of the builders of the enclosure, considered to be Hopewell, actually lived within its walls, at least for a short time.

Among the other mounds within the park are three confirmed or suspected burial mounds that occupy a promontory immediately southwest of the fort. The largest is 6 feet high and 90 feet in diameter at the base. A partial excavation of this mound in 1966 yielded remains of at least 6 human skeletons. An adjacent village site, also excavated in 1966, apparently was occupied during both early Adena (800 BC to 300 BC) and late Adena-Hopewell, or middle Woodland, (AD 1 to AD 700) periods. This information indicates that the upland surface was inhabited before Miami Fort was built, and allows that the enclosure itself could have been built during the second, or middle Woodland, occupation. Twin Mounds Village, located on the upland surface north of the park road no more than one-half mile east of Miami Fort, was a Hopewell site later occupied by Fort Ancient people – as were other parts of the park.

Miami Fort is reached by a foot trail from the southern end of the main park road. The Miami Fort Trail, 1.4 miles in length, leads from a parking lot at the base of Fort Hill through Miami Fort to the west end of the elevated promontory. Nine recorded archeological sites, including the fort itself, are located along the trail. Be certain to take along a copy of the well-written and informative Miami Fort Trail Guide. The vista from Miami Fort is well worth the walk to the summit; once there, it is difficult not to imagine the view of the Ohio and Great Miami valleys that the Hopewell occupants of this place had two thousand years ago and to contemplate the reasons why they surveyed the land below.

Wall panels inside the entrance to the Shawnee Centre provide some basic interpretation of the prehistory of the park and its environs, while the Shawnee Lookout Archeological Museum, open seasonally, contains more extensive exhibits of the region's archeology.

DIRECTIONS: Northbound on I 275 exit at Lawrenceburg, Indiana (Indiana exit 2), then go east on US 50 about 3 miles to Elizabethtown,

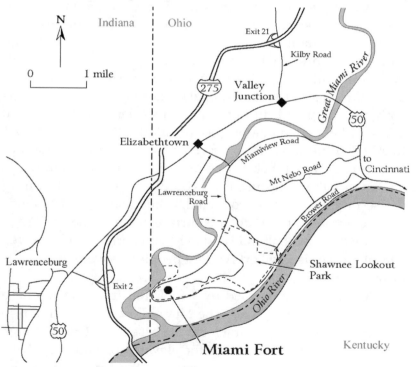

Figure 70. The location of Miami Fort.

then go east and south on Lawrenceburg Road about 2 miles to Shawnee Lookout Park. Southbound on I 275 exit onto Kilby Road (Ohio exit 21), go south on Kilby about 1 mile to US 50, go west on US 50 about 1.5 miles to Elizabethtown, then proceed as above (Figure 70).

PUBLIC USE: Season and hours: *Grounds:* Open year round during daylight hours. *Shawnee Centre:* Lobby open daily, dawn to dusk. Museum open about mid-March to early November, daily, dawn to dusk; closed early November to mid-March. **Fee area:** Admission. **Recreational facilities**.

FOR ADDITIONAL INFORMATION: Contact: Hamilton County Park District, 10245 Winton Road, Cincinnati, OH 45231; 513-521-7275. **Read:** (1) S. F. Starr, 1960. "The Archaeology of Hamilton County, Ohio." (2) S. L. Welsh, n.d. *Miami Fort Trail Guide.*

OHIO - HAMILTON COUNTY

29. Norwood Mound

Norwood Mound is located on the southern end of a ridge that stands more than 150 feet above a lowland drained by Duck Creek, a tributary of the Little Miami River. The structure lies adjacent to the City of Norwood's Water Tower Park, which itself is a tiny space sequestered in a residential neighborhood high above the central part of Norwood. The mound, now supporting several large trees but otherwise clearly visible, is conical with a slightly elliptical base; it is 13.5 feet high and 130 by 100 feet in diameter at the base. A paved driveway circles the base of the structure. The mound has not been excavated.

DIRECTIONS: Follow combined US 22 and SR 3 (Montgomery Road) north from downtown Norwood 0.5 mile, then go southeast on Indian Mound Avenue 0.25 mile to Norwood Mound. The mound is reached by a lane that leads south several yards from Indian Mound Avenue between private residences at 2409 and 2413 Indian Mound Avenue (Figure 71).

PUBLIC USE: Norwood Mound may be viewed from Indian Mound Avenue at any time during daylight hours.

FOR ADDITIONAL INFORMATION: Contact: City of Norwood, 4645 Montgomery Road, Norwood, OH 45212; 513-396-8150.

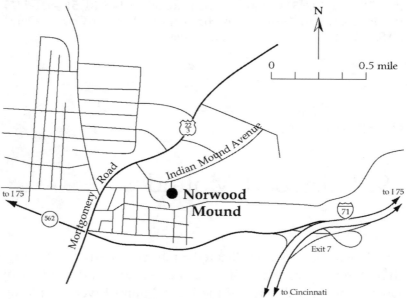

Figure 71. The location of Norwood Mound.

30. Shorts Woods Park Mound

Shorts Woods Park Mound is located in the eastern part of Shorts Woods Park in Sayler Park, a suburb of northwestern Cincinnati. Shorts Woods Park is leased by the Fernbank Golf and Tennis Club; the mound is best viewed from the clubhouse, although it also can be seen from near the intersection of Fernbank and Dahlia avenues or the northwest end of Home City Avenue. The elliptical mound is about 8 feet high and 113 feet by 90 feet in basal diameters; it is situated upon the third terrace of the Ohio River near the crest of the ridge separating the Ohio River and Muddy Creek.

This mound is not known to have been excavated, but it is considered to be Adena because of its shape and location, and its proximity to the better known Sayler Park Mound. Sayler Park Mound was large (38 feet high and 175 feet in diameter), was started about 2,000 years ago, and contained at least 39 burials, most of which were located in log tombs. The mound was completely excavated by the Cincinnati Museum of Natural History in 1957, and no visible trace of it remains today.

DIRECTIONS: Follow US 50 west from downtown Cincinnati about 9 miles to Sayler Park, then go northeast on Wilkins Shore Road 0.25 mile, then go southeast on Fernbank Avenue to the Fernbank Golf and Tennis Club office (Figure 72).

PUBLIC USE: Season and hours: Fernbank Golf and Tennis Club is open from mid-March to late October. At other times of the year, the park is open during daylight hours. **Restrictions:** Visitors are discouraged from walking on the grounds when golfers are at play. Do not go onto the golf course without checking at the club office.

FOR ADDITIONAL INFORMATION: Contact: Cincinnati Park Board, 950 Eden Park Drive, Cincinnati, OH 45202; 513-352-4080, *www.cinci-parks.org.* **Read:** S. F. Starr, 1960. "The archaeology of Hamilton County, Ohio."

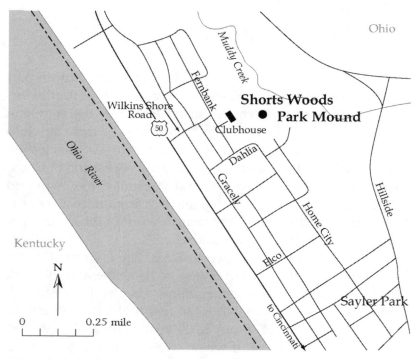

Figure 72. The location of Shorts Woods Park Mound.

31. Fort Hill

Fort Hill, located in Fort Hill State Memorial, is a major Ohio Hopewell hilltop enclosure whose earthen and stone walls lie tumbled in the tracks of their former order (Plate 9). Such a presentation duplicates the probable appearance and condition of many of the mounds and earthworks when they were discovered by American settlers in the late eighteenth and early nineteenth centuries. As is typical of Hopewell hilltop enclosures, the walls of Fort Hill follow the irregular contour of the upland surface, here some 400 feet above the valley of Ohio Brush Creek on the deeply eroded western edge of the Appalachian Plateau. About 1.6 miles in total length, the walls are 6 to 15 feet high and 40 to 45 feet wide at the base. There are 33 irregularly spaced openings, each about 20 feet wide. The fort walls enclose somewhere between 40 and 48 acres (Figure 73).

The excavation of a part of the wall near the southern end of the enclosure in 1964 revealed that the wall had been built in two stages. The first embankment was built of subsoil and decaying rocks along the edge of the hilltop and then was covered with tightly fitting slabs of quarried sandstone, the largest of which measured up to almost 3 feet square. Some time after the initial bank was completed, a second phase of building took place. A retaining wall of stones laid one upon another was put in place along the inside base of the old wall, then the old wall and the new retaining wall were covered with subsoil and decaying rock. Next, the entire new surface was covered with multiple layers of quarried sandstone slabs, and finally a layer of humus was spread across the rock surface.

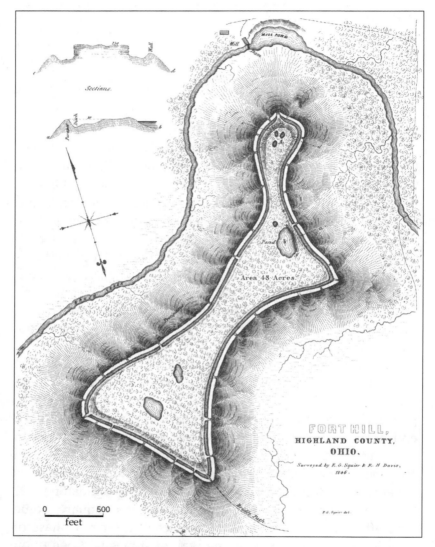

Figure 73. Fort Hill. (From Squier and Davis, 1848)

Earlier, during the summers from 1952 to 1954, an occupation area at the base of the hill south of the enclosure had
been excavated and had yielded evidence of three large structures and scattered cultural debris. The structures included

two circular earthen enclosures and one rectangular wooden enclosure without an associated mound. One of the circular enclosures contained evidence of an associated wooden structure with a diameter of 174 feet, possibly the outline of a residential or dormitory compound in which visitors lived or worked while at the site. The rectangular structure, of double post construction, measured 120 by 80 feet and might have been a workshop area. These buildings have been interpreted as having been periodically occupied structures associated with the ceremonial use of the site, and that interpretation has suggested to some archeologists that Fort Hill was also primarily a ceremonial site rather than a defensive one. To others, however, the primary function of the fort was defensive — a place of secure retreat when faced with danger. All agree, however, that both the lowland site and the enclosure are Hopewell in origin.

Fort Hill State Memorial, all 1,200 acres of which have been designated a nature preserve, is as significant for its natural history as for its human prehistory. The park lies at the junction of several physiographic regions, each with a distinctive environmental history, one result of which is that the geological and biological diversity of the region is unusually high. The memorial's new museum, which opened during the spring of 2001, features the area's natural history and Hopewell archeology. Included among the exhibits are models and floor plans of the circular and rectangular structures that were excavated at the base of the hill, a description of the geology and natural history of Fort Hill and environs, and a suite of five interpretive videos dealing with aspects of Hopewell culture and the region's natural history. In addition, more than 10 miles of trails traverse the park. Fort Trail, 2 miles long, goes up to the fort from the picnic area, over the walls, and along the full length of the enclosure. Gorge Trail and Deer Trail, 4 and 5 miles in length, respectively, circle the base of Fort Hill.

DIRECTIONS: From US 50, go south on SR 41 about 11 miles, then go west on Fort Hill Road 0.75 mile to park entrance on south side of road. Parking is available at the museum and the picnic area (Figure 74).

PUBLIC USE: Season and hours: *Grounds:* The memorial grounds are open daily during daylight hours. *Museum:* The museum is open 9:30 AM to 5 PM, Wednesday through Saturday, noon to 5 PM, Sunday and holidays, Memorial Day through Labor Day; noon to 5 PM, weekends only, Labor Day through October. Closed November through Memorial Day. **Fee area:** Museum. **Recreational facilities.**

FOR ADDITIONAL INFORMATION: Contact: Ohio Historical Society, 1982 Velma Road, Columbus, OH 43211; 800-686-1535, *www.ohiohistory.org*. **Read:** (1) E. G. Squier and E. H. Davis, 1848. *Ancient Monuments of the Mississippi Valley*, pp. 14-16. (2) R. S. Baby, 1954. "Archaeological explorations at Fort Hill." (3) M. A. Potter and E. S. Thomas, 1970. *Fort Hill.* (4) O. H. Prufer, 1997. "Fort Hill 1964: New data and reflections on Hopewell hilltop enclosures in southern Ohio."

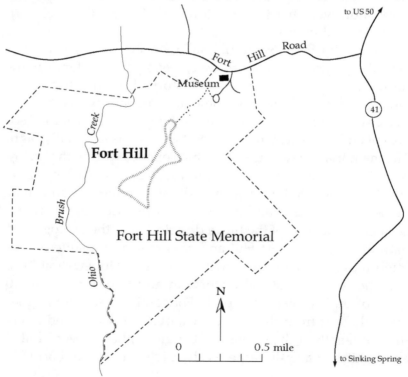

Figure 74. The location of Fort Hill.

32. Tiltonsville Cemetery Mound

Tiltonsville, or Hodgen's, Cemetery Mound is located near the corner of Walden Street and Arn Avenue in the Tiltonsville Cemetery. This simple and quietly beautiful conical mound

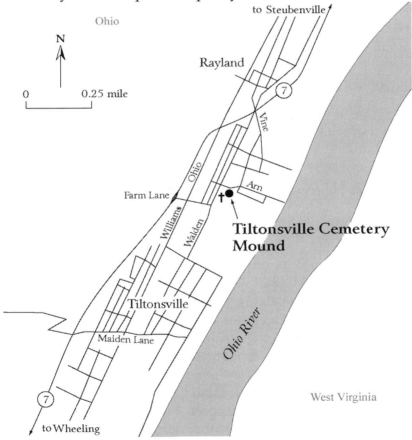

Figure 75. The location of Tiltonsville Cemetery Mound.

13 feet high and 80 feet in basal diameter occupies a prominent position in this picturesque cemetery which is situated on a high terrace of the Ohio River flood plain about 1,000 feet west of the Ohio River.

DIRECTIONS: Exit SR 7 at Tiltonsville (Farm Lane), go 0.15 mile east to Walden Street (old SR 7), then go north on Walden Street 0.1 mile to Arn Avenue, then go east on Arn Avenue 250 feet. The cemetery is on the south side of Arn Avenue, but it also can be viewed from just south of the intersection of Walden and Arn (Figure 75).

PUBLIC USE: The Tiltonsville Cemetery Mound may be viewed from Walden Street or Arn Avenue at any time.

FOR ADDITIONAL INFORMATION: Contact: Village of Tiltonsville, P. O. Box 127, Tiltonsville, OH 43963; 740-859-2730.

OHIO - LICKING COUNTY

33. Alligator Mound

Why should an effigy mound in central Ohio bear the name Alligator Mound? Doubt about the appropriateness of this name has been thinly veiled, at best, for more than 150 years. Squier and Davis remarked that "It is known in the vicinity as 'the Alligator;' which designation has been adopted, for want of a better, although the figure bears as close a resemblance to the lizard as any other reptile" (p. 99). Paul Hooge noted that the brothers James and Charles Salisbury surveyed the mound in 1862 and observed that it was "undoubtedly intended to represent the panther, king of the American forest" (pp. 69-70), while other observers saw it as more likely representing such other animals as an opossum or a raccoon. Quite recently, Bradley Lepper of the Ohio Historical Society has suggested that the mound represents the underwater panther, one of the most powerful supernatural spirits among Native Americans of the Ohio Valley during the Late Prehistoric and early Historic periods:

> *The earliest white traders and settlers who came to the Raccoon Creek valley had the opportunity to ask the local Indians what creature the mound was intended to represent. There, in the translation of an alien concept by alien tongues, lay the road to misunderstanding. If they had been told it was an "Underwater Panther" they surely would have been dumbfounded, and further attempts at explanation could only have added to their confusion. The literal-minded Europeans would have known that panthers do not live in the water; the only American animal they knew that seemed to fit the description of a ferocious, four-legged, long-tailed monster was the American alligator.* . . . . (Lepper, p. 25).

Alligator mound is located at the end of a promontory that protrudes from a ridge running along the north side of Raccoon Valley. Lying about 150 feet above the valley, the Alligator faces to the southwest overlooking the lowland. The mound was described by Squier and Davis (Figure 76) as being about 250 feet long, with its body about 40 feet wide and each limb about 36 feet long. The head, shoulders, and rump were higher than the other parts of the body; the shoulders were 6 feet high and the average height was 4 feet. The mound was built of clay, silt, and stone. About 30 feet north of the effigy's midsection was a raised circular space covered with rocks which showed evidence of burning. A graded path about 10 feet wide connected the elevated circle and the effigy.

Squier and Davis noted that quarrying at the base of the promontory was threatening the effigy; the slope below the mound was so steep that the hillside was beginning to collapse. They reported that the owner of the land had agreed to stop the quarrying, but they also expressed their hopes that the citizens of nearby Granville would find a way to permanently protect the site. The site remained in agricultural use, primarily as pasture land, and the mound continued to be reduced in height. George Frederick Wright of Oberlin College noted in 1888 that:

> *One of the most vivid things in my memory is the picture of the sheep, cattle and horses which I saw stamping flies under the shade cast by a solitary tree upon the Alligator Mound. Their busy hoofs will not long suffer any remnant of it to continue visible* (Lepper, p. 21).

Memory of the Alligator slipped into relative oblivion, however, until concern about it was revived in the 1980s as residential development began to reach into Raccoon Valley. Fortunately, the developer and preservation interests worked together in a way that allowed both parties to realize their goals. Today, Alligator Mound is preserved on a 1.5-acre tract

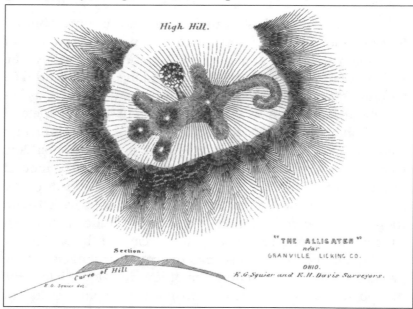

Figure 76. Alligator Mound. (From Squier and Davis, 1848)

174

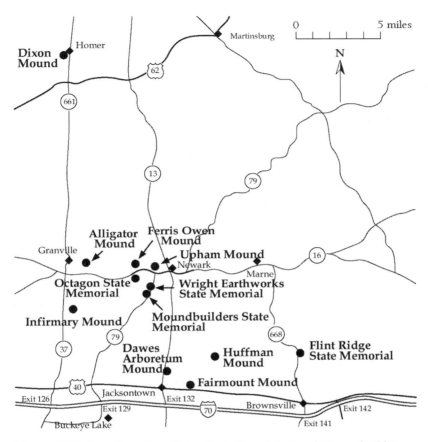

Figure 77. Mounds and earthworks in the vicinity of Newark, Ohio.

of greenspace owned by the Licking County Historical Society that is located in a cul-de-sac within an upscale residential neighborhood.

Until recently, Alligator Mound was considered to be but one example of the numerous architectural features that dotted the Adena and, especially, Hopewell landscapes of Newark and its immediate environs (figures 23, 77). One result of Lepper's excavation of part of the Alligator in 1999, however, was a radiocarbon date which indicated that the mound was only a little more than 700 years old. Invoking Native Ameri-

175

can traditions as well as archeological, ethnographic, geologic, and geographic evidence, Lepper concluded that the Alligator is probably a product of the Fort Ancient culture, and that it represents one of the two most powerful spirits among Native Americans of the region — the Underwater Panther, master of all underwater and underworld creatures.

DIRECTIONS: From Granville, go east on CR 539 (East Broadway/Newark-Granville Road) about 1.1 miles to Bryn du Woods estate, go north on Bryn du Drive about 1.25 miles to Alligator Mound. From Newark, go west on SR 16 to CR 539 (Newark/Granville Road) exit, continue west on CR 539 about 2.0 miles to Bryn du Woods and proceed as above (Figures 77, 78).

PUBLIC USE: Season and hours: Alligator Mound can be viewed from Bryn du Drive at any time. **Restrictions:** Walking on the mound is not permitted.

FOR ADDITIONAL INFORMATION: Contact: Licking County Historical Society, P. O. Box 785, Newark, OH 43055; 740-345-4898. **Read:** (1) E. G. Squier and E. H. Davis, 1848. *Ancient Monuments of the Mississippi Valley*, pp. 98-100. (2) I. Smucker, 1885. "Alligator Mound: An effigy or symbolic mound in Licking County, Ohio." (3) P. E. Hooge, 1992. "The Alligator Mound: A case study of archaeology and preservation in Licking County." (4) B. T. Lepper, 2001. "Ohio's 'alligator'."

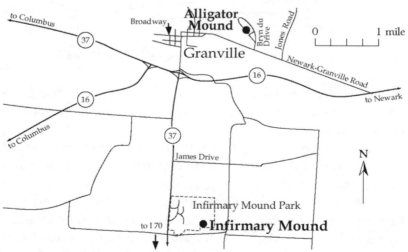

Figure 78. The location of Alligator Mound and Infirmary Mound.

34. Infirmary Mound

Infirmary Mound Park is a 326-acre unit of the Licking Park District; the mound and the park take their names from the fact that this property formerly was the Licking County Infirmary Farm. Samuel Park, once the owner of the land that became the county infirmary farm and a surveyor in the mid-1800s, apparently conducted some of his survey work from atop Infirmary Mound.

Infirmary Mound (Figure 31) occupies the southern edge of the highest point in the southern half of this park and over-looks Ramp Creek. This mound and the land around it was cultivated for years before it was acquired by the park district. As a result, the structure is greatly reduced in height and its profile is quite subtle, almost to the point of being unnoticeable. At present, it is about 2 to 3 feet high and 70 feet in diameter. This mound and the field in which it is located are mowed regularly. The mound is located a short distance south of the horse arena and can be identified by a wooden rail fence along its north side. The remaining contour of the feature is most easily noticed from the west, near the base of the hill, while looking upslope toward it; from the north, the mound blends almost imperceptibly with the natural summit of the hill.

DIRECTIONS: Follow SR 37 north from I 70 Exit 126 for about 6 miles or south from the SR 16/SR 37 intersection in Granville for about 2.5 miles to the southern entrance to Infirmary Mound Park, then enter the park and follow the paved road to the parking area for shelter #4. On foot, follow the gravel road at the north end of the parking area to the horse arena, then walk south of the arena to find the mound (Figures 77, 78).

PUBLIC USE: Season and hours: Infirmary Mound Park is open daily during daylight hours.

FOR ADDITIONAL INFORMATION: Contact: Licking Park District, 4309 Lancaster Road, P. O. Box 590, Granville, OH 43023; 740-587-2535, *www.msmisp.com/lpd*; e-mail: *lpd@msmisp.com*.

35. Dawes Arboretum Mound

The Dawes Arboretum, founded in 1929, presently contains some 1,149 acres of land on the western edge of the Appalachian Plateau. About one-third of this property is occupied by the arboretum's large and diverse plant collection and associated landscapes, another third is used for silviculture and agriculture, and the remaining third is natural. Much of the arboretum's eastern unit is naturally vegetated, and it is in that area, amidst a regenerating hardwood forest, where the Dawes Arboretum Mound is located.

This mound is a low, subconical structure about 4 feet high and some 30 feet across, and it occupies the highest point on the grounds of the arboretum. The mound probably has been lowered by plowing, and it might have been explored by amateur curiosity seekers. It has been identified as Adena based on artifacts expelled by groundhog burrowing.

Dawes Arboretum Mound is accessible only on foot. It is located on the Indian Mound Loop in Arboretum East. Arboretum East is available only on a restricted basis and a written permit, which can be obtained at the visitor center, is required.

Plate 1. The first light of day penetrates the morning mist at Mound City in Chillicothe, Ohio. Mound City, a unit of Hopewell Culture National Historical Park, is one of the many earthworks found in Ross County, arguably at one time the cultural center of the Ohio Hopewell world. (Photograph by Joe E. Murray)

Plate 2. The large Shawnee Reservation Mound in Institute, West Virginia, is one of the few surviving structures from the many Adena mounds and earthworks that once occurred along the Kanawha River.

Plate 3. Grave Creek Mound in Moundsville, West Virginia, is the largest Adena burial mound. This mound exemplifies the substantial investment of human labor that went into building these burial monuments and territorial markers. (Photograph by Richard W. Pirko/Rudinec and Associates)

Plate 4. Williamson Mound in Cedarville, Ohio, occupies a ridge crest above Massies Creek. The symbolic authority of such a monumental structure is reinforced when the mound is approached from below.

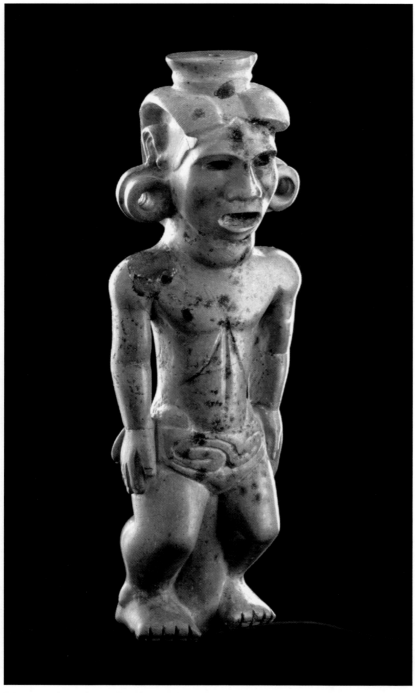

Plate 5. The Adena pipe from Adena Mound in Chillicothe, Ohio — a unique expression of Adena craftsmanship. (Photograph by Ohio Historical Society)

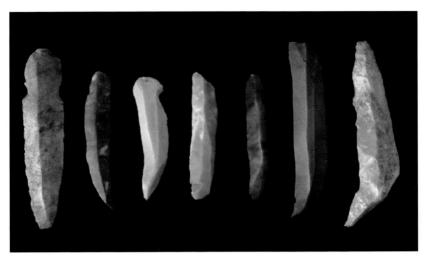

Plate 6. Flint bladelets from the Hopewell Mound Group in the North Fork of Paint Creek Valley west of Chillicothe, Ohio. Bladelets were distinctive tools of the Ohio Hopewell and, like these examples, were most often made of the colorful Vanport Flint from Flint Ridge, Ohio. The longest bladelet shown here is about 2.5 inches long. (Photograph by Ohio Historical Society)

Plate 7. A water-filled quarry pit at Flint Ridge near Brownsville, Ohio. For thousands of years Indians quarried Vanport Flint from Flint Ridge, but the most intensive extraction appears to have taken place during early and middle Woodland time by the Adena and, especially, Hopewell people.

Plate 8. Octagon and Observatory Circle earthworks in Newark, Ohio, illustrate clearly the great size, geometric precision, and variety of structures that characterized many of the lowland enclosures built by the Ohio Hopewell. This site has the unusual distinction of accommodating a golf course. (Photograph by Richard W. Pirko/Rudinec and Associates)

Plate 9. The west wall of Fort Hill, a Hopewell hilltop enclosure in southcentral Ohio, is still distinct nearly two thousand years after it was built. The wall extends completely around the perimeter of this isolated upland on the western edge of the Appalachian Plateau.

Plate 10. This raven effigy was cut from a sheet of hammered copper by a Hopewell artisan. The eye is represented by an inset pearl. The specimen is 13.75 inches long and is one of two copper raven effigies that were found in a deposit beneath Mound 25 of the Hopewell Mound Group. (Photograph by Ohio Historical Society)

Plate 11. Shannon Mound, near Shannon, Kentucky, is representative of many mounds that have received at least some level of protection by virtue of their being located within historical cemeteries.

Plate 12. Excavation trench T in the embankment north of the central gateway at Pollock Works. The reddened clay soil and whitened limestone rocks are evidence that fire occurred at the site, probably when the wooden fence and stockade burned around AD 225. (Photograph by Robert V. Riordan)

The Indian Mound Loop is about 0.9 mile round trip from the parking area nearest the trailhead.

DIRECTIONS: Follow SR 13 about 5 miles south from Newark or 1.5 miles north from the intersection of SR 13 and US 40 in Jacksontown. Dawes Arboretum lies astride SR 13 (Figures 77, 79).

PUBLIC USE: Season and hours: *Grounds:* Open daily, dawn to dusk. *Visitor Center:* Monday to Saturday, 8 AM to 5 PM, Sundays and holidays, 1 PM to 5 PM. **Restrictions:** As posted; written permit required to hike into Arboretum East to view the mound.

FOR ADDITIONAL INFORMATION: Contact: Dawes Arboretum, 7770 Jacksontown Road SE, Newark, OH 43056; 1-800-44-DAWES, *www.dawesarb.org*.

36. Fairmount Mound

Fairmount Mound, on the grounds of the Fairmount Presbyterian Church and adjoining the Fairmount Cemetery, is a conical structure about 15 feet high and 80 feet in diameter at the base that is located on the crest of a ridge overlooking the rolling hills of the western Appalachian Plateau (Figure 30). The cultural affiliation of this feature has not been determined.

DIRECTIONS: Exit I 70 at Exit 132, go north on SR 13 1 mile to US 40, go east on US 40 1.5 miles, then north on CR 323 (Fairmount Road) 0.15 mile to top of hill. The mound is located immediately east of Fairmount Church. Limited parking is available near the church (Figures 77, 79).

PUBLIC USE: Season and hours: The mound may be viewed from CR 323 at any time. **Restrictions:** This mound is on private property and trespassing is prohibited.

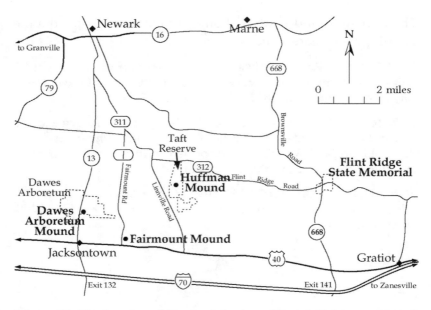

Figure 79. The location of Dawes Arboretum Mound, Fairmount Mound, Flint Ridge, and Huffman Mound.

OHIO - LICKING COUNTY

37. Flint Ridge

Flint Ridge State Memorial is a 525-acre cultural and natural preserve created in 1933 to protect part of a significant natural area and prehistoric flint quarry (Plate 7). Flint Ridge is a natural, elongate chain of narrow hills extending roughly east-west for about 7 miles through the southeastern part of

Licking and the western part of Muskingum counties. The ridge is formed of resistant Vanport Flint which typically occurs as pockets or beds from 1 to 5 feet in thickness. Near Flint Ridge State Memorial, however, the deposits reach 12 feet in thickness. The gem quality flint is translucent and variously colored, including white, yellow, pink, salmon, red, blue, green, and black. The different colors are caused by the presence of iron or other minerals and organic impurities. Flint Ridge flint is the official gemstone of Ohio.

The Vanport Flint outcrops along Flint Ridge constitute one of the most extensive surface deposits of high quality flint in the eastern part of the United States. As a result, this material was exploited by Indians from the Paleo-Indian period up into the early historic period, as well as by the Anglo-Americans who settled the Muskingum Valley. The surface of the ridge is pitted from thousands of years of human activity. The weathered surface exposures of flint were of little or no value for use as tools, so prehistoric people had to quarry the deeper, unweathered subsurface deposits. This quarrying was done with heavy stone or wooden hammers and wood or bone wedges. The wedges were driven into natural cracks in the flint to separate large blocks. These blocks were then reduced in size for transport away from the quarry or were worked into tools at the site. Most tools made from the hard flint were intended for cutting, scraping, drilling or puncturing uses in the form of projectile points, scrapers, drills, knives, awls, and bladelets, among others. The relative abundance and high quality of Vanport Flint also made it an item of regular and extensive trade; the material has been found in prehistoric sites throughout Ohio and the Midwest, and as far away as New York, Maryland, Georgia, Louisiana, and Kansas.

Vanport Flint has been found in many Adena and, especially, Hopewell sites and appears to have been the single most important source of flint for these mound-building people since it has been found throughout their range and often is the most frequently represented type of flint at their sites (Plate 6). Since the Vanport Flint was important in the region's prehistoric economy, questions have been raised as to what control, if any, native populations living in or near Flint Ridge might have had over the exploitation of the resource and how the extraction and removal of flint was organized and managed. Control over this raw material by populations in the Licking River drainage might have allowed the Newark Hopewell center to achieve a place of power and prominence during the middle Woodland period. Local populations could have either mined the flint and reduced it to workable blanks or finished tools before releasing it into the exchange network, or they could have extracted tolls or rents from visiting miners who would remove the flint themselves. Even the most simple answers to these basic questions about control and production are lacking, but the questions remain as intriguing legacies of a very valuable raw material utilized for millennia by Native Americans.

Today, Flint Ridge offers visitors an opportunity to walk the hills and valleys of the ridge within a maturing hardwood forest amidst quarry pits that are representative of the hundreds of points of extraction created by the prehistoric miners. Three nature trails extend through the wooded nature reserve and provide access to the upland forest, the ridge itself, many prehistoric quarry pits, and the outcrops of flint. The quarry pits range from those that are barely discernable to depressions 20 feet deep and 60 feet in diameter. Millions of flakes lie scattered across the surface, often near the depressions, testifying to the reduction of newly mined flint to more convenient blanks, preforms, or finished tools.

A centerpiece of the memorial is its museum that has been built over one of the quarry pits at one of the highest points on the memorial grounds. First opened in 1968 and renovated in 1999, this museum interprets the geological and human history of Flint Ridge. Central among the exhibits is a life-sized diorama depicting an Indian quarrying flint from an authentic quarry pit. Other exhibits describe the natural formation and distribution of flint at Flint Ridge and elsewhere in Ohio; flint-working techniques and the products produced; and the distribution of flint as a trade item across the eastern United States. Interactive video monitors allow the visitor to explore selected cultural and natural themes.

Flint Ridge serves as an excellent example of a source of raw material that was important to the Woodland economy and technology of the Adena and Hopewell homeland and beyond.

DIRECTIONS: Eastbound on I 70 exit at Exit 141 (Brownsville exit) onto SR 668, go north on SR 668 about 3.75 miles to Flint Ridge State Memorial on east side of road. Westbound on I 70 exit at Exit 142 (Gratiot exit) onto US 40, go west on US 40 1.75 miles to Brownsville, then go north on SR 668 3.0 miles to the memorial (Figures 77, 79).

PUBLIC USE: Season and hours: *Grounds:* Open daily during daylight hours. *Museum:* 9:30 AM to 5 PM, Wednesday through Saturday, Noon to 5 PM, Sundays and holidays, Memorial Day through Labor Day; same hours, weekends only, Labor Day through October. Closed November through Memorial Day. **Fee area:** Museum. **Recreational facilities. For people with disabilities:** Of special significance at Flint Ridge State Memorial is a 1,100-foot-long nature trail for handicapped persons. The trail is paved and has a hand rope. Interpretive signs are in Braille as well as printed in English. This award winning facility was the first of its kind in the state. **Restrictions:** Flint must not be removed from the memorial grounds.

FOR ADDITIONAL INFORMATION: Contact: Ohio Historical Society, 1982 Velma Avenue, Columbus, OH 43211; 800-686-1535, *www.ohiohistory.org.* **Read:** (1) W. C. Mills, 1921. "Flint Ridge." (2) W. Stout and R. A. Schoenlach, 1945. *The Occurrence of Flint in Ohio.* (3) R. M. DeLong, 1972. *Bedrock geology of the Flint Ridge area, Licking and Muskingum Counties, Ohio.* (4) K. D. Vickery, 1996. "Flint raw material use in Ohio Hopewell." (5) B. T. Lepper, R. W. Yerkes, and W. H. Pickard, 2001. "Prehistoric flint procurement strategies at Flint Ridge, Licking County, Ohio."

38. Huffman Mound

The Taft Reserve is a 425-acre property of the Licking Park District that presently offers hiking and horseback riding, and houses the William C. Kraner Nature Center. This reserve contains two prehistoric earthen structures, but only one of these is readily visible from established trails on the property.

Huffman Mound, also known as Tippet or Tippett Mound, is a well preserved mound located on the crest of a ridge in the southern part of the Taft Reserve. This structure is near one of the established hiking trails and, being located in a cultivated field and covered with trees, it is easily recognized. The mound is about 20 feet high and 200 feet in diameter at the base.

Around 1860, David Wyrick excavated this mound by removing a section from the edge to the center of the mound. Multiple burials were encountered at the base of the mound, and these were overlain by several layers of charcoal and ash. A tubular pipe was found at a depth of about 6 feet from the top. Today, the summit shows signs of this — or some later — excavation. The size, shape, and location of this mound, and the evidence recovered by Wyrick, suggest that it is an Adena burial mound.

DIRECTIONS: From I 70 at Exit 132, go north on SR 13 1 mile to US 40, then go east on US 40 3.5 miles to CR 311 (Linnville Road), then north on CR 311 3.4 miles to CR 312 (Flint Ridge Road), then east on CR 312 0.8 mile to Taft Reserve on south side of road. From parking area, take the hiking/horseback riding trail to the earthworks (Figures 77, 79).

PUBLIC USE: Season and hours: *Grounds*: Taft Reserve is open daily dawn to dusk. *Nature center:* 8:30 AM to 4:30 PM, Tuesdays through

Sundays. **Restrictions:** Examination of the mound and earthworks is by permit only; permits may be acquired from the Licking Park District.

FOR ADDITIONAL INFORMATION: Contact: Licking Park District, 4309 Lancaster Road, P. O. Box 590, Granville, OH 43023; 740-587-2535, *www.msmisp.com/lpd*; e-mail: *lpd@msmisp.com*.

OHIO - LICKING COUNTY

39. Dixon Mound

Dixon Mound, also known as Williamson Mound, is a privately owned structure lying within the village of Homer in northcentral Licking County. This single conical mound is 15 feet high and has a basal diameter of about 80 feet. It is located on a higher terrace of the flood plain of the North Fork of Licking River, about 1,000 feet from the river and 40 feet higher than the river level. The mound presently is covered with low-growing brushy vegetation and a few small trees.

The mound has not been excavated, so the cultural identity of the builders has not been determined. The size, shape, and context of the mound, however, suggest that it is probably an Adena mound. Early in the twentieth century, William C. Mills of the Ohio Historical Society considered this feature to be one of the most important conical mounds in the valley of the North Fork.

DIRECTIONS: Follow SR 661 14 miles north from Granville or 10 miles south from Mount Vernon to the center of Homer, then go west on South Street for 0.35 mile. The mound is on the south side of South Street behind the large yellow house between the Homer Public Library and the Homer Presbyterian Church (Figures 77, 80).

PUBLIC USE: Season and hours: The mound can be viewed from South Street at any time. **Restrictions:** This mound is on private property and trespassing is prohibited.

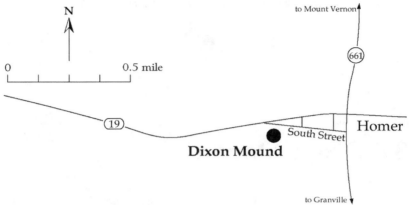

Figure 80. The location of Dixon Mound.

OHIO - LICKING COUNTY

40. Ferris Owen Mound

The conical Ferris Owen Mound stands sentinel at the entrance to the main building at Newark High School's Evans Athletic Complex. This mound was originally described as being 14 feet high and from 59 to 62 feet in diameter at the base. Today the mound is only about 10 feet high, a result of having been lowered dramatically when this area was a showplace potato farm. The feature was subsequently restored to its current size when the land was acquired by Newark High

School.

The mound has not been dated or assigned to a specific culture, but its location on an upper terrace of the North Fork of Licking River flood plain, and its physical characteristics, are typically Adena.

DIRECTIONS: In western Newark, exit SR 16 at 21st Street, go north on 21st Street 0.2 mile to Granville Road, then go west on Granville Road 0.15 mile to Sharon Valley Road, then go north and west on Sharon Valley Road 1 mile to the Evans Athletic Complex on the north side of the road, then enter the complex and drive 0.1 mile to the mound at the head of the turning circle (Figures 77, 81).

PUBLIC USE: Season and hours: This mound may be viewed at any time.

FOR ADDITIONAL INFORMATION: Contact: Newark City Schools, 85 East Main Street, Newark, OH 43055; 740-345-9891.

OHIO - LICKING COUNTY

41. Newark Earthworks

The Newark Earthworks was one of the most extensive and diverse assemblages of prehistoric earthen architecture in the eastern United States when American settlers first settled in the Licking River Valley at the very beginning of the nineteenth century (Figure 23). This complex of circles, squares, octagons, parallel embankments, and circular and elliptical mounds covered about 4 square miles; it was primarily if not exclusively of Hopewell origin and probably was constructed between about 100 BC and AD 500. Most of these earthworks

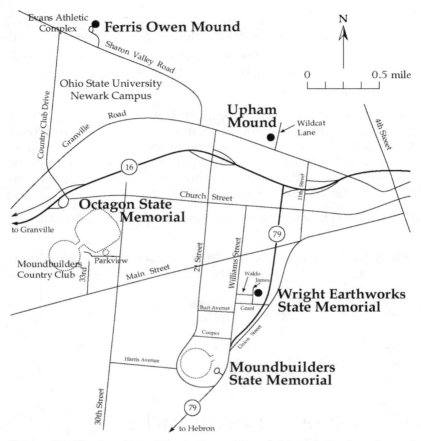

Figure 81. The location of Ferris Owen Mound, Newark Earthworks, and Upham Mound.

were located on the second terrace above the three tributaries of the Licking River which converge at Newark. This site, like many other Hopewell earthworks complexes, lies near the boundary of the relatively level glaciated Central Lowland and the hilly unglaciated Appalachian Plateau regions of Ohio. In addition, the Newark Earthworks are near Flint Ridge, and people living at or near the earthworks may have benefited as a result of their relative proximity to such an important economic resource. During the past two centuries, most of the Newark Earthworks have been destroyed by agriculture, transportation developments, and urban growth, but three parts of the complex, including most of its two largest units, remain. These units were transferred from the City of Newark to the Ohio Historical Society in 1933.

One of the two remaining large features and a few associated structures are incorporated in Moundbuilders State Memorial. This partly wooded tract of 66 acres includes a large circular embankment, Great Circle Earthworks, which encloses nearly 30 acres and measures about 1,200 feet in diameter with walls 8 to 14 feet high. A ditch encircles the interior base of the wall. An opening in the circular wall faces east-northeast. A cluster of 4 small conjoined mounds, sometimes referred to as an eagle or some other bird-like effigy, and an arcuate mound are located at the center of the circle. The conjoined mounds cover the former site of a Hopewell great house (Figure 22). Two parallel walls extend northeastward from either side of the opening in Great Circle to the edge of the memorial grounds.

Great Circle became the site of the Licking County Fairgrounds around 1853 and for several decades thereafter served variously as county fairground, state fairground, amusement park, horse-racing venue, and military drill field. Consequently, some of the prehistoric features in and near Great Circle were altered or destroyed, but some have since been restored.

A second large tract, the 120-acre Octagon Earthworks (Plate 8), contains an interconnected large octagon and circle earthworks and a small circle located just beyond the southeastern edge of the octagon. Octagon, enclosing 50 acres, was the largest single feature in the Newark complex; the circle connected to it encompasses 20 acres. Octagon was used as a National Guard encampment between 1892 and 1908, at which time control of the property reverted to the City of Newark which, two years later, leased the property to Moundbuilders

Country Club. Today the memorial is owned by the Ohio Historical Society and is leased to the Moundbuilders Country
Club, which maintains the grounds as a private golf course.

Wright Earthworks consists of the only surviving corner
of what was once a large square enclosure of 20 acres.

Recent archival work and archeological excavations in
and near Newark Earthworks have shed light on the content,
age, and construction history of the complex as well as the
nature of Hopewell occupation of the vicinity. The discovery
of a long lost map made in 1862 by James and Charles
Salisbury, and the manuscript accompanying this map, revealed that a previously unknown square enclosure had existed above and immediately southeast of the point where the
South Fork of Licking and Raccoon Creek join; that the large
circular earthworks in the Cherry Valley district northeast of
Great Circle was, in fact, a complete oval; and that a polygo-
nal earthen wall surrounded both Great Circle and Octagon-
and-Circle. The Salisbury map also showed that the parallel
walls extending southwest from Octagon continued for a much
greater distance than had previously been illustrated.

The unexpectedly long segment of parallel walls extending to the southwest, combined with archival records refer-
ring to such a road, stimulated Bradley Lepper of the Ohio
Historical Society to search for surviving evidence of the parallel walls. His search turned up encouraging results that have
led him to conclude that a great road might indeed have extended between, and connected, Newark Earthworks and
those in the Chillicothe area. Lepper has called this feature
the Great Hopewell Road; he considers it to have been an avenue used by pilgrims moving between two of the great
Hopewell ceremonial centers.

Excavations at Great Circle in 1992 provided evidence
that the embankment had been built in at least three stages,
with the first step beginning no earlier than about 160 BC.
Apparently the location of Great Circle was marked by plac-

ing piles of clay where the embankment would be located. Then, dark brown loam from immediately inside the circle was excavated and placed over the piles of clay. This excavation created an embankment and left a ditch. A shelf remained between the embankment and the edge of the ditch, and this was covered by placing bright yellow-brown gravelly soil upon it and on the inside of the embankment.

Excavation of a small area within the Octagon in 1994 produced two radiocarbon dates from an artificial basin and a post mold that indicated the features were in use at AD 180 and AD 300, respectively. Investigations of Hopewell habitation sites at several places near the Newark Earthworks confirmed that there were indeed small groups of people living in the vicinity of the earthworks, at least at times, during the active life of the monumental structures. The amount of information collected was not sufficient, however, to determine the overall pattern of Hopewell occupation of the area during the entire middle Woodland period.

The first museum in the United States devoted exclusively to the art of prehistoric Native Americans was opened at Moundbuilders State Memorial in 1971. Today, this museum contains exhibits of Indian art in copper, stone, and ceramic media, along with artifacts from the Paleo-Indian through the Mississippian periods. A life-sized diorama depicts Indians working with a cache of Flint Ridge flint. Outside, near the museum entrance, is a bronze relief map based on the survey of the Newark Earthworks published by Squier and Davis showing how the earthworks appeared in 1847. The parts of the earthworks that survive are burnished on the map. A garden is maintained in the northeastern part of the memorial which contains many plants that were either domesticated or selectively encouraged by the middle Woodland Indians (Table 1).

DIRECTIONS: All of the sites are located in the western part of Newark (Figures 77, 81). (1) The main entrance to Great Circle Earthworks is from Ohio Route 79, but access to the back of the park and the picnic area is possible at the corner of 21st and Cooper streets. (2) To reach Wright Earthworks take 21st Street to Cooper Avenue, then go east on Cooper Avenue to Williams Street, then north on Williams Street to Grant, then east on Grant to James Street, and then turn north on James. The site lies on the east side of James Street, directly across from the end of Waldo Street (which is now permanently closed to traffic). (3) Octagon Earthworks is reached via 30th Street either from Route 79 or Route 16 (via Church Street). Follow 30th Street to Parkview, then go west on Parkview (one-way) to the memorial grounds. Parking is ahead and to the right at the end of Parkview. Alternatively, from West Main Street, take 33rd Street north for 0.3 mile to Octagon Mound parking area.

PUBLIC USE: Season and hours: *Grounds:* The grounds of Great Circle Earthworks are open during daylight hours April through October. Octagon Earthworks and Wright Earthworks are open during daylight hours daily throughout the year. *Museum:* 9:30 AM to 5 PM, Wednesday through Saturday, Noon to 5 PM, Sunday and holidays, Memorial Day through Labor Day; same hours, weekends only, Labor Day through October. **Fee area:** Museum. **Recreational facilities:** Available only at Great Circle Earthworks; enter from corner of 21st and Cooper streets. **Restrictions:** Octagon Earthworks is privately managed as a private golf course by the Mound Builders Country Club. Regulations regarding access to the grounds are posted at the site.

FOR ADDITIONAL INFORMATION: Contact: Ohio Historical Society, 1982 Velma Avenue, Columbus, OH 43211; 800-686-1535, *www.ohiohistory.org.* **Read:** (1) E. G. Squier and E. H. Davis, 1848. *Ancient Monuments of the Mississippi Valley.* (2) P. Hooge and others, n.d. *Discovering the Prehistoric Mound Builders of Licking County, Ohio* (map). (3) B. T. Lepper, 1995. "Tracking Ohio's great Hopewell road." (4) B. T. Lepper, 1996. "The Newark Earthworks and the geometric enclosures of the Scioto Valley: Connections and conjectures."(5) B. T. Lepper, 1998. "The archaeology of the Newark Earthworks."

OHIO - LICKING COUNTY

42. Upham Mound

The Upham Mound is located in Newark on private property adjacent to the main entrance to Newark High School. The mound is about 4 feet high and is located on a wooded ridge west of the high school access road. It has not been excavated.

The Upham-Wright-Jones House adjoining the mound to the west is acknowledged as an outstanding example of Gothic Revival domestic architecture.

DIRECTIONS: In the western part of Newark, exit SR 16 at 21st Street, go north on 21st Street 0.2 mile, then east on Granville Road 0.6 mile to the entrance to Newark High School. The mound is located about 75 yards north of Granville Road (Figures 77, 81).

PUBLIC USE: Season and hours: The mound is visible from Granville Road at any time. **Restrictions:** The mound is on private property and trespassing is prohibited.

OHIO - LOGAN COUNTY

43. Dunns Pond Mound

Dunns Pond Mound is located at the north end of Dunns Pond, a small embayment near the southeast corner of Indian

Lake. Dunns Pond Mound is subconical, about 7 feet high and 70 feet in diameter. It occupies a small wooded tract of about 1 acre in size that is surrounded by a wooden fence.

The cultural identity of the originators of this mound is not known. A limited excavation by curiosity seekers in the 1940s discovered, high up in the mound, the skeleton of one individual who had been buried in the flesh. When this mound was surveyed in 1974 for nomination to the National Register of Historic Places, it was considered tentatively to be a Hopewell mound and the skeleton discovered in the 1940s was interpreted as an intrusive burial.

Dunns Pond Mound is public space owned by Washington Township and is located adjacent to Indian Lake State Park.

DIRECTIONS: From Russells Point at the intersection of US 33 and SR 708, go north on SR 708 1 block to SR 366, then east on SR 366 2.1 miles to SR 368, then north on SR 368 0.8 mile to Edgewater Avenue at the Moundwood Marina launch ramp, then go west on Edgewater 0.75

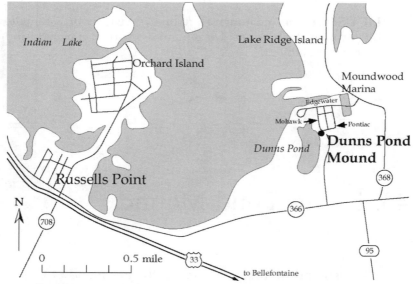

Figure 82. The location of Dunns Pond Mound.

mile to Mohawk, then south on Mohawk 0.1 mile to Dunns Pond Mound. Parking is available at the mound site (Figure 82).

PUBLIC USE: Season and hours: Dunns Pond Mound can be viewed from Mohawk at any time.

FOR ADDITIONAL INFORMATION: Contact: Indian Lake State Park, 12774 State Route 235 N, Lakeview, OH 43331; 937-843-2717, *www.dnr.state.oh.us.*

OHIO - MEIGS COUNTY

44. Buffington Island Mound 1

Buffington Island Mound 1, also known as Price Mound, is the focal point of the Ohio Historical Society's Buffington Island State Memorial, a small tract of land set aside both to preserve this relatively large mound and to commemorate the Battle of Buffington Island that occurred during the Civil War on July 19, 1863.

Buffington Island Mound 1 is about 20 feet high and 125 feet in diameter at the base. Thirty-four concrete steps lead to the top, from which a semi-panoramic view of the Ohio River flood plain may be obtained. Two other, considerably lower, mounds were located in this area but they have been significantly reduced by plowing. This mound reportedly was excavated near the beginning of the twentieth century, but no record or other results of that effort are known to exist. The mound was restored to its current condition in 1931.

DIRECTIONS: This mound is located immediately west of SR 124 in the small community of Portland (Figure 83).

PUBLIC USE: Season and hours: Buffington Island State Memorial is open daily during daylight hours.

FOR ADDITIONAL INFORMATION: Contact: Ohio Historical Society, 1982 Velma Road, Columbus, OH 43211; 800-686-1535, *www.ohiohistory.org.*

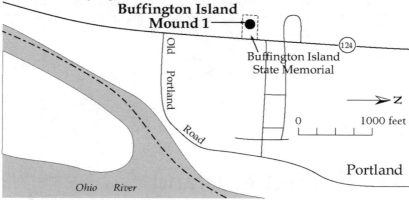

Figure 83. The location of Buffington Island Mound 1.

OHIO - MEIGS COUNTY

45. Mound Cemetery Mound

Mound Cemetery Mound (Figure 84) is located about 2 miles north of Chester in the center of Mound Cemetery, itself perched on the east side of a ridge overlooking a small tributary of Middle Branch of Shade River. This handsome mound is about 12 feet high and 75 feet in diameter at the base, and is conspicuously visible inside an extensively cleared area that includes the cemetery and nearby agricultural land. The cul-

Figure 84. Mound Cemetery Mound is an unusually well-presented conical mound located in open space on a hilltop in southeastern Ohio.

tural affiliation of the mound is not known. Graves of early American settlers in the cemetery date from the 1820s.

DIRECTIONS: From the village of Chester, follow SR 7 north for 1.5 miles to CR 36 (Sumner Road), then go northwest on TR 36 for 0.4 mile to cemetery on west side of road (Figure 85).

PUBLIC USE: The mound may be viewed from CR 36 at any time.

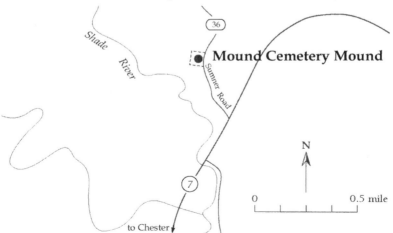

Figure 85. The location of Mound Cemetery Mound.

46. Calvary Cemetery Enclosure

Calvary Cemetery Enclosure was presumably a Hopewell hilltop enclosure and single mound that occupied an estimated 24 acres on top of a prominent ridge known as the Bluffs which is situated immediately south of the Great Miami River in what is now the City of Dayton, Ohio (Figure 86). The west and northwest side of the Bluffs were extremely steep and dropped some 160 feet to the flood plain of the river; the north, east, and south slopes were progressively less steep. Several nearly

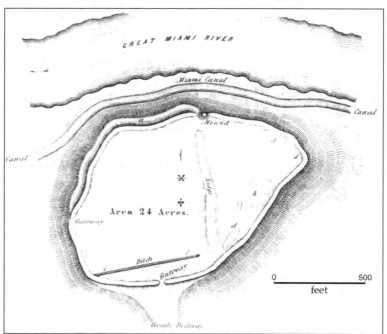

Figure 86. Calvary Cemetery Enclosure. (From Squier and Davis, 1848)

parallel ridges of glacial debris extended across the top of this ridge in a roughly north-south direction, the highest and most prominent of which was named Calvary Ridge. The enclosure was subcircular in shape; its walls were located adjacent to the steep slopes of the north and west sides and lay across more gentle slopes on their south and east sides. The wall was breached in at least three places by planned openings through the south, west, and north walls. A small conical mound was located immediately outside the opening on the north side. The area encompassed by the walls was an irregular surface of ridges and hollows.

Calvary Cemetery was established in 1872 as Dayton's second Catholic cemetery. The headstones that predate 1872 identify many of the nearly 6,000 reinterments that were brought from St. Henry's Cemetery after it ceased to function in 1895. As the Bluffs were converted to a cemetery, the surface of the ridge was graded to smooth the contours and, in the process, parts of the Hopewell enclosure and the glacial ridges were destroyed. By 1915, the east section of the enclosure's wall was gone as was much of Calvary Ridge and the other glacial features. Today, those parts of the enclosure and most of the ridges that were within the cemetery grounds have been removed. Calvary Monument, however, stands atop what was the highest part of Calvary Ridge.

The northernmost part of this enclosure, however, was located outside Calvary Cemetery on land now owned by Carillon Historical Park. As a result, a small section of the enclosure has been preserved within Carillon Historical Park between the north edge of the cemetery and the steep slope descending to the flood plain below. The tree line along the north edge of the cemetery marks the boundary between the cemetery and the park. Also falling on this boundary is the exposed south face of the north end of Calvary Ridge – a graded cut that provides an interesting view of the structure and composition of the largest of the glacial ridges that formerly occupied this hilltop location.

The most conspicuous part of the remaining wall is about 7 feet high and 10 feet in width and crosses the second hollow east of Calvary Ridge. The walls continue up the ridges on either side of the hollow, but as much lower features, and they become indistinguishable at or near the tops of those ridges. In 1915, August Foerste wrote of this site, "Where the wall crosses the head of a much smaller gully, the earth-wall may be distinguished even from a distance" (p. 39). This observation remains valid nearly a century later. The surviving section of the wall is most conveniently viewed from Saint Joseph Drive. From between the Froendhoff and Eyler monuments, look about 10 yards into the woods, in the gully, and you will be looking at the remaining section of the Calvary Cemetery Enclosure. The wall is not on the grounds of the cemetery but on adjoining private property, so please do not walk into the woods to view it without the prior permission of Carillon Historical Park.

DIRECTIONS: Calvary Cemetery is located at the intersection of Calvary and South Dixie avenues, along the west side of South Dixie Avenue, immediately south of Carillon Historical Park. Northbound Exit I-75 at Exit 47 and proceed north on South Dixie Avenue about 3.75 miles to Calvary Cemetery. Southbound Exit US 35 onto South Patterson and proceed south about 1.9 miles to Calvary Avenue. South Patterson becomes South Dixie immediately north of Calvary Cemetery (Figure 87).

PUBLIC USE: Season and hours: October to March, 7 AM to 5:30 PM; April to September, 7 AM to 7:30 PM.

FOR ADDITIONAL INFORMATION: Contact: The Calvary Cemetery Association, Calvary and South Dixie Avenues, Dayton, OH 45409; 937-293-1221. **Read:** (1) E. G. Squier and E. H. Davis, 1848. *Ancient Monuments of the Mississippi Valley*, pp. 23-24. (2) A. F. Foerste, 1915. *An Introduction to the Geology of Dayton and Vicinity.*

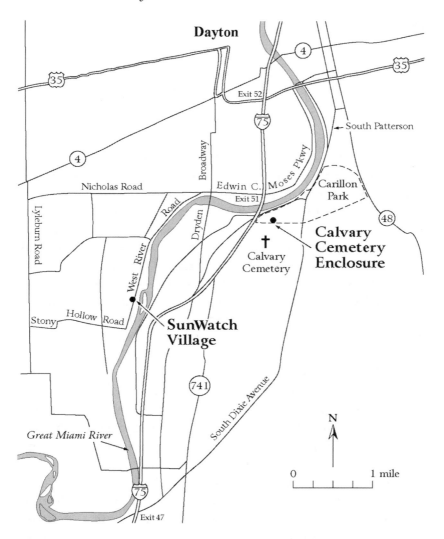

Figure 87. The location of Calvary Cemetery Enclosure and SunWatch Village.

47. SunWatch Village

The SunWatch site, also known as the Incinerator site, lies on the flood plain of the Great Miami River in southern Dayton. SunWatch is an important site of a middle Fort Ancient village that has been extensively excavated by James M. Heilman and associates of the Boonshoft Museum of Discovery, formerly the Dayton Museum of Natural History. Formal excavation of the Incinerator site started in 1971 and continued to 1989, although much of the work was completed during the first few years when the site was threatened with imminent destruction. When the importance of the site became evident, the City of Dayton agreed not to expand its sewage treatment facilities into the area but, instead, to lease the site to the Dayton Museum of Natural History for its continued excavation and conversion to an educational center.

The excavation exposed more than half of the village and provided important information about its shape, size, contents, and the organization and use of space within (Figure 28). The village was nearly circular in outline and measured almost 450 feet in diameter north and south and 380 feet in diameter east and west. The village was surrounded by a stockade and, inside, the dwellings, other buildings, and use areas were arranged in concentric rings and further subdivided into districts with distinct social, political, or other specialized characteristics.

Generally, the stockade that delimited and enclosed the village consisted of upright posts 8 to 10 inches in diameter and placed roughly 10 to 12 inches apart in shallow post holes. Branches were woven between these posts in basket-like fashion. The entrance to the village was toward the northwest through an internal passageway that terminated at what might have been a gatekeeper's house. Elsewhere around the inside perimeter of the stockade was an open zone, and inside that area was a circle of rectangular wooden structures, mostly houses, the floor area of which ranged from 295 to 665 square feet. Inside the circle of structures was a zone of bell-shaped storage and refuse pits, and inside that zone was an area in which many burials were located. At the center of the village was a plaza organized around a large upright post — a post more than 2 feet in diameter that had been sunk nearly 4 feet into the ground. This great center post and two clusters of smaller stakes associated with it apparently constituted the village's solar calendar and served the important function of identifying critical dates in the annual cycle of village life. The western district of the village appears to have contained several specialized corporate buildings, whereas other districts seem to have contained only domestic structures. In the west, for example, were what have been identified as the council house, the men's lodge, and devices coordinated with the solar calendar in the plaza.

In addition to information about the organization and use of space, SunWatch Village has provided abundant and diverse information about a relatively short period of time in the history of one group of Fort Ancient people, a snapshot of the 25 or so years that they spent at a single village in the valley of the Great Miami River during the thirteenth century. Their diet was composed of more than 50 percent maize. The population of the village might have fluctuated seasonally, with the highest population levels occurring during the summer. The people living here suffered from numerous health problems, infant mortality was high, and few lives extended beyond 35 years. Social status and the division of wealth was relatively egalitarian.

The name SunWatch came into use when plans were

made to develop an educational and interpretive center at the site, plans that included the reconstruction of a portion of the village. After several years of preparation, SunWatch Village was opened to the public in 1988 and continues to be the premier publicly accessible site interpreting Fort Ancient culture. SunWatch Village contains about 65 acres and includes a visitor center and a partial reconstruction of the village site. The archeology of the SunWatch site, and the Fort Ancient culture in general, are interpreted in the visitor center, and an outside observation deck lets visitors survey the entire site from a treetop perspective. Representations of several buildings and other important architectural elements of SunWatch have been reconstructed or recreated in the places, and at the scale, suggested by the archeological evidence. A large area of native prairie is being restored in the vicinity of the village.

DIRECTIONS: In downtown Dayton, exit I 75 at Exit 51, go west on Edwin C. Moses Boulevard (which becomes Nicholas Road) about 1 mile to West River Road, then go south on West River Road 1.25 miles to SunWatch Village on the west side of the road (Figure 87).

PUBLIC USE: Season and hours: 9 AM to 5 PM, Tuesday through Saturday, 12 Noon to 5 PM, Sundays. **Fee area:** Admission.

FOR ADDITIONAL INFORMATION: Contact: SunWatch Indian Village, 2301 West River Road, Dayton, OH 45418; 937-268-8199, *www.sunwatch.org,* www.boonshoftmuseum.org. **Read:** (1) J. M. Heilman, M. C. Lileas, and C. A. Turnbow (eds.), 1988. *A History of 17 Years of Excavation and Reconstruction — A Chronicle of 12th Century Human Values and the Built Environment.* (2) J. P. Nass, Jr., and R. W. Yerkes, 1995. "Social differentiation in Mississippian and Fort Ancient societies."

48. Miamisburg Mound

Miamisburg Mound, built on a high bluff east of the Great Miami River and serving as the centerpiece of Miamisburg's Mound Park, is one of the largest conical burial mounds in eastern North America, being rivaled only by the Grave Creek Mound in Moundsville, West Virginia. Originally the mound was at least 68 feet high and 877 feet in circumference at the base. It is now 65 feet high, covers about 1.5 acres, and contains an estimated 54,000 cubic yards of earth. A wooded grassland surrounds the mound. A stairway containing 117 steps leads to the summit which, at 391 feet above the river, provides an excellent view of the City of Miamisburg and the Great Miami River Valley.

Miamisburg Mound (Figure 1) was partly excavated in 1869. At that time a vertical shaft was sunk from the top through the mound to a level 2 feet below the base. Two horizontal tunnels were extended outward from the central shaft. The details of this investigation are sketchy and not entirely consistent. Burials appear to have been found at the 8-foot and 36-foot levels; the upper burial contained a single skeleton covered with bark, and the lower burial consisted only of a log tomb with no sign of human remains. Any interments in the tomb may, of course, have decomposed completely over time. A stone feature, identified as an altar, was reportedly found at a depth of 24 feet. Throughout, layers of ash, stones, and earth were encountered attesting to the fact that the mound had been used at different times and built in increments.

DIRECTIONS: Exit I 75 at Exit 44 (Miamisburg exit), go west on SR 725 for about 3 miles, then south on South Sixth Street approximately 0.4

mile to Mound Avenue, then south on Mound Avenue about 0.6 mile (passing Mound Golf Course) to south end of Mound Park. The well marked entrance is to the left (Figure 88).

PUBLIC USE: Season and hours: Open year round during daylight hours. **Recreational facilities.**

FOR ADDITIONAL INFORMATION: Contact: Miamisburg Parks and Recreation Department, 10 North First Street, Miamisburg, OH 45342; 937-866-4532, *or* Ohio Historical Society, 1982 Velma Avenue, Columbus, OH 43211; 800-686-1535, *www.ohiohistory.org*.

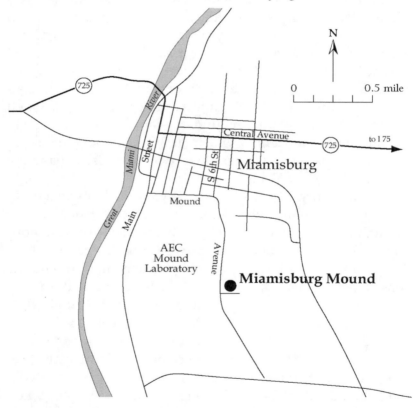

Figure 88. The location of Miamisburg Mound.

OHIO - MONTGOMERY COUNTY

49. Wright Brothers Memorial Mound Group

Much of the pioneering research and development of early aviation was carried out northeast of Dayton, Ohio, and Orville and Wilbur Wright were important participants in that effort. A memorial to the Wright brothers and the advancement of aviation during the industry's early years is located on a hilltop on the north side of what is today one part of Wright-Patterson Air Force Base.

Also on that hilltop, near the north and west sides, one hundred feet above the valley of the Mad River, is a cluster of six mounds that collectively constitute the Wright Brothers Memorial Mound Group (Figure 89). The mounds are low and rounded or conical in shape; they vary in size from 1.7 feet high and 20 feet across at the base to 4.2 feet high and 50 feet across at the base. These mounds are considered to be Adena because of their upland location, size, shape, and number, but this has not been confirmed by excavation.

The mounds are located to the right of the parking lot in the mowed area along the edge of the woods and the hill. This group is one of the finer examples of clustered mounds accessible to the public.

DIRECTIONS: Exit SR 444 onto Kauffman Road (at light near Huffman Dam) eastbound, go 0.15 mile to Skyline Road, then about 250 feet south to entrance to Wright Brothers Memorial west of Wright-Patterson Air Force Base Gate 16B. Park on top of hill; mounds are ahead and to the right (Figure 90).

PUBLIC USE: Season and hours: Open 8 AM to 8 PM daily.

FOR ADDITIONAL INFORMATION: Contact: Office of Environmental Management, 88th Air Base Wing (88 ABW/EM), Wright Patterson Air Force Base, OH 45433, 937-257-5535, extension 254.

Figure 89. Part of the Wright Brothers Memorial Mound Group.

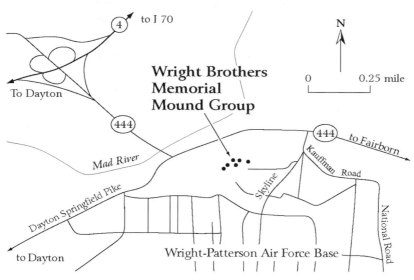

Figure 90. The location of the Wright Brothers Memorial Mound Group.

OHIO - PERRY COUNTY

50. Glenford Fort

Glenford Fort encloses a little more than 27 acres on a ridgetop 200 feet above Jonathan Creek in the Muskingum River drainage system. Unrestored and undeveloped, this fort is significant as one of only a few surviving hilltop enclosures. Its 6,610-foot-long walls are constructed solely of stone from the sandstone caprock of the ridge. Originally the walls could have been 7 feet or more in height and several feet thick, but today they average only 1 to 1.5 feet high.

As is typical of Hopewell hilltop enclosures, the walls of Glenford Fort follow the outline of the hilltop and are absent where natural barriers — in this case an overhanging ledge — provided adequate obstruction to uncontrolled entry. An entrance with re-entrant walls opened onto a narrow neck connecting the fort hill to the adjacent upland.

Apparently, stone was used to some degree in the construction of all hilltop enclosures. Glenford Fort is unique among the hilltop enclosures described in this book in that it is constructed entirely of stone. There were other hilltop enclosures made primarily of stone, perhaps most notably the one at Spruce Hill in Ross County, Ohio.

DIRECTIONS: Follow SR 757 south from Glenford about 0.5 mile, then go east on TR 19 0.2 mile to the Cooperrider farm on the south side of the road. The fort is reached by a primitive footpath located east of the house. Cars may be parked near the foot trail (Figure 91).

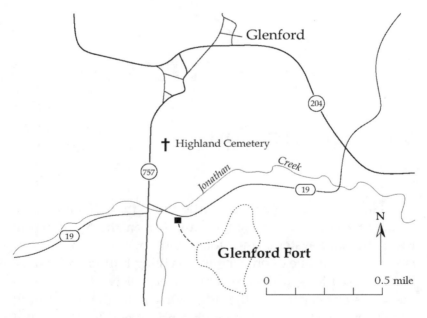

Figure 91. The location of Glenford Fort.

PUBLIC USE: Restrictions: This is an undeveloped site on private property. Visitors enter the property at their own risk. Visitors are requested to ask permission from the landowner before visiting the fort, but may proceed if no one is at the house to extend permission.

FOR ADDITIONAL INFORMATION: Contact: The Cooperrider Family, 4265 Twp Rd. 19, N. W., Glenford, OH 43739; e-mail: *lizcoop1@juno.com.*

OHIO - PIKE COUNTY

51. Piketon Mounds

The four mounds in Mound Cemetery, located on the third terrace near the eastern edge of the Scioto River flood plain about 1 mile south of Piketon, exemplify the many clusters of conical mounds which dotted the Scioto Valley at the time of early American settlement. Squier and Davis, writing in 1848, said:

> *It is common to find two or three, sometimes four or five, sepulchre mounds in a group. In such cases it is always to be remarked that one of the group is much the largest, twice or three times the dimensions of any of the others; and that the smaller ones, of various sizes, are arranged around its base, generally joining it, thus evincing a designed dependence and intimate relation between them* (p. 170).

The largest of the Piketon mounds is about 25 feet high and 75 feet in diameter; the 3 smaller mounds vary between 2 and 5 feet in height. In 1 of the small mounds the skeleton of a girl wrapped in bark was found.

The cultural affiliation of this mound group has not been determined by excavation.

Near the Piketon Mounds cluster was a significant earthwork, one of the most magnificent of known Hopewell graded ways (Figure 92). The Piketon graded way passed in a generally north-south direction from the second terrace to the third terrace, a difference in elevation of 17 feet. When Squier and Davis surveyed this graded way, it was 1,080 feet long

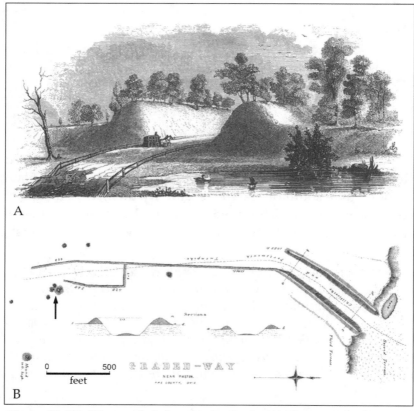

Figure 92. The Piketon graded way and mounds. (A) The upper, northern end of the graded way as it might have appeared in 1848. (B) A plan view of the graded way and the Piketon Mounds (arrow) as portrayed in 1848. (From Squier and Davis, 1848)

and over 200 feet wide. The lower edge of the third terrace had been excavated to create the slope, and the dirt thrown up to level the passage formed an embankment 22 feet above the graded surface. The embankment created along the eastern side of the way continued to the south more than 2,580 feet to a point beyond the cluster of four mounds. Most of this impressive earthwork has been destroyed by farming, modern highway construction, and gravel extraction.

DIRECTIONS: Follow US 23 south from Piketon, exit onto SR 124, go east 0.4 mile (cross Big Beaver Creek), then go north on CR 84 for 0.4 mile to Mound Cemetery on the east side of the road (Figure 93).

PUBLIC USE: Season and hours: Open year round during daylight hours.

FOR ADDITIONAL INFORMATION: Contact: Town of Piketon, 109 Third Street, Piketon, OH 45661; 740-289-8137. **Read:** E. G. Squier and E. H. Davis, 1848. *Ancient Monuments of the Mississippi Valley*, pp. 88-90, 170-171.

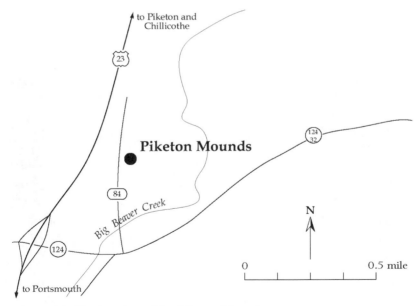

Figure 93. The location of the Piketon Mounds.

52. Hueston Woods Park Mound

Hueston Woods Park Mound is a conical structure, approximately 15 feet high, that lies about 100 yards west of Row B in the Class A camping section of the Hueston Woods State Park campground (Figure 94). The feature has not been excavated so its actual cultural affiliation is not known, but it is similar in size, configuration, and location to other Adena burial mounds. The mound is located in a grove of old beech trees on a narrow terrace between two tributaries of Four Mile Creek. A log fence encloses the feature, and a foot path encircles the fenced mound. The site is reached by walking along a mowed pathway. The 200-acre beech forest in Hueston Woods State Park has been designated a National Natural Landmark.

Figure 94. Hueston Woods Park Mound sits on the edge of a wooded tract at the end of a trail from the park's camping area.

DIRECTIONS: Follow US 27 to Oxford, then go north on SR 732 about 5 miles to park entrance. Signs along road provide directions to the park, and signs in the park provide directions to the campground. There is no established parking area near the mound. Visitors wishing to see the mound must park in the visitors parking lot near the entrance to the campground and walk to the mound (Figure 95).

PUBLIC USE: Season and hours: The park and campground are open year round; grounds close to non-campers at 11 PM.

FOR ADDITIONAL INFORMATION: Contact: Division of Parks and Recreation, 1952 Belcher Drive, C-3, Columbus, OH 43224; 614-265-6561, *www.dnr.state.oh.us.*

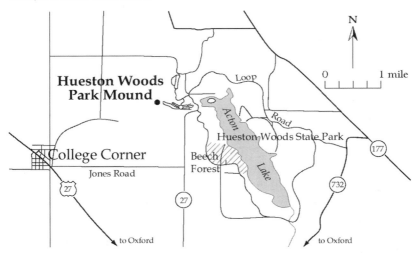

Figure 95. The location of Hueston Woods Park Mound.

53. Adena

Chillicothe and its immediate environs contain an unusually rich concentration of some of Ohio's most significant prehistoric and historic landmarks. Just as one of the great concentrations of Adena and Ohio Hopewell earthworks are located in this middle part of the Scioto River Valley, so too are several key sites related to the emergence of Ohio as a modern political entity from out of the vast Northwest Territory during the decades following the Revolutionary War. Adena, home of Thomas Worthington, commemorates one of Ohio's staunchest advocates of statehood and early economic development. Adena also unites the prehistory and history of the region in a unique way.

Thomas Worthington was born in Virginia and, in the 1790s, moved to Chillicothe where he rose to social, financial, and political prominence. Active in efforts to obtain statehood for Ohio in 1803, Worthington served as one of Ohio's two first US senators and later became the state's sixth governor, and was a strong proponent of canal development in the new state. Worthington was a principal in conceiving Ohio's Coat of Arms, a symbolic image that had its birth in the view of the morning sun rising over the crest of Mount Logan immediately east of the Scioto Valley, as seen from Adena.

In 1805, Worthington commissioned Benjamin Henry Latrobe, one of the most distinguished architects in America at the time, to design a home that would be built on top of the plateau bordering the west side of the Scioto Valley immediately north of Chillicothe, the new state capital of Ohio. Latrobe produced plans for a crisp, modified Georgian structure consisting of a central two-story unit with two wings, one to the front of each end of the central unit, each wing having 1 ½ stories. Formal gardens were to the east with supporting structures to the west. The home was built between 1806 and 1807 out of local sandstone and, when finished, was known as Mount Prospect Hall. While reading ancient history in 1811, however, Worthington came across the name "Adena" which, in Hebrew, means "places remarkable for the delightfulness of their situations." Thereafter, Worthington referred to his estate — a property that contained 5,000 acres, including land on both the plateau and the valley below, much of which had been developed into pastures, orchards, and cultivated fields — as Adena.

Located on the second terrace of the valley floor, near the west edge of the Scioto Valley and northeast of the manor house, was a small lake that Worthington called Ellensmere, and immediately east of this lake and north of Adena Road was a large conical prehistoric mound about 27 feet high and 140 feet in diameter (figures 8 and 12). This mound was surrounded by a circular embankment and it is possible that a wooden structure occupied the site before the mound was built.

Decades after Worthington's death, in 1901, William C. Mills of the Ohio Archaeological and Historical Society excavated much of the mound near Lake Ellensmere. Mills found that the mound had been built in two stages. The first mound was about 20 feet high and 90 feet in diameter, and contained 21 burials. The initial burials were placed in a large rectangular log tomb approximately 13 feet long by 11 feet wide that had been sunk 7 feet into the natural surface. An extended burial of an adult male was made on the bottom of this grave, the cremated remains of an adult and a child were above the male, and above them was the extended skeleton of another adult male who was placed at the foot of, and at right angles to, the lower adult skeleton. All of the remaining 17 burials in the first mound were in log tombs on or within 5 feet of the natural surface. Twelve burials were found in the second mound; these occurred throughout the mound and none was associated with long tombs or bark coverings.

Grave goods were associated with most burials in both stages of the mound, but were more numerous in the first stage. These goods included blades and points of Flint Ridge flint, tubular pipes, copper jewelry, worked shell, beads, and one of the most famous of Adena artifacts, a tubular effigy pipe in the likeness of a human dwarf (Plate 5). Mills' work at the Adena Mound constituted the first systematic archeological investigation of a mound of this type and his report was the first description by an archeologist of the structure and content of an Adena mound. Consequently, Adena Mound on the Adena estate became the type site for the Adena culture.

Today, the Adena estate consists of 320 acres and is owned by the State of Ohio and administered by the Ohio Historical Society as a state memorial. The manor house, one of only 3 houses designed by Latrobe that still survive in the United States, is undergoing extensive restoration under the direction of William Seale. The house will reopen to the public in 2003, along with a new visitor center that will include exhibits on the life of Thomas Worthington, frontier life in Ohio, and Ohio's statehood monument. That part of the ancestral estate that included the Adena Mound is not a part of the present state property. The site now lies invisible beneath a road and house lots east of Lake Ellensmere.

DIRECTIONS: From US 23/US 35 intersection north of Chillicothe, go west on US 35 about 2.0 miles to SR 104, then north 0.1 mile to CR 127 (Pleasant Valley Road), then west 0.4 mile to Adena Road, then west 0.5 mile to Adena State Memorial (Figure 95).

PUBLIC USE: Season and hours: Adena State Memorial is closed for restoration at the time of this writing and will reopen to the public in the spring of 2003.

FOR ADDITIONAL INFORMATION: Contact: *For mound information:* Ohio Historical Society, 1982 Velma Road, Columbus, OH 43211;

800-686-1535, *www.ohiohistory.org*. *For estate information:* Adena State Memorial, P. O. Box 831, Chillicothe, OH 45601-0831; 800-319-7248. **Read:** (1) W. C. Mills, 1902. "Excavations of the Adena Mound." (2) A. B. Sears, 1958. *Thomas Worthington, Father of Ohio Statehood.*

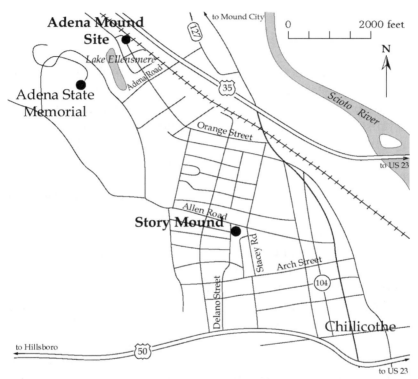

Figure 96. The location of Adena State Memorial, Adena Mound, and Story Mound.

219

OHIO - ROSS COUNTY

54. Story Mound

Story Mound is a conical Adena burial mound owned by the Ohio Historical Society and located on a tract of fenced green space approximately one acre in size within a residential district on the north side of Chillicothe. The mound today is about 19.5 feet high and 95 feet in diameter; although several trees are now growing on the mound, it and the remainder of the fenced area are mowed regularly.

Clarence Loveberry excavated this mound in 1897, at which time it was around 25 feet high, about the same size as the Adena Mound which then lay about 1 mile to the northwest on what had been Thomas Worthington's Adena estate. Loveberry's excavation was carried out by tunneling into the cone from the sides, an activity that located, near the north wall of the mound, a single extended skeleton of a young male with associated grave goods. Loveberry's excavation is particularly significant, however, because it uncovered post holes of a circular structure some 15 feet in diameter, the first documentation of the circular building structure used by the Adena.

DIRECTIONS: Exit US 35 onto SR 104 southbound, go south on SR 104/High Street 0.8 mile to Allen Avenue, then west on Allen Avenue 0.5 mile to Delano Avenue, then south on Delano Avenue one block to Story Mound on east side of road. Curbside parking is available on Delano Avenue (Figure 96).

PUBLIC USE: Season and hours: The mound and interpretive sign can be viewed year round during daylight hours. **Restrictions:** The site is fenced and visitors are not permitted on the grounds.

FOR ADDITIONAL INFORMATION: Contact: Ohio Historical Society, 1982 Velma Road, Columbus, OH 43211; 800-686-1535, *www.ohiohistory.org*.

55. Hopewell Culture National Historical Park

Mound City, a Hopewell embankment and burial mound complex located north of Chillicothe, has long attracted the varied interests of a curious and inquisitive public fascinated with the Hopewell, their architectural monuments, their artistic expression, and their mortuary practices (Plate 1). It is fitting, therefore, that this unique, important, and long appreciated site should now be the anchor property of Hopewell Culture National Historical Park, the primary federal entity devoted to preserving, studying, and interpreting the culture of the people who influenced so much of eastern North America during the middle Woodland period.

Hopewell Culture National Historical Park was established in 1992 at which time the former Mound City Group National Monument's name was changed and the park's geographic and programmatic scope was broadened considerably. Today, the park administers five properties that include some of the most historically and culturally important earthworks of the Scioto Valley Hopewell. Mound City is the administrative center of the park and the principal unit that is managed for public visitation. Portions of Hopewell Mound Group (Figure 17) and Seip Earthworks (Figure 99) west of Chillicothe, and Hopeton Earthworks and High Banks Earthworks east of the Scioto near Chillicothe, also are parts of the park. Hopewell Mound Group provides a parking area, an observation area, and a 1-mile paved trail, and an interpretive kiosk is to installed during the spring of 2002. High Bank, Hopeton, and the park's portion of Seip are not open to the public.

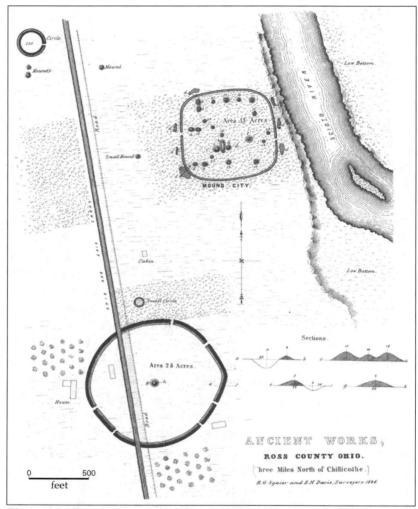

Figure 97. Mound City and environs. (From Squier and Davis, 1848)

The rectangular enclosure at Mound City (Figure 97), the outline of which resembles that of a typical Hopewell wooden structure, is 2,050 feet long and from 2.5 to 3 feet high. The 15.6 acres within this embankment contained at least 23 mounds, one of the greatest concentrations of Hopewell burial mounds known (Figure 96). Squier and Davis, both residents of nearby Chillicothe, excavated parts of most of the mounds — and so did other people. When Squier and Davis investigated these mounds in 1846, the land was in a farmer's woodlot, but within 10 years the woodlot had been cleared, the area was under cultivation, and the mounds and embankments continued to be damaged. In 1917, the US Army constructed Camp Sherman, a World War I training and detention facility, at Mound City. All mounds except the large Central Mound were leveled during the time that Camp Sherman occupied the grounds. Fortunately, the floors of most of the altered mounds were left intact. After the war, in 1920, William C. Mills of the Ohio State Archaeological and Historical Society directed an excavation of the remaining large mound. Later, after Camp Sherman was dismantled, the other mound sites were excavated under the direction of Mills and Henry C. Shetrone. Based on the surveys, descriptions, and excavations of Squier and Davis, Mills, Shetrone, and others, the Mound City Group has been extensively restored. The site was established as a National Monument in 1923.

Generally, each mound within the enclosure covered a site that had contained a wooden structure with a prepared ceremonial surface upon which a variety of ritual activities probably had been carried out. When the ceremonial use of an area had been completed, the structure was burned or taken down and the space it occupied was mounded over with earth, sand, and gravel. The outer surface of the mound was frequently capped with stones and gravel. The mounds were not identical in shape, size, or contents. The diversity found among them, such as their shape, the number of burials they covered, or the presence of unusual types or amounts of grave goods or other deposits, have often been the inspiration for the names the mounds bear today.

A self-guided tour of this site takes visitors through the enclosure and introduces them to selected aspects of the

Hopewell ceremonial activities that took place on these grounds two thousand years ago. Several mounds are featured on this tour. Mica Grave Mound covered a basin 6 feet square that was lined with mica and contained the remains of at least 4 individuals; another 16 burials were located elsewhere at the site. Squier and Davis found nearly 200 effigy pipes, along with copper and beads, in a special deposit near the sole clay basin beneath Mound of the Pipes (Plate 1). These pipes, along with other objects in the Squier and Davis collection, were sold by Davis in 1864 to William Blackmore, a British collector. The collection eventually was acquired by the British Museum. Central Mound, the largest and most complexly structured mound of the group, covered the site of two former wooden structures and the graves of 13 cremated skeletons. Among the artifacts recovered from the Central Mound were fragments of what appears to be a headpiece made of human skull bones. Squier and Davis's "long mound" near the center of the enclosure was the only distinctly elongate mound at Mound City. An outline of the base of a typical wooden ceremonial structure is located south of Central Mound and provides a sense of the size and shape of these structures.

In addition to its importance as a Hopewell site, Mound City is also the type site for the Intrusive Mound Culture, a late Woodland culture that occupied the Scioto Valley between the time that Hopewell disappeared and Fort Ancient appeared. William C. Mills described and named this culture based on material he had found during excavations at Mound City as well as on material that previously had been found at Mound City and two sites in Portsmouth. The name stems from the practice of burying the dead in mounds that had been built earlier by the Adena or Hopewell (Figure 27).

The visitor center houses exhibits describing facets of Hopewell ceremonial practices and screens a video that provides an overview of Hopewell culture. In addition, the center offers the largest and best selection of books available in the middle Ohio Valley on mound builders and other Native Americans of the region, and it is a conduit for *Hopewell Archeology: The Newsletter of Hopewell Archeology in the Ohio River Valley*. The park's web site, given below, is an excellent source of information about Hopewell Culture National Historical Park and the Hopewell culture.

DIRECTIONS: From US 35 at Chillicothe, take SR 104 north 1.6 miles to the monument on the east side of the road (Figure 98). *Note:* If traveling southbound on US 23 north of Chillicothe, exit onto SR 159 north of Hopetown. There is no direct exit onto US 35 from US 23 southbound.

PUBLIC USE: Season and hours: *Grounds:* Open year round during daylight hours. *Museum:* Open daily, 8:30 AM to 5 PM with extended hours in summer; closed Thanksgiving, Christmas, and New Year's

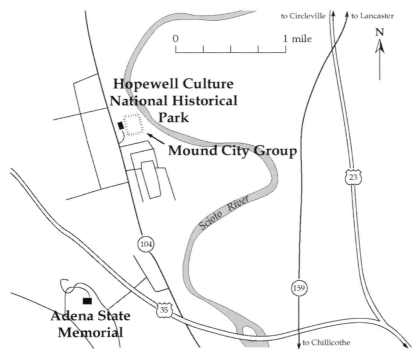

Figure 98. The location of Mound City Group, Hopewell Culture National Historical Park, and Adena State Memorial.

Day. **Fee area:** Admission. **Recreational facilities. For people with disabilities:** Most trails, exhibits, and recreational facilities are accessible.

FOR ADDITIONAL INFORMATION: Contact: Superintendent, Hopewell Culture National Historical Park, 16062 State Route 104, Chillicothe, OH 45601; 740-774-1126, *www.nps.gov/hocu*. **Read:** (1) E. G. Squier and E. H. Davis, 1848. *Ancient Monuments of the Mississippi Valley*, pp. 26-29, 51-52, 54-55. (2) W. C. Mills, 1922. "Exploration of the Mound City Group." (3) H. C. Shetrone, 1926. "Explorations of the Hopewell Group of Prehistoric Earthworks." (4) N. B. Greber and K. C. Ruhl, 2000. *The Hopewell Site: A Contemporary Analysis Based on the Work of Charles C. Willoughby.*

OHIO - ROSS COUNTY

56. Seip Mound

Seip Earthworks was one of several major Hopewell earthworks complexes that were located in the scenic Paint Creek Valley of southcentral Ohio. Situated on the second and third terraces north of Paint Creek, Seip (pronounced *sipe*) consisted of a square and a complete circle joined by a larger polygon which included elements of both circle and rectangle (Figure 99). The area within these combined enclosures is estimated to have been about 121 acres. The walls were up to 10 feet high, 50 feet wide at the base, and 10,000 feet long. Within the embankment were several small mounds, 3 large conjoined mounds, a small circle with a mound in the center, and the exceptionally large oblong central mound – Seip, or Seip-Pricer, Mound – that was surrounded by a low earthen wall. Other mounds were located outside the enclosure. Large mounds like Seip-Pricer, which originally measured 240 feet by 160 feet by 30 feet, are unusual in Hopewell sites; indeed, only Mound 25 of the Hopewell Group, which measured 500 feet by 180 feet by 33 feet, was larger than Seip-Pricer Mound, while Carriage Factory Mound, located near Adena and Story mounds in the northwestern part of Chillicothe, was Seip-Pricer's equal.

The Seip-Pricer Mound was excavated from 1925 to 1928 by Henry C. Shetrone and Emerson F. Greenman of the Ohio State Archaeological and Historical Society and, afterwards, was restored to its present form. These investigators reported finding 122 interments, including both cremations and extended burials. Grave goods included mica from the Carolinas, copper from Isle Royale in Lake Superior, effigy pipes made of raw material from the Tennessee River Valley, and some 15,000 freshwater pearls of various sizes and shapes.

Excavations in the 1970s exposed the postmold patterns

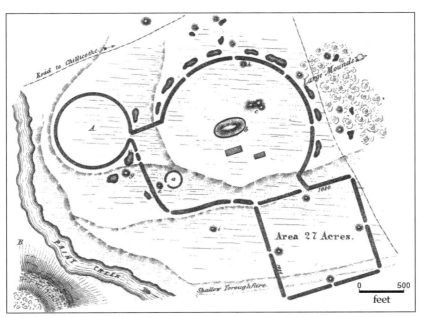

Figure 99. Seip Earthworks and Seip Mound. (From Squier and Davis, 1848)

of 7 Hopewell structures, and the outlines of 3 of these may be seen along the trail that leads to the mound. Most of these structures had 2 opposing walls of double post construction and 2 of single post construction. Most Hopewell structures were square or rectangular.

N'omi Greber of the Cleveland Museum of Natural History has studied Seip and other middle Woodland sites in Paint Creek and Scioto valleys for years and, among other important contributions, has proposed a model according to which Seip and other earthworks complexes in the area might have developed. Greber has determined that Seip was most likely occupied by Hopewell people from around AD 100 to AD 500, during which time, she estimates, the population likely fluctuated from perhaps 4 households of an extended family to perhaps 10 times that number — a range of something like 20 to 200 people. The earliest Hopewell occupants built wooden structures, not enduring monumental earthen ones, but as the population increased, time passed, and needs changed, earthen structures — mounds — came to be placed over the sites where ceremonial structures had once stood. Later, embankments were built to enclose the mounds and their environs. As this earthen architectural landscape evolved, a progressive separation of the location of domestic and corporate activities probably occurred. Accordingly, areas that might have been used in part for habitation during the early history of the site might have become restricted to corporate uses as, or after, the enclosure was built.

Seip was nearly obliterated by decades of farming before a small part of the site was acquired by the Ohio Historical Society. The property, now managed as a state memorial, contains 236 acres, or about 10 percent of the original earthworks area, and is dominated by the large central mound. The Ohio Department of Transportation manages a roadside rest and picnic area adjacent to the site. Exhibits in an outdoor pavilion provide an overview of the archeology of Ohio and more detailed information on Seip and the history of its exploration. The floor plans of some of the houses or workshops have been reconstructed on site, at scale, inside the perimeter of the former earthwork. Other parts of the earthworks have recently been acquired by the National Park Service, but this area is not developed for public access.

DIRECTIONS: Follow US 50 approximately 17 miles west of Chillicothe, 4 miles west of Bourneville, 3 miles east of Bainbridge, or 22 miles east of Hillsboro. Signs identifying the roadside rest appear about 1 mile on either side of the site (Figure 100).

PUBLIC USE: Season and hours: Open year round during daylight hours.

FOR ADDITIONAL INFORMATION: Contact: Ohio Historical Society, 1982 Velma Avenue, Columbus, OH 43211; 800-686-1535, *www.ohiohistory.org*. **Read:** (1) W. C. Mills, 1909. "Explorations of the Seip Mound." (2) H. C. Shetrone and E. F. Greenman, 1931. "Explorations of the Seip Group of prehistoric earthworks." (3) R. S. Baby and S. M. Langlois, 1979. "Seip Mound State Memorial: Nonmortuary aspects of Hopewell." (4) N. B. Greber, 1979. "A comparative study of site morphology and burial patterns at Edwin Harness Mound and Seip mounds 1 and 2." (5) N. B. Greber, 1997. "Two geometric enclosures in the Paint Creek Valley: An estimate of possible changes in community patterns through time."

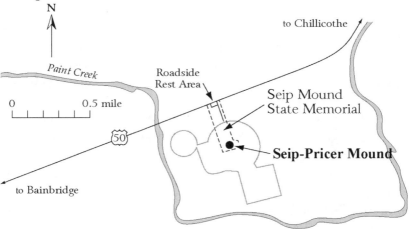

Figure 100. The location of the Seip Earthworks and Seip-Pricer Mound.

57. Portsmouth Mound Park

Near where the Scioto River empties into the Ohio River, extensive level lowlands on both sides of the Ohio and the crossroads function afforded by the convergence of navigable waterways created an ideal setting for the development of a major Woodland earthworks complex. When Squier and Davis provided the first comprehensive description and illustration of the entire Portsmouth system in 1848, they stated that a single integrated network of geometric earthen architecture extended nearly 8 miles alongside the Ohio River and that this network incorporated some 20 miles of earthen embankments in the forms of rectangles, circles, and parallel walls (Figure 23). Other parts of the complex, they explained, had already been destroyed. Not included in the miles of embankments were mounds that were scattered among the embankments — some clearly and directly associated with the walls and enclosures and others that quite possibly stood apart. At present, no other single integrated earthworks complex in the middle Ohio Valley has been shown to extend over a larger area than did the one at Portsmouth, and none has been shown to have included more miles of embankment than did this one.

The Portsmouth complex included three large clusters or centers of geometric earthworks, one in Ohio and two in Kentucky, and all three were located on high terraces near the bordering hills. The geometry of each center was different. The group on the Ohio side (Figure 101) was dominated by a pair of U-shaped embankments, arranged side by side, and partly enclosed by a semi-circle, beyond which were a number of other circles and mounds. Several miles to the south-

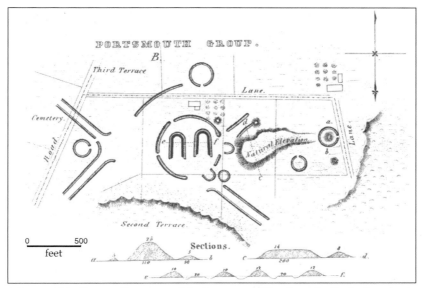

Figure 101. The northern part of the Portsmouth Earthworks, including those features now incorporated within Mound Park. (From Squier and Davis, 1848)

west, on the Kentucky side of the river, was a square enclosure — the Old Fort — from which two nearly identical elongated rectangular enclosures extended to the northeast and the southwest. Almost an equal distance to the southeast of the Ohio center, also on the Kentucky side, was a circular earthwork with a mound in the center. Parallel-walled embankments, uniformly wide and with walls of uniform breadth and height, seemingly connected the three centers. Another set of parallel walls extended to the west of the Ohio center only to vanish as it entered the valley of the Scioto. Squier and Davis conjectured that this embankment might have connected with other Hopewell centers in the Scioto Valley.

Very little of the Portsmouth earthworks has survived, and the only surviving components in public space are those in Mound Park in Portsmouth. The most distinct of these is the eastern U-shaped embankment which, now fenced, occupies the southwestern part of the park. According to Squier and Davis, this feature, which at one time lay at the heart of the earthworks system, measured 80 feet in length by 70 feet in breadth. The picnic pavilion in the southeastern part of the park sits upon what is also, almost certainly, an archeological feature — either a mound or an artificially leveled surface that was ascended by a graded ramp. Atwater felt that this rise was artificial; Squier and Davis considered it geological in origin but to have been modified by those who built and used the Portsmouth earthworks complex. At least two low rises in the northwestern part of Mound Park could be remnants of mounds or embankments that were part of the once-great Portsmouth earthworks.

The Portsmouth earthworks are generally considered to have been built by the Hopewell, but there is an Adena presence at the site. The Biggs Mound (figures 15 and 23, feature D), a circle and ditch with an enclosed burial mound located northwest of the eastern center in Kentucky, is a classic Adena landscape feature, and artifacts from Biggs Mound include objects that are usually considered to be Adena. The circular earthwork of the eastern center (Figure 23, feature C) is structurally not far removed from the basic architectural elements of the Adena circle and mound. The Old Fort that makes up much of the western center in Kentucky (Figure 23, feature A) is Hopewell, but part of the earthwork lies upon what was once an Adena site.

DIRECTIONS: From US 23 in Portsmouth, go east on Kinneys Lane approximately 0.75 mile (to three blocks past Greenlawn Cemetery), then go south on Hutchins Avenue for 0.3 mile (2 blocks) to Mound Park. From US 52, go north on Hutchins Avenue 0.25 mile (3 blocks) to Mound Park. Curbside parking is available at the park (Figure 102).

PUBLIC USE: Season and hours: Open daily. **Recreation facilities.**

FOR ADDITIONAL INFORMATION: Contact: Public Service Department, City of Portsmouth, 55 Mary Ann Street, Portsmouth, OH 45662; 740-354-8807. **Read:** (1) C. Atwater, 1833. *The Writings of Caleb Atwater*, pp. 56-61. (2) E. G. Squier and E. H. Davis, 1848. *Ancient Monuments of*

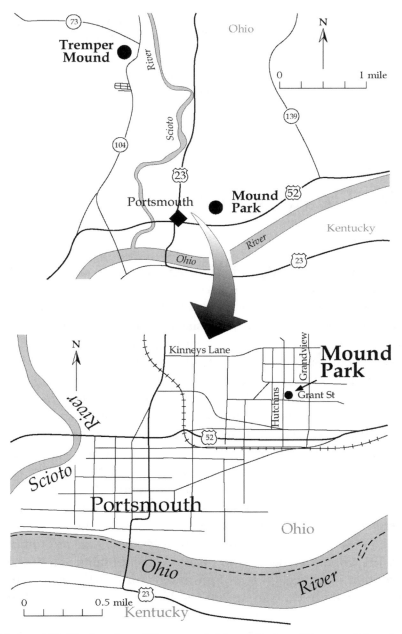

Figure 102. The location of Portsmouth Mound Park and Tremper Mound.

the Mississippi Valley, pp. 77-82. (3) A. G. Henderson, D. Pollack, and D. R. Cropper, 1988. "The Old Fort Earthworks, Greenup County, Kentucky."

OHIO - SCIOTO COUNTY

58. Tremper Mound

The Tremper Mound is located on high ground along the extreme western edge of the lower Scioto Valley, on what was once the property of state senator William D. Tremper of Portsmouth. The site originally consisted of a nearly square enclosure with rounded corners measuring roughly 480 feet by 400 feet, with a single opening to the southwest beyond which was a single elongate mound or segment of embankment (Figure 103). The walls of the embankment were abut 3 feet high and 30 feet across at the base when surveyed by Charles Whittlesey. A large, low amorphous mound was located near the center of the enclosure. The maximum height of the mound was 8.5 feet, with its lowest parts being at the eastern end where the projecting points were only about 1 foot high. Because of its amorphous shape, the interior mound was long referred to as an effigy mound.

William C. Mills excavated the interior mound at Tremper in 1915. Beneath the mound he found the remains of a burned wooden structure. Over 600 postmolds outlined a multichambered oval building some 200 feet long by 100 feet wide (Figure 21), a structure now recognized as a great house. Unique to Tremper Mound were 4 communal graves for the dead and their paraphernalia, a circumstance that contrasted with the individual burials characteristic of other Hopewell burial mounds. Mills estimated that some 375 cremations were contained in the 4 communal graves on the floor of the charnel house.

Tremper is also well known for the large number of beautifully crafted pipes that were found at the site. One group of 9 unbroken pipes, along with a small number of other objects, were found near the center of the mound, about 2.5 feet above its base. A larger group of some 500 objects was found in a deposit in the floor of the mound near the east end of the mound; 136 of these objects were pipes. All of the pipes in this lower deposit had been broken ritually before being covered by the mound, almost all were platform pipes, most were made of Ohio pipestone, and about 90 were effigies carved in the form of native animals, especially birds, and humans.

The mound was completely restored after excavation, but the site is undeveloped, privately owned, and currently being

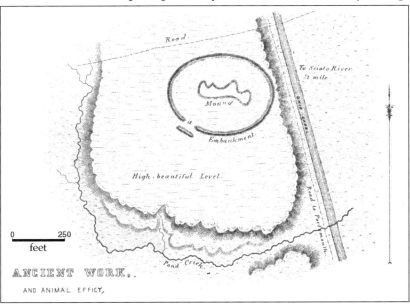

Figure 103. The Tremper Site. (From Squier and Davis, 1848)

used as pasture. The mound is located on a low hill to the west of, and slightly above the level of, SR 73 and 104. It is in an open field and is marked by a small but largely ineffective sign. However, it can be seen from the road immediately south of where SR 73 and 104 converge. The mound is most easily viewed when approaching from the south; there are a few places on the east side of SR 73/104 to pull over, but none is intended for this use. Stop at your own risk!

DIRECTIONS: Combined SR 73/104 pass the mound 0.1 mile south of where they converge. SR 73/104 is a two-lane highway. Caution should be exercised when viewing the mound, as traffic can be heavy at times. No formal parking is available (Figure 103).

PUBLIC USE: Season and hours: The Tremper Mound may be viewed from SR 73/104 at any time. **Restrictions:** The Tremper Mound is located on private property and trespassing is prohibited.

FOR ADDITIONAL INFORMATION: Read: W. C. Mills, 1916. "Exploration of the Tremper Mound." (2) M. P. Otto, 1984. "Masterworks in pipestone: Treasure from Tremper Mound."

OHIO - VINTON COUNTY

59. Hope Furnace Mound

A single, low subconical mound measuring about 3 feet in height and 40 feet in diameter at the base occupies a low ridge overlooking the upper part of Lake Hope, an artificial reservoir that is the main attraction of Lake Hope State Park. Prior to the creation of the reservoir, this mound would have overlooked the confluence of Sandy Run and Habron Hollow

Creek. The site is located about 20 paces west of the Hope Furnace Trail, about one-eighth of a mile from where the White Oak and Hope Furnace trails diverge at the base of the hill below the nature center.

This mound is not a registered archeological site, and it has no excavation history to confirm that it is prehistoric. Yet, there is no compelling reason to suspect that it is not prehistoric. The location of this feature is typical for Adena mounds, many mounds are known to have existed in the vicinity of Lake Hope State Park, and a prehistoric habitation site is nearby. There are no excavation scars or roadways leading to the site that would imply a historic origin for the structure.

Hope Furnace is a relic of the iron industry that flourished in southeastern Ohio during the nineteenth century.

DIRECTIONS: Take SR 278 to the Hope Furnace Picnic Area. Walk northwest 0.5 mile on the Hope Furnace Trail to a point about 0.1 mile beyond the junction with White Oak Trail, then look to the west into an area of pine trees to locate the mound. Alternatively, park at the nature center near the campground and take the White Oak Trail to the base of

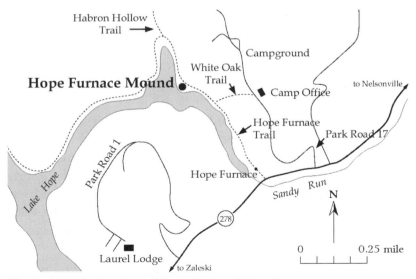

Figure 104. The location of Hope Furnace Mound.

the hill, then go west 0.1 mile to the mound. Be advised that the White Oak Trail is very steep and straight (Figure 104).

PUBLIC USE: Lake Hope State Park is open daily throughout the year.

FOR ADDITIONAL INFORMATION: Contact: Division of Parks and Recreation, Ohio Department of Natural Resources, 1952 Belcher Drive, C-3, Columbus, OH 43224; 614-265-6561, *www.dnr.state.oh.us.*

Оню - Vinton County

60. Ranger Station Mound

     Ranger Station Mound, also known as Zaleski Mound I, is located in Zaleski State Forest, west of the Zaleski Elementary School near the forest manager's residence, about 60 feet above the level of nearby Raccoon Creek. The mound is about 13 feet high and 80 feet in diameter, and it now has several large trees growing upon it. A driveway (State Forest Road 17) loops past the manager's residence and the mound, which is identified with a sign.

     There is no known record of excavation for this mound, but it has traditionally been considered an Adena burial mound. A root cellar was dug beneath the structure during the middle of the nineteenth century and a skeleton reportedly was found but, if a skeleton was found, it has since been lost. Near the mound is the Forest of Honor, a memorial established in 1987 to commemorate those who have made significant contributions to forestry in Ohio.

DIRECTIONS: From the intersection of SR 278 and 677 in Zaleski, follow SR 278 north 0.3 mile, then go west at Zaleski Elementary School for 0.2 mile into Zaleski State Forest (via State Forest Road 17) and the Ranger Station Mound. Parking is available near the mound (Figure 105).

PUBLIC USE: The mound may be viewed at any time from State Forest Road 17, but remember that the nearby structure is a residence.

FOR ADDITIONAL INFORMATION: Contact: Forest Manager, Zaleski State Forest, General Delivery, Zaleski, OH 45698; 740-596-5781, *www.dnr.state.oh.us.*

OHIO - VINTON COUNTY

61. Zaleski Methodist Church Mound

Zaleski Methodist Church Mound is located on a relatively level surface of a ridge spur that extends toward the flood plain of Raccoon Creek. The mound is some 5 feet high and about 60 feet in diameter at the base, and it lies about 60 feet above Raccoon Creek. It is covered with grass and occupies most of the back yard of the Zaleski Methodist Church. The mound is low relative to its breadth, and appears to have been lowered by cultivation.

There is no record that this mound has been excavated and its cultural affiliation is not known. It is presumed to be Adena based on its location, size, and shape, and its proximity to other mounds and earthworks considered or known to be Adena.

DIRECTIONS: From the intersection of SR 278 and 677 in Zaleski, follow SR 278 north 1 block, then go west 1 block. The Zaleski Methodist Church will be directly ahead, on the northwest corner of the intersection. The mound is behind the church (Figure 105).

PUBLIC USE: This mound may be viewed at any time from the streets of Zaleski. **Restrictions:** The mound is on private property and trespassing is prohibited.

FOR ADDITIONAL INFORMATION: Contact: Zaleski United Methodist Church, Broadway Street, Zaleski, OH 45698; 740-596-4202.

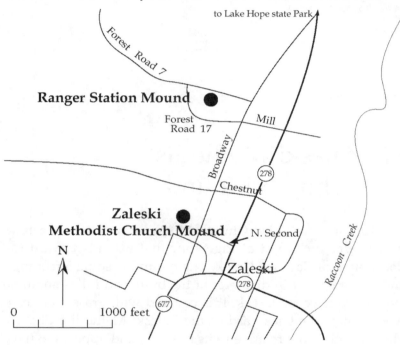

Figure 105. The location of Ranger Station Mound and Zaleski Methodist Church Mound.

62. Fort Ancient

Fort Ancient, one of the most well known prehistoric sites in the United States and Ohio's first state park (1891), is an outstanding example of the Hopewell hilltop enclosure (Figure 106). Winding almost 3.5 miles across a plateau surface in southwestern Ohio, mostly near the precipitous edge of a promontory looking over the Little Miami River 275 feet below, the earth and stone walls of Fort Ancient enclose some 125 acres of nearly level, glaciated upland. The walls range from 4 to 23 feet in height, the highest segment being in the northeast where the promontory connects with the more extensive upland surface and there is no bordering ravine. In some places where the hillside is exceptionally steep, there is no wall at all, most likely a result of erosion rather than design. The embankment is interrupted by 67 broad U-shaped gateways, some shallow and others deeper. Several conical mounds were located in or just outside of the embankment, the most important of which were a pair of mounds east of the northeast entrance and a set of four mounds inside the northeastern part of the enclosure. At least three arcuate mounds were inside the walls. A rectangular earthwork consisting of parallel walls closed with a semi-circle at the east end was located immediately east of the twin mounds at the northeast entrance to the enclosure. The open west end of this feature was in line with the pair of mounds outside the northeast entrance.

The spectacular nature of Fort Ancient attracted the attention of antiquarians and early archeologists. Atwater and Squier and Davis gave this site substantial attention, and

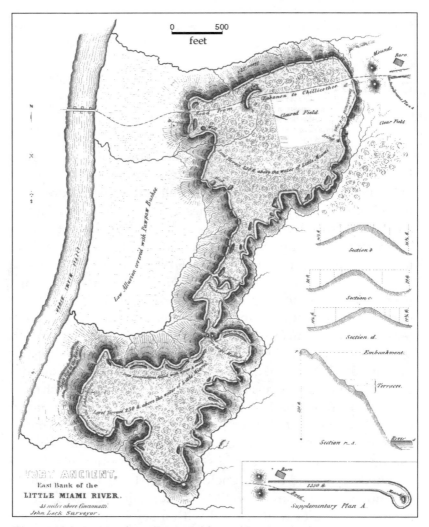

Figure 106. Fort Ancient. (From Squier and Davis, 1848)

Warren K. Moorehead chose Fort Ancient as one of the sites to explore in his search for artifacts to exhibit at the World's Columbian Exposition held in Chicago in 1893. Research into the history of Fort Ancient has continued since Moorehead investigated the site, the most recent surge of attention having started in the early 1980s under the direction of Patricia Essenpreis and continued through the mid-1990s under Robert P. Connolly.

At present, archeological evidence indicates that Fort Ancient was constructed in stages between about 100 BC and AD 300. The oldest part of the embankment complex is the broad southern unit, while the narrow middle section and the northern section appear to have been built at about the same time. Younger still was the parallel-walled feature once located northeast of the main enclosure. The architectural details and construction methods varied somewhat over time as the enclosure grew. The walls in the southern and middle sections are sinuous and they hug the precipice closely. Some parts of the wall in these sections are, in fact, built on surfaces that were created artificially, by building up the surface of the plateau, to allow the walls to be placed in the desired position. The walls of the northern section are less tightly bound to the edge of the plateau and the segments are straighter and longer between gates. The walls of the southern and middle sections were made primarily of clay and reinforced and covered with stone. Some of the walls in the north were laid out with a core of stone and then covered with clay and, again, reinforced and covered with stone; other parts of the northern wall were built without the stone core. At least three phases of construction of the walls have been identified in all major parts of the embankment.

Inside and outside of the walls, other artificial or artificially modified features have been located that add considerable depth to the architectural detail of the design and manifestation of the Fort Ancient landscape. These features include stone circles, ponds, ditches, paved walkways, retaining walls, ramps, and exterior terraces.

Evidence of Hopewell habitation that spanned a considerable period of time has been found both inside and east of the northeastern part of the enclosure. Indications are that the area was used on multiple occasions, in part for domestic activities and in part for other as yet unidentified purposes, but probably it was not occupied for any extended period at any given time. Wooden structures were built, destroyed or allowed to decay, and rebuilt. The largest structure recognized is unusually large for a Hopewell house and therefore suggests that the area was used for some special activity, presumedly related to the use of the enclosure. The four mounds arranged in a square inside the north compound, and correlated gates in the northeastern wall, for example, have been interpreted as being an astronomical chronograph keyed to those celestial events that were critical in Hopewell culture. In general, the current view is that Fort Ancient probably served multiple functions for its Hopewell creators and that it is reasonable to believe that people would assemble periodically, as governing dictums and serendipitous circumstances might warrant, to use this architectural masterpiece in which so much thought, planning, labor, and tradition had been invested.

In addition to its Hopewell originators, archeological evidence indicates that Fort Ancient and its surrounding area were used by the Fort Ancient people for several centuries beginning around AD 1000. Warren K Moorehead explored one village below the enclosure, along the river, and a second village that existed within the southern part of the enclosure itself. The village inside the walls was itself located within a stockade. Moorehead assumed that the people whose remains he was excavating had built the great earthworks known as Fort Ancient. It was not until the 1940s that Fort Ancient was determined to have been built by the Hopewell and not the Fort Ancient people.

Fort Ancient is maintained by the Ohio Historical Society as Fort Ancient State Memorial. The site is readily accessible and easily explored by motor vehicle or bicycle, or on foot. Fort Ancient also serves as the Ohio Historical Society's Gateway to American Indian Heritage and, supporting that role, a new museum opened at the site in 1998. This museum contains 9,000 square feet of exhibit space, and uses contemporary information and concepts to describe and interpret the full span of Native American presence in the Ohio Valley. Emphasis, however, is placed on the original colonization of America some 15,000 years ago, the development of agriculture, and the impact of European culture on American Indian life and culture. An outdoor garden is maintained in which are grown many varieties of food crops which were raised by Native Americans (Table 1).

DIRECTIONS: Southbound, exit I 71 at Exit 36 onto CR 7 (Wilmington Road), go east about 0.25 mile to CR 45 (Middleboro Road), then go south on CR 45 about 2 miles to SR 350, then go west on SR 350 about 0.5 mile to park entrance. Northbound, exit I 71 at Exit 32 onto SR 123, go southeast on SR 123 for several hundred feet, then go east (first left) on SR 350 for 3 miles to Fort Ancient (Figure 107).

PUBLIC USE: Season and hours: *Grounds and museum:* 10 AM to 5 PM daily, May through September; same hours, Wednesday through Sunday, March and April, October and November. **Fee area:** Admission. **Recreational facilities.**

FOR ADDITIONAL INFORMATION: Contact: Ohio Historical Soci-

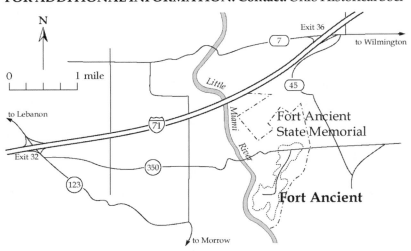

Figure 107. The location of Fort Ancient.

ety, 1982 Velma Avenue, Columbus, OH 43211; 800-686-1535, *www.ohiohistory.org.* **Read:** (1) W. K. Moorehead, 1890. *Fort Ancient: The Great Prehistoric Earthwork of Warren County, Ohio.* (2) P. S. Essenpreis and M. E. Moseley, 1984. "Fort Ancient: Citadel or coliseum." (3) J. Blosser and R. C. Glotzhober, 1995. *Fort Ancient: Citadel, Cemetery, Cathedral, or Calendar?* (4) R. P. Connolly, 1996. "Prehistoric land modification at the Fort Ancient hilltop enclosure: A model of formal and accretive development." (5) R. P. Connolly, 1997. "The evidence for habitation at the Fort Ancient Earthworks, Warren County, Ohio." (6) R. P. Connolly, 1998. "Architectural grammar rules at the Fort Ancient hilltop enclosure."

OHIO - WARREN COUNTY

63. Stubbs Earthworks

The Stubbs Earthworks, also known as the Bigfoot Earthworks after the adjacent Bigfoot Creek, were a Hopewell enclosure and associated features situated on the second terrace along the south side of the Little Miami River (Figure 108). The conjoined semicircular and rectangular enclosure, which appears to have been open along most of its northern side, incorporated some 85 acres of level land. These earthworks were sketched by Charles Whittlesey of the Ohio Geological Survey in 1839 after many years of farming had already reduced individual features and obliterated their details.

Whittlesey noted that the wall of the rectangular section was low, while the larger and better defined wall of the semicircle was some 2 feet high and 20 feet across at the base. The north wall of the rectangle apparently continued from the sec-

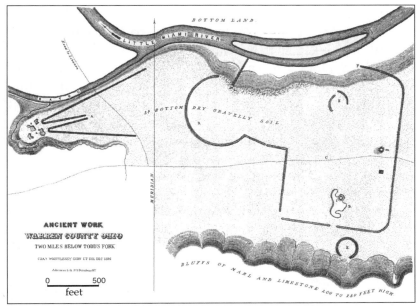

Figure 108. Stubbs Earthworks. (From Whittlesey, 1852)

ond terrace down onto the first terrace, a characteristic unusual for Hopewell earthworks. A graded way descended from
the semicircle to the first terrace. Inside the earthwork were
two crescentic ridges, a low mound, and an irregular mounded
feature toward the southern edge of the rectangle. The irregular mound was about 4 feet high on its western side and 2 feet
high on its eastern side, and a small conical mound sur-
mounted its northeast edge. This feature reminded Whittlesey
of effigy mounds he had seen in Minnesota and Wisconsin,
but he did not conclude that this was in fact an effigy mound.
The association stuck, however, and this feature continues to
be referred to obliquely as an effigy. A small, nearly complete
circle embankment had been constructed immediately south
of the rectangle. West of the semicircle and occupying a peninsula of the second terrace bordered by Bigfoot Creek and a
flood channel of the Little Miami River was a pair of wedge-

shaped embankments.

The earthworks site continued to be farmed after Whittlesey's visit, and the features were progressively obliterated. Archeological excavations of portions of the site were undertaken by Harlan Smith in 1892, about the same time that attention was directed to the wedge-shaped embankments at the west edge of the site. Some thought the features represented a serpent effigy and the debate over their effigy status continued intensely, as a minor footnote in the history of Ohio archeology, until the feature was destroyed in the 1970s. During the 1960s and 1970s, much of the site located north of US 22 was destroyed by gravel quarrying. In an effort to heighten public awareness of the site's value and afford it some protection through recognition, the 110 acres located south of US 22 were placed on the National Register of Historic Places in 1978 and, subsequently, The Archaeological Conservancy acquired easements to some of the remaining parts of the site. The most recent major change in land use affecting this complex was the construction, in 1998, of the new Little Miami High School, now clearly the dominant structure on what once was probably the focal point of a middle Woodland society that extended from this location north and south along the valley of the Little Miami River and into the bordering uplands.

In 1998 and 1999, before and during the construction of Little Miami High School, several areas within the remaining portion of the earthworks site were excavated by Frank L. Cowan and associates from the Cincinnati Museum Center. From this work came important information about the number, size, variety, uses, and ages of wooden structures that occupied the site during Hopewell times (Figure 20). Excavation in the northern and southern parts of the "effigy" mound suggested that a single complex building probably had existed under the mound. The "effigy" mound was likely a number of conjoined mounds, and the resulting shape of the composite mound mimicked the floor plan of the structure. The circular embankment south of the main enclosure was found to cover a circle of very large post molds, evidence suggesting that a monumental wooden structure had been erected here at one time. The vertical logs forming this structure had the diameter, and could have had the length, of telephone poles. Even so, the entire structure was dismantled before the earthen embankment was built over it about AD 180.

Elsewhere across the site, evidence of numerous house-like structures, most built during the second century AD, was found which provided new information about the diversity in shape of Hopewell buildings. Indeed, Stubbs has provided more information about Hopewell wooden structures than has any other site. The scarcity of artifacts related to domestic life or specialized craftsmanship is interpreted to mean that the site was used only periodically and for short periods of time. Wooden architecture would have been an important part of the landscape when the area was in active use by its Hopewell originators. At those certain times in the Hopewell ritual calendar, the site would probably have been quite busy with the people who had come together to participate in what must have been important parts of their cultural calendar.

Today, the only accessible part of the Stubbs Earthworks is the remaining portion of the "effigy" mound that once occupied the southern part of the rectangular enclosure. This feature, a part of The Archaeological Conservancy's easement, is now a low, gently mounded, grass-covered and routinely manicured rise incorporating about 0.5 acre and lying within the central part of the loop drive that leads from Morrow-Cozaddale Road to the main entrance of Little Miami High School.

DIRECTIONS: Little Miami High School is located immediately south of US 22 between the communities of Hopkinsville and Morrow. Northbound exit I 70 at Exit 28, go south on SR 48 to Hopkinsville, then east on US 22 3.5 miles to the school. Southbound, exit I 70 at Exit 32, go south on SR 123 to Morrow, then west on US 22 2.0 miles to the school (Figure 109).

PUBLIC USE: Season and hours: The grounds of Little Miami High School are open to the public during daylight hours.

FOR ADDITIONAL INFORMATION: Contact: The Archaeological Conservancy, 5301 Central Avenue NE, Suite 402, Albuquerque, NM 87108; 505-266-1540 **or** Office of the Principal, Little Miami High School, 3001 East US 22, Morrow, OH 45152; 513-899-3781. **Read:** (1) C. Whittlesey, 1850. *Descriptions of Ancient Works in Ohio.* (2) J. R. White, 1996. "The Stubbs Earthwork: Serpent effigy or simple embankment." (3) R. A. Genheimer, 1997. "Stubbs cluster: Hopewellian site dynamics at a forgotten Little Miami River Valley settlement." (4) F. L. Cowan, T. S. Sunderhaus, and R. A. Genheimer, 1998. "Notes from the field: An update from the Stubbs Earthworks site."

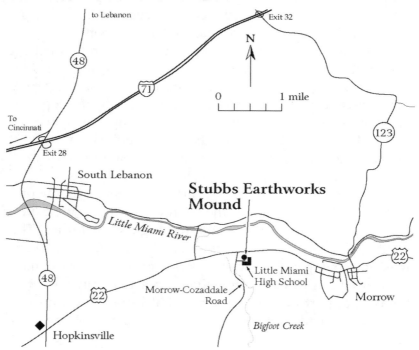

Figure 109. The location of Stubbs Earthworks.

OHIO - WASHINGTON COUNTY

64. Blennerhassett Island Overlook Mound

Beneath a large oak tree near the southwest corner of Hardees' parking lot, on federal property administered by the US Army Corps of Engineers and serving as the agency's Blennerhassett Island Scenic Overlook, lies a low subconical mound that is presumed to be a burial mound — although this fact has not been confirmed and the feature's cultural affiliation is not known. The mound is approximately 4 feet high and 30 to 35 feet in diameter; the oak tree is growing on top of the mound. The structure is identified by a sign erected by the Belpre Historical Society.

DIRECTIONS: From the US 50 / SR 618 intersection in downtown Belpre, go west on SR 618 (Washington Boulevard) to Hardees/ Blennerhassett Island Scenic Overlook on the south side of the road. Parking for the overlook is at the rear of Hardees (Figure 110).

PUBLIC USE: Season and hours: The mound can be viewed at any time. **Recreational facilities.**

Figure 110. The location of Blennerhassett Island Overlook Mound.

65. Marietta Earthworks

In Marietta, Ohio, at the confluence of the Muskingum and Ohio rivers, is an earthworks complex significant for its diverse individual features as well as for the history of its preservation.

Leaders of the Ohio Company of Associates from New England arrived at the future site of Marietta, Ohio, on April 7, 1788. Through the efforts of this visionary group, Marietta would become the first permanent American settlement in what was then the new Northwest Territory of the fledgling United States and the first capital of the Northwest Territory. Awaiting these first American settlers was an extensive earthworks complex consisting of a large conical mound, straight earthen walls, two rectangular enclosures with associated mounds, and a graded way (Figure 111). Impressed with the antiquities, the enlightened and foresighted directors of the Ohio Company acted on July 2, 1788, to preserve the major features of the earthworks as a commons. As decades passed, Marietta grew and the increased use of the commons area destroyed some of the earthworks, while other parts simply deteriorated after being cleared of protective vegetation. Attention to the earthworks was renewed in the 1830s and the citizens of Marietta established a fund to restore and maintain the mounds and the embankments. Early in its history, Marietta demonstrated historic preservation efforts which, if not the first of their kind west of the Appalachian Mountains, were certainly among the vanguard of efforts to preserve prehistoric cultural landscapes on the western frontier of America.

The Marietta Earthworks were situated on a high terrace

above the Muskingum River at its confluence with the Ohio River. This unusual association of earthen features included elements of Adena, Hopewell, and perhaps even Late Prehistoric architecture. Highest and most massive of the features

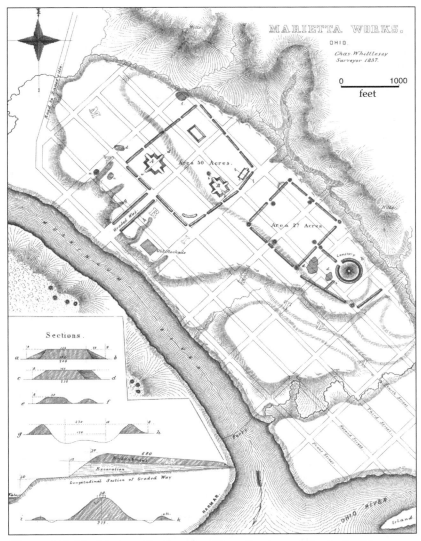

Figure 111. The Marietta Earthworks. (From Squier and Davis, 1848)

was a large conical mound, 30 feet high, surrounded by a low circular embankment with an interior ditch. At least four straight segments of earthen walls occurred near this mound and circle, one of which led northwest to a nearly square enclosure that contained some 27 acres. This enclosure consisted of walls somewhat less than 5 feet in height that were interrupted with 10 gates, 2 pairs of which consisted of gates close to each other; 8 mounds were associated with the gates. Farther to the west was a larger rectangular enclosure containing about 50 acres; its walls were 5 to 6 feet high and interrupted by 16 gates. Four, or perhaps 5, mounds were inside this enclosure, 1 arcuate and 3 or 4 others that were flat-topped rectangular pyramidal mounds, 3 with ramps ascending to their upper surface. The largest of these pyramidal mounds measured 188 feet by 132 feet at the base and was about 10 feet high. Midway along each side of this mound, earthen ramps extended from the ground to the summit. A graded way led 680 feet from the square enclosure on the upper terrace down toward, or to, the bank of the Muskingum River. Parallel earthen walls 150 feet apart lined each side of the graded way and rose above the planed surface from 10 feet at the upper end to as much as 20 feet at the lower end. The directors of the Ohio Company chose classical names for the major features of the earthworks: *Conus* for the conical mound, *Quadranaou* for the larger truncated pyramid, *Capitolium* for the next largest pyramid, and *Sacra Via* for the graded way.

Today, despite the good intentions of the original American settlers, much of the Marietta earthworks has disappeared. The most visible surviving element of the complex is *Conus*, the centerpiece of Mound Cemetery. It is a rare surviving example of a conical mound with an encircling moat, or ditch, and embankment intact. The moat measures 15 feet wide and 4 feet deep. The base of the embankment is 20 feet wide and 585 feet in circumference. Forty-five stone steps lead to the top of *Conus*, where 3 park benches afford visitors the opportunity to sit and survey the cemetery, downtown Marietta, and the land beyond. A time capsule was placed in this mound on July 3, 1976, in commemoration of the US Bicentennial; it is to be opened July 4, 2076. Mound Cemetery, opened in 1801, is the burial place for a large number of the early settlers of Marietta, many of whom were veterans of the Revolutionary War. It is said that more officers of that war are buried here than in any other single place.

The largest 2 pyramidal mounds have been preserved, albeit in vastly different contexts. The larger, *Quadranaou*, also known as Camp Tupper, stands in a park at the head of the graded way between Third Street and Fourth Street. The Washington County Public Library, however, sits atop *Capitolium*, the smaller of the two remaining elevated squares, on Fifth Street. Both of the enclosures are gone, but part of the trace of the graded way is preserved as a parkway leading from Third Street to Sacra Via Park on the banks of the Muskingum River. The houses that line *Sacra Via* today, particularly those on the northwest side, are raised above the graded way's surface, the slight elevation preserving the prehistoric alteration of the second terrace which provided a smooth grade on the path way between the river and the earthworks.

One of the intriguing and unanswered questions about the prehistory of the Marietta Earthworks concerns the possible influence of southern architectural and cultural models on the terminal landscape of this site. The contributions of Adena influence on *Conus* and Hopewell influence on the enclosures and graded way are unquestioned, and the excavation of a small part of *Capitolium* by the Cleveland Museum of Natural History in 1990 found unequivocal evidence of Hopewell involvement in the origin and expansion of the mound. The shape of the truncated pyramids, and their positioning within the larger enclosure, however, are not unlike elements of southern Hopewell, or even Mississippian, structure and site design. Could these structures possibly have been built, or reconfigured, to mimic architecture more typical of another region where truncated pyramids were known, such as the middle Woodland Pinson site in western Tennessee, or perhaps even later Mississippian sites?

Campus Martius Museum in Marietta is the Ohio Historical Society's Gateway to Settlement and Migration History. Exhibits include the early history of Marietta and provide valuable context within which the efforts of the American settlers to preserve the Marietta Earthworks might better be appreciated.

DIRECTIONS: Exit I 77 at Exit 1 onto SR 7 southbound (Pike Street), go 2 miles west into the City of Marietta. Just beyond Marietta College, turn northwest (right) at the traffic lights onto Fourth Street. Go northwest 3 blocks to Scammel Street. Turn northeast (right) and drive one block east to Mound Cemetery. The main entrance to the cemetery is on Fifth

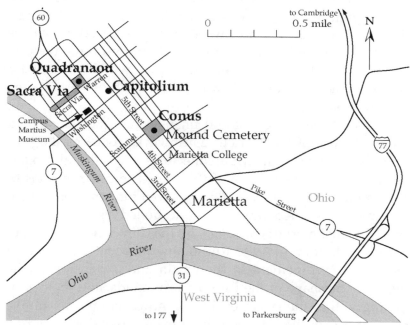

Figure 112. The location of the Marietta Earthworks.

Street at the end of Scammel, but access is also possible from Tupper Street. The other earthworks can be seen by continuing northwest on Fifth Street. Between Washington and Warren streets is the Washington County Public Library, situated on *Capitolium* Mound. Turn southwest (left) at Warren Street and go 1 block to *Quadranaou* (Camp Tupper Mound) in the park ahead to your right. At Third Street, Warren Street becomes a divided parkway designated Sacra Via. Continue on Sacra Via to Sacra Via Park at riverside. Curbside parking is available on most of the streets surrounding the remaining earthworks. There is a parking area at Sacra Via Park at the foot of the graded way (Figure 112).

PUBLIC USE: Season and hours: *Mounds and earthworks:* All of the remnants of the Marietta Earthworks may be viewed from public streets at any time. *Campus Martius:* 9:30 AM to 5 PM, Monday through Saturday and noon to 5 PM Sunday and holidays, May through September; 9:30 AM to 5 PM, Wednesday through Saturday and noon to 5 PM Sunday, March and April, October and November. **Fee area:** Museum. **For people with disabilities:** Campus Martius is accessible for people with disabilities. One wheelchair is available for free use on site.

FOR ADDITIONAL INFORMATION: Contact: Marietta/Washington County Tourist & Convention Bureau, 316 Third Street, Marietta, OH 45750; 614-373-5178, 800-288-2577, *www.mariettaohio.org.* **Read:** (1) C. Atwater, 1833. *The Writings of Caleb Atwater,* pp. 34-42. (2) E. G. Squier and E. H. Davis, 1848. *Ancient Monuments of the Mississippi Valley,* pp. 73-77.(3) J. R. Graybill, 1980. "Marietta Works, Ohio, and the eastern periphery of Fort Ancient." (4) W. H. Pickard, 1996. "1990 excavations at Capitolium Mound (33WN13), Marietta, Washington County, Ohio: A working evaluation."

66. South Charleston Mound

One of the major concentrations of Adena earthen architecture extended for some 5 miles across the upper terraces of both sides of the Kanawha River downstream from what is today Charleston, West Virginia. In the 1894 report of the Bureau of Ethnology's mound explorations, Cyrus Thomas described 50 mounds, at least 8 enclosures, a number of circular clay-lined pits, and many stone cysts in this area (Figure 113). The mounds ranged in size from 3 to 35 feet in height and 35 to 200 feet in diameter; the largest, 175 feet in diameter and 35 feet high, was the Great Smith Mound on the north side of the river, near the base of the bluffs, in what is today Dunbar. The smallest enclosures contained less than an acre, while the largest, located atop Spring Hill, apparently contained 30 acres. Most of these architectural features have been destroyed by farming and urban development, but at least 3 of the mounds have survived and all are in public space. The flagship of the surviving features is South Charleston Mound, also known as Criel Mound and Thomas's Mound 1.

South Charleston Mound was the second largest mound in this Adena landscape when the Bureau of Ethnology conducted its survey of the region in the early 1880s. At that time, the conical mound was 33 feet high and about 165 feet in diameter; years earlier, part of its top had been removed so that a judging platform, associated with a race track that encircled the mound, could be built there. About 300 feet northeast of the mound was a ceremonial circle with walls about 2 to 3 feet high, a diameter of about 177 feet, and an opening that faced south. A ditch bordered the wall on the inside. One

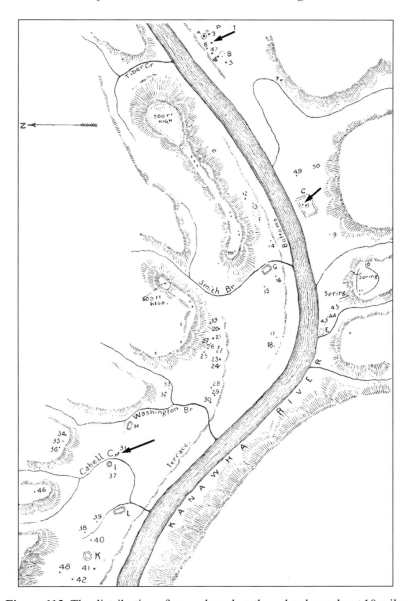

Figure 113. The distribution of mounds and earthworks along about 10 miles of the Kanawha Valley from Charleston to Saint Albans, West Virginia, around 1886. Mounds 1 (South Charleston Mound), 8 (Wilson Mound), and 31 (Shawnee Reservation Mound) are marked with arrows. (From Thomas, 1894)

small burial mound, about 3 feet high, was located in the center of the circle, and another of the same size was located about 75 feet south of the opening. A similar circle and mound was located about 300 feet southwest of South Charleston Mound, but it differed from the one just described in that the opening faced to the northwest and apparently no mound occurred in the center.

South Charleston Mound was excavated by the Bureau of Ethnology under the supervision of Colonel P. W. Norris, one of Thomas's three original field assistants. A vertical shaft was sunk through the center of the mound, from the top to its base. A total of 14 burials were found during the excavation; the first was located within 3 feet of the upper surface, 2 others a short distance lower, and 11 skeletons were found at the base of the mound. The group of 11 consisted of 1 extended skeleton in the center whose head had been crushed. The other 10 bodies were arranged in 2 groups, 5 on each side in a semicircle with the feet facing the central skeleton and the heads radiating outward. Each of the 5 bodies on the east side had been buried with a lance head, and next to the northernmost skeleton were 4 small projectile points and some mussel shells. No artifacts were found with the bodies in the western group. Before these bodies had been put into place, the ground had been packed and hardened, a layer of bark had been put down, and the surface had been covered with what was estimated to have been some 6 inches of fine wood ash. The bodies were then placed on the prepared surface and covered with bark. A vault 4 feet high and 5 feet in diameter was located adjacent to the heads of some of the skeletons, and a pit 2 feet deep and 5 feet across lay beneath the vault. Apparently the entire group had been buried in a circular wooden structure about 16 feet in diameter.

Today, South Charleston Mound is the centerpiece of Staunton Park in downtown South Charleston. The mound and the grounds of the park are for the most part grass-covered and regularly mowed. Some trees have been removed from the mound in recent years and illumination for viewing at night has been improved. A walkway encircles the base of the mound, and 2 spiraling stairways lead to the still-flattened top from where a panoramic view of the Ohio River flood plain is possible. Although the present cultural landscape is much different than that of 2,000 years ago, the flood plain and bordering hills can be seen and some impression of the scale and geometry of the former Adena landscape can be imagined. In the northeast part of the park is a piece of sculpture entitled "The Burial Attendants."

DIRECTIONS: Exit I 64 at Exit 56 onto Montrose Drive, go north about 0.15 mile to the end of Montrose, then west on US 60 (MacCorkle Avenue) 0.5 mile to Seventh Avenue, then southwest onto Seventh Avenue 0.1 mile to South Charleston Mound on north side of street (Figure 114).

PUBLIC USE: Staunton Park is open at all hours.

FOR ADDITIONAL INFORMATION: Contact: South Charleston Convention and Visitors Bureau, P. O. Box 8595, South Charleston, WV 25303; 800-238-9488. **Read:** C. Thomas, 1894. *Report on the Mound Explorations of the Bureau of Ethnology,* pp. 414-418.

---

67. Wilson Mound

Wilson Mound, Thomas's Mound 8, is located on the south side of the Kanawha River in the community of Spring Hill. This mound was surrounded by a rectangular earthwork

(Thomas's Enclosure C, Figure 113) whose walls, 5 to 6 feet high and bordered on the inside by a ditch, enclosed some 20 acres. In the 1880s, when the Bureau of Ethnology surveyed the area, the enclosure had been obliterated and the mound had been excavated. Informants indicated that a human burial and several stone artifacts had been found beneath the mound, near its center. The mound and environs had already been used as a burying ground for several decades by the time of the survey.

Wilson Mound lies immediately west of Sunset Memorial Cemetery on a small tract of land maintained by the City of South Charleston. It is a flat topped feature about 8 feet high, 60 feet in diameter at the top, and 120 feet in diameter at the base. A depression over the center on the top is probably a result of the nineteenth-century excavation. Several old head-stones, small and badly weathered, are visible on top of the mound. Three trees are growing on it now, and it is mowed regularly. Access is through a gate that faces Park Avenue.

DIRECTIONS: Exit I 64 at Exit 54 in South Charleston, go west on US 60 (MacCorkle Avenue) for 0.5 mile, then go south on Park Avenue for

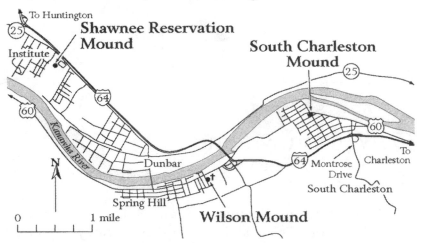

Figure 114. The location of South Charleston Mound, Wilson Mound, and Shawnee Reservation Mound.

0.1 mile. The mound is in a fenced lot on the east side of Park Avenue (Figure 114).

PUBLIC USE: Season and hours: Wilson Mound may be viewed from Park Street at any time.

FOR ADDITIONAL INFORMATION: Contact: South Charleston Convention and Visitors Bureau, P. O. Box 8595, South Charleston, WV 25303; 800-238-9488. **Read:** C. Thomas, 1894. *Report on the Mound Explorations of the Bureau of Ethnology,* p. 418.

68. Shawnee Reservation Mound

Shawnee Reservation Mound (Plate 2) is located north of the Kanawha River on a high terrace near the base of a wall of high hills (Figure 113). This is the only surviving mound of the many mounds and earthworks that existed in this immediate area at the time of the Bureau of Ethnology's mound survey early in the 1880s.

This flat-topped conical mound was about 25 feet high, 40 feet in diameter across the top, and 100 feet in diameter across the base when it was documented and excavated by the Bureau under the supervision of Colonel P. W. Norris. As was done with many mounds, the excavation of this one was carried out by sinking a vertical shaft through the center of the feature from the top to its base. Three feet from the top, 2 extended burials were found with 1 lying immediately above and facing the other. The excavation continued:

Ten feet below these were two very large skeletons in a sitting position, facing each other, with their extended legs interlocking to the knees. Their hands, outstretched and slightly elevated, were placed in a sustaining position to a hemispherical, hollowed, coarse-grained sandstone, burned until red and brittle. This was about 2 feet across the top, and the cavity or depression was filled with white ashes containing fragments of bones burned almost to coals. Over it was placed a somewhat wider slab of limestone 3 inches thick, which had a hemispherical or cup-shaped depression of 2 inches in diameter near the center of the under side, but this bore no trace of heat. Two copper bracelets were on the left wrist of one skeleton, a hematite celt and lancehead with the other (Thomas, 1894: 432).

No other skeletons were found, but the natural surface under the mound had been covered with a clay layer and, in the center, was a ritual basin filled with a thick layer of compressed ash, 1 foot thick in the center and 2 feet thick at the edges. Scattered throughout the ash were waterworn stones 3 to 5 inches in diameter and fragments of bone, all of which had been burned.

McMichael and Mairs (1969: 33) believe that the basin and lance head are more typical of Hopewell than Adena burial practices. Because of this and other information, they consider the Kanawha earthworks to be very late Adena and early Hopewell in origin.

Shawnee Reservation Mound is smaller today than it was when Colonel Norris saw to its excavation. After periodic pot hunting had disfigured the surface, a Kanawha County official had the mound tidied up and made to look like a proper conical mound. The feature is now about 20 feet high and 80 feet in diameter at the base – and is indeed conical in shape. A low stone retaining wall circles the base of the mound, and the feature is mowed regularly. The mound is located on the west side of Shawnee Park, a multipurpose recreational facility that includes a swimming pool, fairgrounds, and golf course.

Other names for this mound include Institute Fairgrounds Mound, Poorhouse Mound, and Thomas's Mound 31.

DIRECTIONS: Exit I 64 at Exit 50 in Institute onto SR 25, go east about 0.75 mile to Shawnee Regional Park on south side of highway. The mound is about 800 feet south of SR 25 (Figure 114).

PUBLIC USE: Season and hours: Shawnee Park is open daily, dawn to dusk. **Recreational facilities.**

FOR ADDITIONAL INFORMATION: Contact: Kanawha County Parks and Recreation Commission, 2000 Coonskin Drive, Charleston, WV 25311; 304-768-7600, *www.kanawhacounty.com/parks*. **Read:** (1) C. Thomas, 1894. *Report on the Mound Explorations of the Bureau of Ethnology*, p. 432. (2) E. V. McMichael and O. L. Mairs, 1969. *Excavation of the Murad Mound, Kanawha County, West Virginia and an Analysis of Kanawha Valley Mounds.*

WEST VIRGINIA - MARSHALL COUNTY

69. Grave Creek Mound

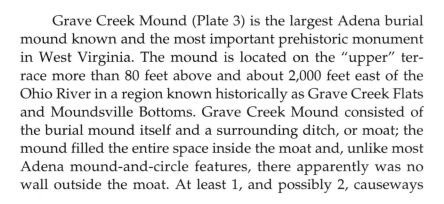

Grave Creek Mound (Plate 3) is the largest Adena burial mound known and the most important prehistoric monument in West Virginia. The mound is located on the "upper" terrace more than 80 feet above and about 2,000 feet east of the Ohio River in a region known historically as Grave Creek Flats and Moundsville Bottoms. Grave Creek Mound consisted of the burial mound itself and a surrounding ditch, or moat; the mound filled the entire space inside the moat and, unlike most Adena mound-and-circle features, there apparently was no wall outside the moat. At least 1, and possibly 2, causeways led across the ditch to the enclosed space. The certain causeway entrance faced to the south. The mound was surveyed by a road engineer in 1838 who measured its height at 69 feet and the diameter of the base at 295 feet. More recent measurements of the mound, following decades of excavation, neglect, and restoration, give the height at between 60 and 65 feet and the diameter at 240 feet. Excavations in 1975 and 1976 located the moat and determined that the encircling ditch was about 40 feet in width, 4 to 5 feet deep, and 910 feet in

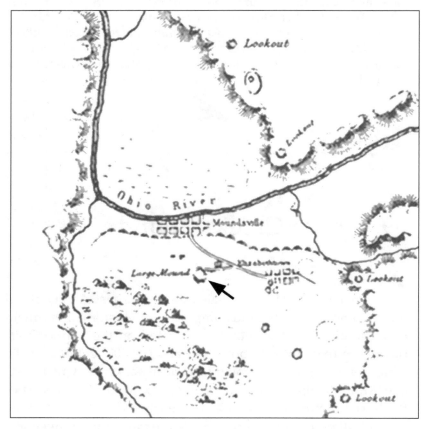

Figure 115. Mounds and earthworks in the vicinity of Moundsville, West Virginia, as depicted in 1851 by H. R. Schoolcraft. Grave Creek Mound, the "large mound" on this map, is marked with an arrow. (From Schoolcraft, 1851)

length when measured at the midline.

Grave Creek Mound was the largest mound among a significant array of mounds and earthworks that existed in the Grave Creek area at the onset of American settlement in the early 1770s, and it is apparently the only feature of the entire complex that survives (Figure 115). Most of the mounds and earthworks in this area appear to have been built during the Adena period, but some are later. Grave Creek Mound was certainly an Adena structure, and the current interpretation of its history is that it was constructed in two major phases between about 300 BC and 100 BC, during the peak of Adena influence in the region. The initial interment apparently consisted of a log tomb placed in the ground at the summit of a natural rise. Once the mounding process got underway, it proceeded without major interruption until the mound was some 27 feet high. Following a defined pause, a second major phase of accumulation began after another log tomb was placed on the summit of the older mound. The moat was constructed during the second major phase of mound building and the earth that was removed from the moat was placed on the mound. When the enlargement of the mound stopped, the feature comprised an estimated 57,000 tons, or some 3 million basket loads, of earth.

Joseph Tomlinson purchased the land upon which Grave Creek Mound was located in the early 1770s. During the next 50 years, as the cultural landscape around Grave Creek changed dramatically, Tomlinson left the mound undisturbed despite recurrent suggestions that he excavate it or allow others to do so. Joseph Tomlinson died in 1826, and his son Jesse continued his father's protection of the mound until, in 1838, he succumbed to pressure to explore the site. Jesse's nephew Abelard Tomlinson was placed in charge of the exploration, which got underway in March. The excavation, which by historical coincidence is the earliest recorded investigation of an Adena mound, consisted of cutting a tunnel from about 4 feet above the base toward the center, a strategy that exposed the log tomb 111 feet into the feature. From this tomb, the excavators probed upward until they hit rocks, following which they cut another horizontal tunnel into the mound at 34 feet above its base. This tunnel, too, encountered a log tomb. Completing the basic exploration, a vertical shaft was sunk from the top of the mound down to the original surface, passing through the points where the log tombs had been discovered (Figure 29). The lower tomb contained skeletons of two adults, one male and one female. The upper tomb contained a single skeleton. Burial goods were found in both tombs. Tomlinson's excavation appears to have obliterated the moat that surrounded the mound.

One of the most intriguing consequences of the 1838 excavation of Grave Creek Mound is the legacy of an object reportedly found in the upper tomb. The object has become known as the Grave Creek Tablet, and it contributed significantly to debates during the nineteenth century as to whether or not Europeans had reached North America before the voyages of Columbus and whether or not Native Americans possessed either an alphabetic or hieroglyphic system of writing. Generally accepted as a fraud, the tablet is now lost.

The driving force behind the 1838 excavation was the commercial potential of the curiosities within the mound. Advocates of excavation had argued that:

> *The minerals of Europe will be poured into our place in copious torrents. . . . [and, after excavation, the owners could] . . . build a staircase up the middle and establish a gentle 'toll' upon the curious* (Norona, 1998: 17, 31).

After the mound had been excavated, a museum was set up inside, at its base, where the lower log tomb had been found. Construction of the museum required that the chamber be enlarged, during which an additional ten skeletons were found, all reportedly in the sitting position. The museum opened in May, 1839, and within a few years a three-story observatory had been built on the summit of the mound. A visitor's description of the museum includes the following:

> . . . *Around the base of this column there is a circular shelf provided with wire cases, in which the bones, bead ornaments, and other objects of interest, found in the vaults are arranged. The place was dark, or but dimly lighted with a few tallow candles, which cast around a sepulchral glare on the wired skeleton and other bones spread around. Silence added its impressive influence to the panoramic display of so profound and humid a recess* (Norona, 1998: 34).

The museum was not commercially successful and it closed around 1846 after part of the tunnel collapsed. For the next 30 years the mound experienced a great range of uses. Soon after the museum closed the observatory was replaced by a saloon. At one time during the Civil War, an artillery emplacement occupied the summit, and over a period of years the Fourth of July was celebrated by hauling a cannon to the top and discharging it. In 1876, the site was purchased by a former superintendent of the West Virginia State Penitentiary who, two years later, offered the mound to the state as a good place to situate a water tank to supply the penitentiary — which was located immediately east of the mound. The state did not acquire the property at that time and, during the ensuing years, a dancing platform was built on the summit, children continued to dig in and play on the mound, and the idea of placing a water tank on top of the mound persisted.

In 1909, following continuing threats that the mound would be destroyed by its owner, the State of West Virginia purchased the mound and placed it under the jurisdiction of the Penitentiary Board. The mound was cleaned up and once again made symmetrical, a process that in part required hauling earth to the top to fill in the concave summit. A stone building was constructed on the south side of the mound in 1915 for the purpose of selling souvenirs made by inmates at the penitentiary, and a spiraling stone walkway was built from the base to the top of the mound. Thirty-five years later, the building was enlarged and a museum operated by the West Virginia Archeological Society was established in the addition. The museum opened in 1952 and continued in use until the Delf Norona Museum was built. In the meantime, ownership of the site has remained with the state, but departmental responsibility for its administration has changed frequently. The site is presently administered by the West Virginia Department of Education and the Arts, Division of Culture and History, and is home to both the state curation center and the state archeological collection.

The Delf Norona Museum and Cultural Centre opened to the public in December, 1978. The museum exhibits include an overview of archeology in West Virginia; the Adena culture; and the discovery, uses, and excavations of the Grave Creek Mound by Americans. A diorama shows the mound being enlarged during the early part of the second phase of its

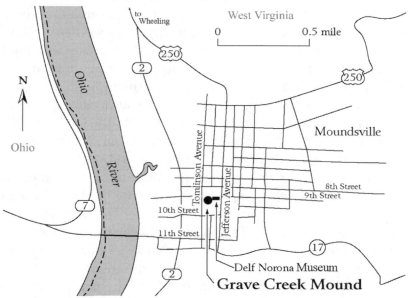

Figure 116. The location of Grave Creek Mound.

construction. The museum will provide special lectures to groups if arrangements are made in advance. Access to Grave Creek Mound is through the museum. The modern architecture of the building, with its pyramidal skylights and earth tones, is well matched to the subject and site for which it provides access and about which it provides enlightenment.

DIRECTIONS: From SR 2 in Moundsville, go east on 8th Street 1 block to Grave Creek Mound Historic Site. Parking is available on the east side of the museum off of Jefferson Avenue (Figure 116).

PUBLIC USE: Season and hours: Sunday, 1 to 5 PM; Monday to Saturday, 10 AM to 4:30 PM. The mound may be viewed from outside the fence at any time. **Fee area:** Admission to site. **For people with disabilities:** A wheelchair ramp provides access to the exhibits and the area at the base of the mound. Wheelchairs are available for public use.

FOR ADDITIONAL INFORMATION: Contact: Delf Norona Museum, Grave Creek Mound Historic Site, P. O. Box 527, Moundsville, WV 26041; 304-843-1410. **Read:** (1) D. Norona, 1998. *Moundsville's Mammoth Mound.* (2) E. T. Hemmings, 1984. "Investigations at Grave Creek Mound 1975-76: A sequence for mound and moat construction." (3) T. A. Barnhart, 1986. "Curious Antiquity? The Grave Creek controversy revisited."

WEST VIRGINIA - PLEASANTS COUNTY

70. Reynolds Mound

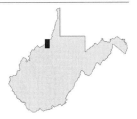

Reynolds Mound (Figure 33) is a prominent conical mound situated on a higher terrace of the Ohio River flood plain northeast of Saint Marys. The mound is about 16 feet high and stands guard at the entrance to Mound Estates, a small housing development on the south side of State Route 2.

The area bordering the entrance to the development, and the mound, are mowed regularly, so the feature is clearly visible. This site is privately owned by The Archaeological Conservancy and is open to the public only with the written permission of the conservancy.

Little is known about the archeology of the feature, but based on its size and location it has long been considered to be an Adena burial mound.

DIRECTIONS: Follow SR 2 northeast from the Saint Marys-Newport Bridge for about 3 miles, then go south on Mound Manor into Mound Estates. The entrance road loops around the mound (Figure 117).

PUBLIC USE: Season and hours: This mound can be viewed from SR 2 at any time.

FOR ADDITIONAL INFORMATION: Contact: The Archaeological Conservancy, 5301 Central Avenue NE, Suite 402, Albuquerque, NM 87108; 505-266-1540.

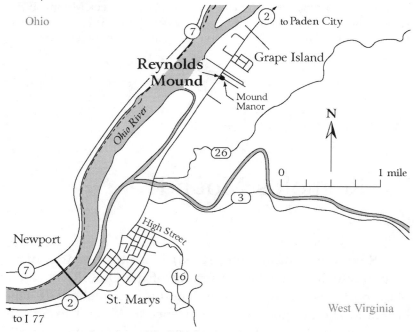

Figure 117. The location of Reynolds Mound.

WEST VIRGINIA - RANDOLPH COUNTY

71. Hyer Mound

Hyer Mound, also known as Hyre Mound, is located on the top of a low ridge in the upper Tygart Valley of eastern West Virginia. The crest of this ridge is about 30 feet above, and immediately southeast of, Elkwater Fork near where that stream enters Tygart Valley River. The mound is about 75 yards south of US 219 on the ridge in a pasture between the road and the old Hyer log cabin, and can be seen easily from the highway. The nearly circular mound was about 5 feet high and 40 feet in diameter at the base, and was constructed of stone and sandy clay. The panoramic view afforded of this mound and its environs gives an unusually clear view of the physical setting typical of many small upland burial mounds of the Woodland period.

When this mound was excavated by the West Virginia Geological Survey in 1963, 20 burials were found in or beneath the mound. The single skeleton found beneath the mound had been cremated, while those found within the mound included 3 that appeared to have been buried in the flesh and 16 that were bundle burials. Artifacts found in the mound included rolled copper beads, a ceramic elbow pipe, an Armstrong cord-marked ceramic vessel, a fragment of a polished stone tubular pipe, and a large cache blade of Flint Ridge flint. Although this mound has been considered representative of the middle Woodland period, the contents of the mound included some artifacts that are more typical of Adena than Hopewell. The mound was restored to its original dimensions after excavation.

DIRECTIONS: Hyer Mound lies about 75 yards south of US 219, 9 miles south of Huttonsville and 5.1 miles north of the SR 15/US 219 intersection in Valley Head (Figure 118).

PUBLIC USE: Season and hours: Hyer Mound can be viewed from US 219 at any time. **Restrictions:** This mound is located on private property and trespassing is prohibited.

FOR ADDITIONAL INFORMATION: Contact: Archeologist, West Virginia Division of Culture and History, The Cultural Center, 1900 Kanawha Boulevard East, Charleston, WV 25305; 304-558-0220. **Read:** B. J. Broyles, 1964. (Abstract) "Mounds in Randolph County, West Virginia."

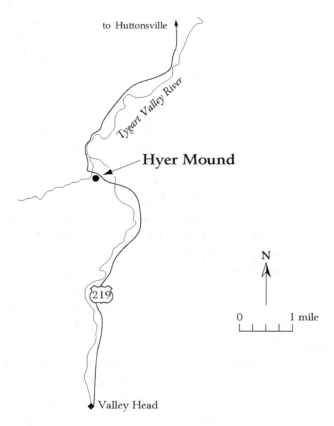

Figure 118. The location of Hyer Mound.

WEST VIRGINIA - WAYNE COUNTY

72. Camden Park Mound

Camden Park is a rare survivor of the golden age of America's suburban amusement parks. The recreational use of this site began in 1903 when the Camden Interstate Railway opened service between Huntington, West Virginia, and Ashland, Kentucky. The railway had an exchange point close to where Twelvepole Creek entered the Ohio River. A pavilion for picnicking, holding reunions, and square dancing was built in a shaded area nearby, and the site was named Camden Park after Senator J. N. Camden, one of the owners of the railway. Within the next few years, the present merry-go-round and some other amusement rides were added, and the park continued to expand its attractions for the next two decades. Camden Park reeled during the Great Depression, but survived, and rebounded after World War II as new roads and the automobile brought increasing numbers of visitors. The park continues to expand and diversify its attractions and educational offerings as it nears completion of its first century of existence, but it retains an unmistakable imprint of American amusement history that disappeared across most of the country fifty years ago.

Located on the Ohio River flood plain near the center of Camden Park is Camden Park Mound, a conical feature some 15 feet high and 100 feet in diameter. Although this mound has never been excavated, its size, shape, and location suggest that it is an Adena burial mound.

When Camden Park was young, a bandstand was located on top of the mound and visitors were entertained by a variety of music that emanated from its summit. Later, the

Figure 119. Camden Park Mound lies adjacent to the midway of Camden Park, a relic of the golden age of suburban amusement parks. This mound has been a part of the recreational use of the Camden Park area since the first decade of the twentieth century.

bandstand was removed and a fence was erected around the base of the mound. The mound is still fenced with a chain barrier but it is fully visible to visitors at the park (Figure 119). The mound presently has a flat top, a circumstance that suggests the top might have been artificially leveled to accommodate the bandstand and, perhaps later, park benches for visitors.

DIRECTIONS: Camden Park is located on the north side of US 60 west of Huntington. Westbound traffic on I 64 should use Exit 6, going north 0.8 mile to Madison Avenue, then west about 2.5 miles on Madison (becomes Piedmont Road) to Camden Park. Traffic entering Huntington from Ohio via US 52 should exit onto US 60 (Adams Avenue) westbound and follow US 60 about 2.5 miles to Camden Park. Eastbound traffic on I-64 should use Exit 1, going north on SR 75 0.7 mile to US 60 (Oak Street), then east on US 60 about 2.5 miles to Camden Park (Figure 120).

PUBLIC USE: Season and hours: Schedule and hours change annually. Generally, Camden Park is open from the last weekend in April to

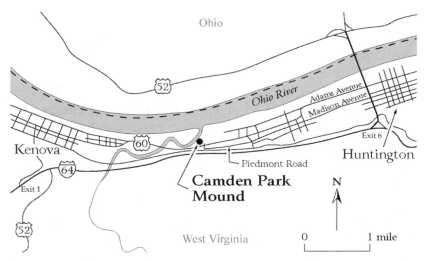

Figure 120. The location of Camden Park Mound.

mid-October, 11 AM to 9 PM, Wednesday through Sunday, and week-ends only mid-August to mid-October. Closed mid-October through April. **Fee area:** Admission. **Recreational facilities.**

FOR ADDITIONAL INFORMATION: Contact: Camden Park, P. O. Box 1778, Huntington, WV 25718; 304-522-8320, *info@camdenpark.com; www.camdenpark.com.* **Read:** J. Platania, 1987. "The sign of the happy clown,"

WEST VIRGINIA - WOOD COUNTY

73. Boaz Mound

Boaz Mound, also known as the Mayo Mound, is located in the community of Boaz near the bluff that forms the western edge of a high terrace overlooking the Ohio River. The conical mound is some 8 to 10 feet high and 30 feet in diameter at the base and lies within what is believed to have been an Adena village site.

Boaz Mound is located in the second lot east of CR 21/2 and can be viewed easily from either Kellar Lane or Pine Street. It is covered with high grasses and scattered shrubs and has a conifer tree growing on its summit. The site is privately owned by The Archaeological Conservancy and is open to the public only with the written permission of the conservancy.

DIRECTIONS: Boaz Mound lies about 0.3 mile west of SR 14 on the south side of Kellar Lane (CR 6), an unusually narrow paved street (Figure 121). The mound also can be seen from Pine Street.

PUBLIC USE: Season and hours: This mound may be viewed from Kellar Lane and Pine Street at any time. **Restrictions:** This mound is located on private property. Trespassing is strictly prohibited.

FOR ADDITIONAL INFORMATION: Contact: The Archaeological Conservancy, 5301 Central Avenue NE, Suite 402, Albuquerque, NM 87108; 505-266-1540.

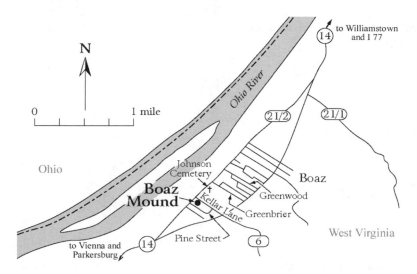

Figure 121. The location of Boaz Mound.

Section III

Sources of Additional Information

Museum Exhibits

The museums listed below are not connected directly to any of the sites identified in Section II, but they do have exhibits that include specific information about mounds, earthworks, and the mound-building cultures. The scope, focus, and level of information provided varies considerably from one museum to another. Visitors should check with the museum directly for days and hours of operation, admission fees, holiday schedules, and other logistical information.

1. **Ohio Historical Center,** 1982 Velma Avenue, Columbus, OH 43211-2497; 800-686-1535, *www.ohiohistory.org*

    The Ohio Historical Center's "The First Ohioans" exhibit contains the most extensive museum exhibit devoted to the mound-building Indians of the middle Ohio Valley. If you visit only one museum to see exhibits dealing with Woodland or Late Prehistoric mound-building Indians, this is the one to choose.

2. **Glenn A. Black Laboratory of Archaeology,** 9th and Fess Streets, Indiana University, Bloomington, IN 47405; 812-855-0022, *www.gbl.indiana.edu/exhibit.html*

    The exhibit hall of Black Laboratory describes and interprets the sequence of prehistoric cultures that occurred in the Midwest and illustrates different aspects of the practice of archeology. These exhibits rely significantly on artifacts from the institution's collections. Visitors on weekends enter the Black Laboratory exhibit hall through the William Hammond Mathers Museum.

3. **Indiana State Museum,** 202 North Alabama Street, Indianapolis, IN 46204; 317-232-1637, *www.state.in.us/ism/museum*

    In May, 2002, the Indiana State Museum will open in new facilities at White River State Park immediately west of downtown Indianapolis. The early Woodland Anderson Mounds and Mississippian Angel Mounds will be featured parts of the exhibit on Native American prehistory.

4. **Behringer-Crawford Museum,** Devou Park, 1600 Montague Road, Covington, KY 41012; 859-491-4003

    Behringer-Crawford is a general museum with exhibits that include one gallery on the prehistory of northern Kentucky. Aspects of Adena, Hopewell, and Fort Ancient cultures receive special attention.

5. **Kentucky History Center,** 100 West Broadway, Frankfort, KY 40601; 502-564-1792, *www.state.ky.us/agencies/khs*

    The Kentucky History Center opened in 1999, and its "First Kentuckians" exhibit is devoted to the prehistoric people of Kentucky.

6. **William S. Webb Museum of Anthropology,** 211 Lafferty Hall, University of Kentucky, Lexington, KY 40506; 859-257-8208, *www.uky.edu/AS/Anthropology/Museum.htm*

    The Webb Museum includes exhibits devoted to the prehistoric people of Kentucky.

7. **Cleveland Museum of Natural History,** 1 Wade Oval, University Circle, Cleveland, OH 44106; 216-231-4600, *www.cmnh.org*

    The Cleveland Museum of Natural History has one gallery devoted to the prehistory of North America. A cut-away model of a mound is included.

8. **Johnson-Humrickhouse Museum,** Roscoe Village, 300 North Whitewoman Street, Coshocton, OH 43812; 740-622-8710, *jhmuseum@clover.net*

    Johnson-Humrickhouse is a general museum with exhibits that include galleries on Native American prehistory and art. Three cabinets are devoted to the archeology of the Woodland period.

9. **Indian Museum of Lake County Ohio,** Lake Erie College, 391 West Washington, Painesville, OH 44077; 440-352-1911

    Indian Museum has a small permanent exhibit devoted to Native American prehistory, and each year presents a special exhibit devoted to Native Americans of one region of North America.

Web Sites

Each of the web sites listed below provides information or products relative to the prehistory of the middle Ohio Valley.

1. **Cleveland Museum of Natural History** — *www.cmnh.org*

   The Cleveland Museum web site contains an outline of Ohio's prehistory, with special reference to northeastern Ohio.

2. **EarthWorks, The Center for the Electronic Reconstruction of Archaeological and Historical Sites,** University of Cincinnati — *www.cerhas.uc.edu/earthworks*

   EarthWorks employs interactive multi-media technology to create public consciousness of Native American cultural landscapes that are located in the middle Ohio Valley.

3. **Hopewell Culture National Historical Park** — *www.nps.gov/hocu*

   This site offers the most extensive information available on the internet for the Hopewell culture. Be certain to go to *www.nps.gov/hocu/indepth.htm* for links to other sites containing information about Adena, Hopewell, and other mound-building groups.

4. **Kentucky Heritage Council** — *www.state.ky.us/agencies/khc/prehist1.html* or *www.kyheritage.org.*

   The Kentucky Heritage Council site provides an impressive list of resources for teachers and others interested in teaching about archeology, prehistory, and native peoples, as well as for those using archeology and local history sources in teaching history.

5. **Native American Studies, Northern Kentucky University** — *www.nku.edu/~nas/resources.html*

   The Native American Studies site identifies members of the NKU faculty and staff who have expertise in Native American studies, including their areas of specialization and e-mail addresses.

6. **Ohio Historical Society** — *www.ohiohistory.org/resource/collect.html*

The Ohio Historical Society's collections pages provide a brief overview of the society's collections and curatorial comments about the Wray figurine from the Newark Earthworks.

7. **Ohio Junction** — *www.ohiojunction.net/hopewell*

The Great Hopewell Road serves as a forum from which additional information about the Hopewell in particular and Native Americans in general is presented.

8. **Ohiokids** — *www.ohiokids.org*

Ohiokids is an interactive, educationally oriented site with substantial coverage of Ohio's prehistory on the "Ohio History Central" pages. There is much information available on these pages that will inform adults as well as children.

9. **Pictures of Record** — *www.picturesofrecord.com*

Pictures of Record offers sets of slides organized around themes that include North American prehistory and protohistory.

10. **Southeast Archaeological Research Center, National Park Service** — *www.cr.nps.gov/seac/links3.htm*

The Southeast Archaeological Research Center site contains extensive information about the prehistory of the southeastern United States and some of the Caribbean islands, and provides links to numerous web sites with significant archeological content.

11. **Voyageur Media Group/Pangea Productions Ltd.** — *www.voyageurmedia.org*

Voyageur Media Group and Pangea Productions produce documentaries about science, history, and culture, including several documentaries about the prehistoric cultures of the middle Ohio Valley.

12. **West Virginia State Museum** — *www.wvculture.org/shpo/archindex.html*

The West Virginia State Museum web site contains reviews of the cultural stages of West Virginia prehistory.

13. **William S. Webb Museum of Anthropology, University of Kentucky** — *www.uky.edu/AS/Anthropology/Museum.htm*

The Webb Museum web site contains reviews of the cultural stages of Kentucky prehistory.

Graphic Resources

Listed here are CD-ROMs, slide sets, and videos that provide pictorial representation of many aspects of the mound-building Indians and the mounds and earthworks they built. Web sites are provided to facilitate contact with the publisher.

Slides

Adena Mounds of Kentucky, 2001. Pictures of Record. *www.picturesofrecord.com.* Color slides and commentary.

Ohio Hopewell, 1989. Pictures of Record. *www.picturesofrecord.com.* Color slides and commentary.

Videos

Earthworks: Touring the Newark Complex, 1998. CERHAS. *www.earthworks.uc.edu.* A bird's-eye view of a virtual reconstruction of the Newark Earthworks.

Kentucky Archaeology is an on-going series of short documentaries about Kentucky's prehistory. Four episodes are now either available or will be available soon. These include *Ancient Fires at Cliff Palace Pond*, 2000; *The Adena People: Moundbuilders of Kentucky*, 2000; *Saving a Kentucky Time Capsule*, 2000; and *WPA Archaeology: Legacies of an Era*, 2001. Kentucky Heritage Council. *www.state.ky.us/agencies/khc/ prehist1.html* or *www.kyheritage.org.*

Legacy of the Mound Builders, 1994. Hopewell Culture National Historical Park / Camera One. *www.nps.gov/hocu.*

Searching for the Great Hopewell Road, 1998. Pangea Productions Ltd. *www.voyageurmedia.org.*

CD/ROMs

The Hopewell Mound Group: Its People and Their Legacy, 1995. Ohio Historical Society.

Bibliography

The books and articles listed here are representative of professional and popular publications that contain information about North American prehistory. This list includes most of the important publications dealing with the Woodland and Late Prehistoric mound-building cultures of the middle Ohio Valley. The actual list of publications that are relevant to the mound builders of the Ohio Valley is quite lengthy, but the use of the publications listed here will introduce the reader to the literature on prehistoric Native Americans in general and the mound-building people of the middle Ohio Valley in particular.

Abrams, E. M. 1992. "Archaeological investigations of the Armitage Mound (33At434), The Plains, Ohio." *Midcontinental Journal of Archaeology* 17: 80-111.

Abrams, E. M. 1992. "Woodland settlement patterns in the southern Hocking River Valley, southeastern Ohio." Pp. 19-23 in M. F. Seeman (ed.), *Cultural Variability in Context: Woodland Settlements of the Mid-Ohio Valley* (MCJA Special Paper 7). Kent: Kent State University Press.

Andrews, E. B. 1877. "Report of exploration of mounds in southeastern Ohio." *The Peabody Museum, Tenth Annual Report:* 51-74.

Atwater, C. 1820. "Description of the antiquities discovered in the State of Ohio and other western states." *Archaeologia Americana: Transactions and Collections of the American Antiquarian Society* 1, 109-251.

_____. 1833. *The Writings of Caleb Atwater.* Columbus: Scott and Wright (privately printed).

Baby, R. S. 1954. "Archaeological explorations at Fort Hill." *Museum Echoes* 27: 86-87.

Bibliography

Baby, R. S., and S. M. Langlois. 1979. "Seip Mound State Memorial: Nonmortuary aspects of Hopewell." Pp. 16-18 in D. S. Brose and N. B. Greber (eds.), *Hopewell Archaeology: The Chillicothe Conference*. Kent: The Kent State University Press.

Baby, R. S., M. A. Potter, and A. Mays, Jr. 1966. "Exploration of the O. C. Voss Mound, Big Darby Reservoir area, Franklin County, Ohio." *Papers in Archaeology of the Ohio Historical Society* 3.

Balthazar, R. 1992. *Remember Native America: The Earthworks of Ancient America*. Santa Fe: Five Flower Press.

Barnhart, T. A. 1985. "An American Menagerie: The cabinet of Squier and Davis." *Timeline* 2 (6): 2-17.

_____. 1986. "Curious antiquity? The Grave Creek controversy revisited." *West Virginia History* 46, 103-124.

_____. 1998. "Forgotten archaeologist: James McBride." *Timeline* 15 (2): 2-15.

Black, G. A. 1934. "Archaeological survey of Dearborn and Ohio counties." *Indiana History Bulletin* 11 (7).

Blosser, J., and R. C. Glotzhober. 1995. *Fort Ancient: Citadel, Cemetery, Cathedral, or Calendar?* Columbus: Ohio Historical Society.

Boewe, C. (ed.) 2000. *John D. Clifford's Indian Antiquities: Related Material by C. S. Rafinesque*. Knoxville: The University of Tennessee Press.

Bradford, A. W. 1841. *American Antiquities and Researches into the Origin and History of the Red Race*. New York: Dayton and Saxton.

Bridges, M. 1988. "Above the mounds: A photographic portfolio." *Timeline* 5 (3): 37-47.

Brose, D. S., and N'omi B. Greber (eds.). 1979. *Hopewell Archaeology: The Chillicothe Conference*. Kent: The Kent State University Press.

Broyles, B. J. 1964. (Abstract) "Mounds in Randolph County, West Virginia." *Eastern States Archeological Federation Bulletin* 23, 9.

Clay, R. B. 1985. "Peter Village 164 years later: 1983 excavations." Pp. 1-41 in D. Pollack, T. N. Sanders, and C. D. Hockensmith (eds.), *Woodland Period Research in Kentucky*. Frankfort: Kentucky Heritage Council.

_____. 1986. "Adena ritual spaces." Pp. 581-595 in K. B. Farnsworth and T. E. Emerson (eds.), *Early Woodland Archeology*. Kampsville, IL: Center for American Archeology Press.

_____. 1987. "Circles and ovals: Two types of Adena space." *Southeastern Archaeology* 6: 46-56.

_____. 1988. "Peter Village: An Adena enclosure." Pp. 19-30 in R. C. Mainfort, Jr. (ed.), *Middle Woodland Settlement and Ceremonialism in the Mid-South and Lower Mississippi Valley.* Jackson: Mississippi Department of Archives and History, Archaeological Report 22.

_____. 1991. "Adena ritual development: An organizational type in a temporal perspective." Pp. 30-39 in C. Stout and C. K. Hensley (eds.), *The Human Landscape in Kentucky's Past: Site Structure and Settlement Patterns.* Lexington: Kentucky Heritage Council.

_____. 1998. "The essential features of Adena ritual and their implications." *Southeastern Archaeology* 17 (1): 1-21.

Cochran, D. R. 1992. "Adena and Hopewell Cosmology: New Evidence from East Central Indiana." Pp. 26-40 in R. Hicks (ed.), *Native American Cultures in Indiana: Proceedings of the First Minnetrista Council for Great Lakes Native American Studies.* Muncie: Minnetrista Cultural Center and Ball State University.

_____. 1996. "The Adena/Hopewell convergence in east central Indiana." Pp. 340-352 in P. J. Pacheco (ed.), *A View from the Core: A Synthesis of Ohio Hopewell Archaeology.* Columbus: The Ohio Archaeological Council, Inc.

Coe, M., D. Snow, and E. Benson. 1986. *Atlas of Ancient America.* New York and Oxford: Facts on File Publications.

Connolly, R. P. 1996. "Prehistoric land modification at the Fort Ancient hilltop enclosure: A model of formal and accretive development." Pp. 258-273 in P. J. Pacheco (ed.), *A View from the Core: A Synthesis of Ohio Hopewell Archaeology.* Columbus: The Ohio Archaeological Council, Inc.

_____. 1997. "The evidence for habitation at the Fort Ancient Earthworks, Warren County, Ohio." Pp. 251-281 in W. S. Dancey and P. J. Pacheco (eds.), *Ohio Hopewell Community Organization.* Kent: Kent State University Press.

_____. 1998. "Architectural grammar rules at the Fort Ancient hilltop enclosure." Pp. 85-113 in R. C. Mainfort, Jr., and L. P. Sullivan (eds.), *Ancient Earthen Enclosures of the Eastern Woodlands.* Gainesville: University Press of Florida.

Converse, R. N. 1979. *The Glacial Kame Indians.* Worthington: The Archaeological Society of Ohio.

Bibliography

Cowan, C. W. 1987. *First Farmers of the Middle Ohio Valley: Fort Ancient Societies, A.D. 1000–1670.* Cincinnati: The Cincinnati Museum of Natural History.

Cowan, F. L. 2000. "A mobile Hopewell? Questioning assumptions of Ohio Hopewell sedentism." Unpublished manuscript presented at the Center for American Archeology, Perspectives on Middle Woodland at the Millennium conference.

Cowan, F. L., T. S. Sunderhaus, and R. A. Genheimer. 1998. "Notes from the field: An update from the Stubbs Earthworks site." *OAC Newsletter* 10 (2): 6-12.

_____. 2000. "Wooden architecture in Ohio Hopewell sites: Structural and spatial patterns at the Stubbs Earthworks site." Unpublished manuscript presented at the 65th Annual Meeting, Society for American Archaeology.

Dancey, W. S. 1992. "Village origins in central Ohio: The results and implications of recent middle and late Woodland research." Pp. 24-29 in M. F. Seeman (ed.), *Cultural Variability in Context: Woodland Settlements of the Mid-Ohio Valley* (MCJA Special Paper 7). Kent: Kent State University Press.

_____. 1996. "Putting an end to Ohio Hopewell." Pp. 394-405 in P. J. Pacheco (ed.), *A View from the Core: A Synthesis of Ohio Hopewell Archaeology.* Columbus: The Ohio Archaeological Council, Inc.

Dancey, W. S., and P. J. Pacheco. 1997. "A community model of Ohio Hopewell settlement." Pp. 3-40 in W. S. Dancey and P. J. Pacheco (eds.), *Ohio Hopewell Community Organization.* Kent: Kent State University Press.

Dancey, W. S., and P. J. Pacheco (eds.). 1997. *Ohio Hopewell Community Organization.* Kent: Kent State University Press.

DeLong, R. M. 1972. *Bedrock Geology of the Flint Ridge Area, Licking and Muskingum Counties, Ohio.* Ohio Division of Geological Survey Report of Investigations 95.

Dragoo, D. W. 1963. "Mounds for the dead." *Annals of Carnegie Museum* 37.

Drooker, P. B. 1997. *The View from Madisonville: Protohistoric Western Fort Ancient Interaction Patterns.* University of Michigan Museum of Anthropology Memoir 31.

_____. 2000. "Madisonville Focus revisited: Reexcavating southwestern Ohio Fort Ancient from museum collections." Pp. 228-270 in R. A. Genheimer (ed.), *Cultures before Contact: The Late Prehistory of Ohio and Surrounding Regions.* Columbus: The Ohio Archaeological Council.

Durham, M. S. 1995. "Mound country." *American Heritage* 46 (2): 118-129.

Essenpreis, P. S., and M. E. Moseley. 1984. "Fort Ancient: Citadel or coliseum." *Field Museum of Natural History Bulletin* 55 (6): 5-26.

Fagan, B. M. 1977. *Elusive Treasure: The Story of Early Archaeologists in the Americas.* New York: Charles Scribner's Sons.

_____. 1995. *Ancient North America: The Archaeology of a Continent.* Second edition. London and New York: Thames and Hudson Ltd.

_____. 1998. *From Black Land to Fifth Sun: The Science of Sacred Sites.* Reading: Perseus Books.

Fenton, J. P., and R. W. Jeffries. 1991. "The Camargo Mound and Earthworks: Preliminary findings." Pp. 40-55 in C. Stout and C. K. Hensley (eds.), *The Human Landscape in Kentucky's Past: Site Structure and Settlement Patterns.* Lexington: Kentucky Heritage Council.

Fletcher, R. V., T. L. Cameron, B. T. Lepper, D. A. Wymer, and W. Pickard. 1996. "Serpent Mound: A Fort Ancient icon?" *Midcontinental Journal of Archaeology* 21 (1): 105-143.

Foerste, A. F. 1915. *An Introduction to the Geology of Dayton and Vicinity, with Special Reference to the Gravel Ridge Area South of the City, Including Hills and Dales and Moraine Park.* Indianapolis: The Hollenbeck Press.

Genheimer, R. A. 1997. "Stubbs Cluster: Hopewellian site dynamics at a forgotten Little Miami River Valley settlement." Pp. 283-309 in W. S. Dancey and P. J. Pacheco (eds.), *Ohio Hopewell Community Organization.* Kent: Kent State University Press.

Genheimer, R. A. (ed.). 2000. *Cultures before Contact: The Late Prehistory of Ohio and Surrounding Regions.* Columbus: The Ohio Archaeological Council.

Gibson, J. L., and J. R. Shenkel. 1988. "Louisiana earthworks: Middle Woodland and predecessors." Pp. 7-18 in R. C. Mainfort, Jr. (ed.), *Middle Woodland Settlement and Ceremonialism in the Mid-South and Lower Mississippi Valley.* Jackson: Mississippi Department of Archives and History, Archaeological Report 22.

Bibliography

Glotzhober, R. C., and B. T. Lepper. 1994. *Serpent Mound: Ohio's Enigmatic Effigy Mound.* Columbus: Ohio Historical Society.

Graybill, J. R. 1980. "Marietta Works, Ohio, and the eastern periphery of Fort Ancient." *Pennsylvania Archaeologist* 50 (1-2): 51-60.

Greber, N. B. 1979. "A comparative study of site morphology and burial patterns at Edwin Harness Mound and Seip mounds 1 and 2." Pp. 27-38 in D. S. Brose and N. B. Greber (eds.), *Hopewell Archaeology: The Chillicothe Conference.* Kent: The Kent State University Press.

_____. 1983. *Recent Excavations at the Edwin Harness Mound, Liberty Works, Ross County, Ohio* (MCJA Special Paper 5). Kent: Kent State University Press.

_____. 1991. "A study of continuity and contrast between central Scioto Adena and Hopewell sites." *West Virginia Archeologist* 43 (1 and 2): 1-26.

_____. 1996. "A commentary on the contexts and contents of large to small Ohio Hopewell deposits." Pp. 150-172 in P. J. Pacheco (ed.), *A View from the Core: A Synthesis of Ohio Hopewell Archaeology.* Columbus: The Ohio Archaeological Council, Inc.

_____. 1997. "Two geometric enclosures in the Paint Creek Valley: An estimate of possible changes in community patterns through time." Pp. 207-229 in W. S. Dancey and P. J. Pacheco (eds.), *Ohio Hopewell Community Organization.* Kent: The Kent State University Press.

Greber, N. B., and K. C. Ruhl. 2000. *The Hopewell Site: A Contemporary Analysis Based on the Work of Charles C. Willoughby.* N.p.: Eastern National.

Greenman, E. F. 1932. "Excavation of the Coon Mound and an analysis of the Adena culture." *Ohio State Archaeological and Historical Quarterly* 41: 366-523.

Hanson, M. C. 1998. "The Serpent Mound disturbance." *Timeline* 15 (5): 46-51.

Hawkins, Rebecca A. 1996. "Revising the Ohio middle Woodland ceramic typology: New information from the Twin Mounds West site." Pp. 70-91 in P. J. Pacheco (ed.), *A View from the Core: A Synthesis of Ohio Hopewell Archaeology.* Columbus: The Ohio Archaeological Council, Inc.

Heilman, J. M., M. C. Lileas, and C. A. Turnbow (eds.). 1988. *A History of*

17 Years of Excavation and Reconstruction — A Chronicle of 12ᵗʰ Century Human Values and the Built Environment. 2 volumes. Dayton: Dayton Museum of Natural History.

Hemmings, E. T. 1984. "Investigations at Grave Creek Mound 1975-76: A sequence for mound and moat construction." *West Virginia Archeologist* 36 (2): 3-49.

Henderson, A. G. 1992. "Dispelling the myth: Seventeenth- and eighteenth-century Indian life in Kentucky." *The Register of the Kentucky Historical Society* 90: 1-25.

_____. 1992. *Kentuckians Before Boone.* Lexington: University Press of Kentucky.

Henderson, A. G. (ed.). 1992. *Fort Ancient Cultural Dynamics in the Middle Ohio Valley.* Madison: Prehistory Press, Monographs in World Archaeology 8.

Henderson, A. G., D. Pollack, and D. R. Cropper. 1988. "The Old Fort Earthworks, Greenup County, Kentucky." Pp. 64-81 in D. Pollack and M. L. Powell (eds.), *New Deal Era Archaeology and Current Research in Kentucky.* Lexington: Kentucky Heritage Council.

Hicks, R. 1992. *Native American Cultures in Indiana: Proceedings of the First Minnetrista Council for Great Lakes Native American Studies.* Muncie: Minnetrista Cultural Center and Ball State University.

Hively, R., and R. Horn. 1982. "Geometry and astronomy in prehistoric Ohio." *Archaeoastronomy* 4, S1-S20.

Hooge, P. E. 1992. "The Alligator Mound: A case study of archaeology and preservation in Licking County." Pp. 65-73 in P. E. Hooge and B. T. Lepper (eds.), *Vanishing Heritage: Notes and Queries about the Archaeology and Culture History of Licking County, Ohio.* Newark: Licking County Archaeology and Landmarks Society.

Hooge, P. E., and others. n.d. *Discovering the Prehistoric Mound Builders of Licking County, Ohio.* Newark: The Licking County Archaeological and Landmarks Society. (One sheet, color, text with maps and other illustrations.)

Hooge, P. E., and B. T. Lepper (eds.). 1992. *Vanishing Heritage: Notes and Queries about the Archaeology and Culture History of Licking County, Ohio.* Newark: Licking County Archaeology and Landmarks Society.

Hooton, E. A., and C. C. Willoughby. 1920. "Indian village site and cemetery near Madisonville, Ohio." *Peabody Museum of American Archaeology and Ethnology Papers* 8 (1).

Kellar, J. H. 1960. "The C. L. Lewis Stone Mound and the Stone Mound Problem." *Indiana Historical Society Prehistory Research Series,* 3 (4).

Kennedy, R. G. 1994. *Hidden Cities: The Discovery and Loss of Ancient North American Civilization.* New York: Free Press.

Lepper, B. T. 1992. "The Newark Earthworks." Pp. 41-50 in P. E. Hooge and B. T. Lepper (eds.), *Vanishing Heritage: Notes and Queries about the Archaeology and Culture History of Licking County, Ohio.* Newark: Licking County Archaeology and Landmarks Society.

_____. 1995. "Tracking Ohio's great Hopewell road." *Archaeology* 48 (6): 52-56.

_____. 1996. "The Newark Earthworks and the geometric enclosures of the Scioto Valley: Connections and conjectures." Pp. 224-241 in P. J. Pacheco (ed.), *A View from the Core: A Synthesis of Ohio Hopewell Archaeology.* Columbus: The Ohio Archaeological Council, Inc.

_____. 1998. "Great Serpent." *Timeline* 15 (5): 30-45.

_____. 1998. "The archaeology of the Newark Earthworks." Pp. 114-134 in R. C. Mainfort, Jr., and L. P. Sullivan (eds.), *Ancient Earthen Enclosures of the Eastern Woodlands.* Gainesville: University Press of Florida.

_____. 1999. *People of the Mounds: Ohio's Hopewell Culture.* Columbus: Ohio Historical Society.

_____. 2000. "The Great Hopewell Road and the role of pilgrimage in the Hopewell Interaction Sphere." Unpublished manuscript presented at the Center for American Archeology, Perspectives on Middle Woodland at the Millennium conference.

_____. 2001. "Ohio's 'Alligator.'" *Timeline* 18 (2): 18-25.

_____. 2001. "Saving the Serpent." *American Archaeology* 5 (1): 11-13.

Lepper, B. T., C. E. Skinner, and C. M. Stevenson. 1998. "Analysis of an obsidian biface fragment from a Hopewell occupation associated with the Fort Hill (33HI11) hilltop enclosure in southern Ohio." *Archaeology of Eastern North America* 25: 33-39.

Lepper, B. T., R. W. Yerkes, and W. H. Pickard. 2001. "Prehistoric flint procurement strategies at Flint Ridge, Licking County, Ohio."

Midcontinental Journal of Archaeology 26: 53-78.

Lewis, R. B. (ed.). 1996. *Kentucky Archaeology.* Lexington: The University Press of Kentucky.

Lilly, E. 1937. *Prehistoric Antiquities of Indiana.* Indianapolis: Indiana Historical Society.

Mainfort, R. C., Jr., and L. P. Sullivan (eds.). 1998. *Ancient Earthen Enclosures of the Eastern Woodlands.* Gainesville: University Press of Florida.

Marschall, W. 1972. "Exploration of Glen Helen Mound." *Atti del XL Congresso Internazionale degli Americanisti,* 89-97.

Maslowski, R. F. 1989. *Prehistoric People of the Kanawha Valley: Resource Guide.* Charleston: Sunrise Museum.

McConaughy, M. A. 1990. "Early Woodland mortuary practices in western Pennsylvania." *West Virginia Archeologist* 42 (2): 1-10.

McDonald, J. N. 1989. "A collection of fossils from an Adena mound in Athens County, Ohio, and notes on the collecting and uses of fossils by Native Americans." Pp. 295-306 in B. C. Roper (ed.), *In the Light of Past Experience: Papers in Honor of Jack T. Hughes.* Panhandle Archeological Society Publication 5.

McDonald, J. N., and S. L. Woodward. 1987. *Indian Mounds of the Atlantic Coast: A Guide to Sites from Maine to Florida.* Blacksburg: The McDonald & Woodward Publishing Company.

McMichael, E. V. 1968. *Introduction to West Virginia Archeology.* Second edition. Educational Series, West Virginia Geological and Economic Survey.

McMichael, E. V., and O. L. Mairs. 1969. *Excavation of the Murad Mound, Kanawha County, West Virginia and an Analysis of Kanawha Valley Mounds.* West Virginia Geologic and Economic Survey, Report of Archeological Investigations No. 1.

Meltzer, D. J. 1998. "Introduction: Ephraim Squier, Edwin Davis, and the making of an American archaeological classic." Paginated separately 1-98 in the 1998 reprint of E. G. Squier and E. H. Davis, *Ancient Monuments of the Mississippi Valley.* Washington: Smithsonian Institution Press.

Metz, C. L. 1878. "The prehistoric monuments of the Little Miami Valley." *Journal of the Cincinnati Society of Natural History* 1 (3).

Mills, W. C. 1902. "Excavations of the Adena Mound." *Ohio Archaeological and Historical Society Publications* 10: 451-479.

_____. 1906. "Baum prehistoric village." *Ohio Archaeological and Historical Publications* 15: 44-136.

_____. 1909. "Explorations of the Seip Mound." *Ohio Archaeological and Historical Quarterly* 18: 269-321.

_____. 1914. *Archaeological Atlas of Ohio.* Columbus: Fred J. Heer for the Ohio State Archaeological and Historical Society.

_____. 1916. "Exploration of the Tremper Mound." *Ohio Archaeological and Historical Quarterly* 25: 262-389.

_____. 1921. "Flint Ridge." *Ohio Archaeological and Historical Quarterly* 30: 90-161.

_____. 1922. "Exploration of the Mound City Group." *Ohio Archaeological and Historical Quarterly* 31: 423-584.

Moorehead, W. K. 1890. *Fort Ancient: The Great Prehistoric Earthwork of Warren County, Ohio, Compiled from a Careful Survey with an Account of its Mounds and Graves.* Cincinnati: Robert Clarke & Co.

_____. 1897. "Report of field work carried on in the Muskingum, Scioto and Ohio valleys during the season of 1896." *Ohio Archaeological and Historical Publications* 5: 165-274.

Morgan, W. N. 1999. *Precolumbian Architecture in Eastern North America.* Gainesville: University Press of Florida.

Murphy, J. L. 1989. *An Archeological History of the Hocking Valley.* Revised edition. Athens: Ohio University Press.

Nass, J. P., Jr., and R. W. Yerkes. 1995. "Social differentiation in Mississippian and Fort Ancient societies." Pp. 58-80 in J. D. Rogers and B. D. Smith (eds.), *Mississippian Communities and Households.* Tuscaloosa: University of Alabama Press.

Norona, D. 1998. *Moundsville's Mammoth Mound.* Hurricane, WV: West Virginia Archeological Society. (Reprint, with new introduction, of the 1962 edition.)

O'Connor, M. McC. 1995. *Lost Cities of the Ancient Southeast.* Gainesville: University Press of Florida.

Otto, M. P. 1979. "Hopewell antecedents in the Adena heartland." Pp. 9-14 in D. S. Brose and N. B. Greber (eds.), *Hopewell Archaeology: The Chillicothe Conference.* Kent: The Kent State University Press.

_____. 1984. "Masterworks in pipestone: Treasures from Tremper Mound." *Timeline* 1 (1: October): 18-33.

Pacheco, P. J. (ed.). 1996. *A View from the Core: A Synthesis of Ohio Hopewell Archaeology*. Columbus: The Ohio Archaeological Council, Inc.

Park, Samuel. 1870. *Pioneer Paper No. 5: Notes of the Early History of Union Township, Licking County, Ohio*. Terre-Haute: O. J. Smith & Co.

Pickard, W. H. 1996. "1990 excavations at Capitolium Mound (33WN13), Marietta, Washington County, Ohio: A working evaluation." Pp. 274-285 in P. J. Pacheco (ed.), *A View from the Core: A Synthesis of Ohio Hopewell Archaeology*. Columbus: The Ohio Archaeological Council, Inc.

Platania, J. 1987. "The sign of the happy clown," Goldenseal Magazine 13 (2:Summer): 9-18.

Peck, G. R. 1980. *The Rise and Fall of Camp Sherman: Ohio's World War One Soldier Factory*. Privately printed.

Pollack, D., and A. G. Henderson. 1992. "Toward a model of Fort Ancient Society." Pp. 281-294 in A. G. Henderson (ed.), *Fort Ancient Cultural Dynamics in the Middle Ohio Valley*. Madison: Prehistory Press, Monographs in World Archaeology 8.

_____, and _____. 2000. "Insights into Fort Ancient culture change: A view from south of the Ohio River." Pp. 194-227 in R. A. Genheimer (ed.), *Cultures before Contact: The Late Prehistory of Ohio and Surrounding Regions*. Columbus: The Ohio Archaeological Council.

Potter, M. A., and E. S. Thomas. 1970. *Fort Hill*. Columbus: Ohio Historical Society.

Prufer, O. H. 1997. "Fort Hill 1964: New data and reflections on Hopewell hilltop enclosures in southern Ohio." Pp. 311-327 in W. S. Dancey and P. J. Pacheco (eds.), *Ohio Hopewell Community Organization*. Kent: Kent State University Press.

Putnam, F. W. 1890. "The Serpent Mound of Ohio." *Century Illustrated Magazine* 39: 871-888.

Railey, J. A. 1991. "Woodland settlement trends and symbolic architecture in the Kentucky Bluegrass." Pp. 56-77 in C. Stout and C. K. Hensley (eds.), *The Human Landscape in Kentucky's Past: Site Structure and Settlement Patterns*. Lexington: Kentucky Heritage Council.

_____. 1996. "Woodland Cultivators." Pp. 79-125 in R. B. Lewis (ed.), *Kentucky Archaeology*. Lexington: The University Press of Kentucky.

Randall, E. O. 1905. *The Serpent Mound, Adams County, Ohio.* Columbus: Ohio State Archaeological and Historical Society.

_____. 1908. *The Masterpieces of the Ohio Mound Builders: The Hilltop Fortifications including Fort Ancient.* Columbus: The Ohio Archaeological and Historical Society.

Riordan, R. V. 1995. "A construction sequence for a middle Woodland hilltop enclosure." *Midcontinental Journal of Archaeology* 20: 62-104.

_____. 1996. "The enclosed hilltops of southern Ohio." Pp. 242-256 in P. J. Pacheco (ed.), *A View from the Core: A Synthesis of Ohio Hopewell Archaeology.* Columbus: The Ohio Archaeological Council, Inc.

_____. 1998. "Boundaries, resistance, and control: Enclosing the hilltops in middle Woodland Ohio." Pp. 68-84 in R. C. Mainfort, Jr., and L. P. Sullivan (eds.), *Ancient Earthen Enclosures of the Eastern Woodlands.* Gainesville: University Press of Florida.

Romain, W. F. 2000. *Mysteries of the Hopewell: Astronomers, Geometers, and Magicians of the Eastern Woodlands.* Akron: University of Akron Press.

Russo, M. 1994. "A brief introduction to the study of Archaic mounds in the Southeast." *Southeastern Archaeology* 13 (2): 89-93.

Schoolcraft, H. R. 1851. *Historical and Statistical Information Respecting the History, Conditions, and Prospects of the Indian Tribes of the United States.* Six volumes. Philadelphia: Lippincott, Grambo and Co.

Sears, A. B. 1958. *Thomas Worthington, Father of Ohio Statehood.* Columbus: Ohio State University Press for the Ohio Historical Society.

Seeman, M. F. 1979. *The Hopewell Interaction Sphere: The Evidence for Interregional Trade and Structural Complexity.* Indianapolis: Indiana Historical Society.

_____. 1986. "Adena 'houses' and their implications for Early Woodland settlement models in the Ohio Valley." Pp. 564-580 in K. B. Farnsworth and T. E. Emerson (eds.), *Early Woodland Archeology.* Kampsville, IL: Center for American Archeology Press.

_____. 1992. "The bow and arrow, the Intrusive Mound Complex, and a late Woodland Jack's Reef horizon in the Mid-Ohio Valley." Pp. 41-51 in M. F. Seeman (ed.), *Cultural Variability in Context: Woodland Settlements of the Mid-Ohio Valley* (MCJA Special Paper 7). Kent: Kent State University Press.

_____. 1992. "Woodland traditions in the midcontinent: A comparison of three regional sequences." *Research in Economic Anthropology,* Supplement 6: 3-46.

Seeman, M. F. (ed.). 1992. *Cultural Variability in Context: Woodland Settlements of the Mid-Ohio Valley* (MCJA Special Paper 7). Kent: Kent State University Press.

Shaffer, L. N. 1992. *Native Americans before 1492: The Moundbuilding Centers of the Eastern Woodlands.* Armonk, NY and London, England: M. E. Sharpe.

Shetrone, H. C. 1926. "Explorations of the Hopewell Group of Prehistoric Earthworks." *Ohio Archaeological and Historical Society Publications* 35: 5-227.

_____. 1930. *The Mound-builders.* New York: Appleton-Century.

Shetrone, H. C., and E. F. Greenman. 1931. "Explorations of the Seip Group of prehistoric earthworks." *Ohio Archaeological and Historical Quarterly* 40: 343-509.

Silverberg, R. 1986. *The Mound Builders.* Athens: Ohio University Press.

Smith, B. D. 1992. "Hopewellian farmers of eastern North America." Pp. 201-248 in B. D. Smith (ed.), *Rivers of Change: Essays on Early Agriculture in Eastern North America.* Washington, DC: Smithsonian Institution Press.

Smucker, I. 1885. "Alligator Mound: An effigy or symbolic mound in Licking County, Ohio," *The American Antiquarian* 7 (6): 349-355.

Squier, E. G., and E. H. Davis. 1848. *Ancient Monuments of the Mississippi Valley.* Washington, DC: Smithsonian Contributions to Knowledge 1. (Reprinted 1998 with an introduction and notes by D. J. Meltzer.)

Starr, S. F. 1960. "The archaeology of Hamilton County, Ohio." *Journal of the Cincinnati Museum of Natural History* 23 (1).

Stout, W., and R. A. Schoenlach. 1945. *The Occurrence of Flint in Ohio.* Ohio Division of Geological Survey, fourth series — Bulletin 46.

Swartz, B. K., Jr. 1976. "Mounds State Park." *Central States Archaeological Journal* 23: 26-32.

_____. 1981. *Indiana's Prehistoric Past.* Muncie: Ball State University.

Swartz, B. K., Jr. (ed.). 1971. *Adena: The Seeking of an Identity.* Muncie: Ball State University.

Bibliography

Tanner, H. H. (ed.). 1995. *The Settling of North America: The Atlas of the Great Migrations into North America from the Ice Age to the Present.* New York: Macmillan.

Thomas, C. 1894. *Report on the Mound Explorations of the Bureau of Ethnology.* Washington, DC: Bureau of American Ethnology, Twelfth Annual Report, 1890-91. (Reprinted 1985 with an introduction by B. D. Smith.)

Vickery, K. D. 1970. "Preliminary report on the excavation of the 'Great Mound' at Mounds State Park in Madison County, Indiana." *Proceedings of the Indiana Academy of Science for 1969,* 79:75-82.

_____. 1996. "Flint raw material use in Ohio Hopewell." Pp. 110-127 in P. J. Pacheco (ed.), *A View from the Core: A Synthesis of Ohio Hopewell Archaeology.* Columbus: The Ohio Archaeological Council, Inc.

Webb, W. S. 1940. "The Wright Mounds: Sites 6 and 7, Montgomery County, Kentucky." *University of Kentucky Reports in Anthropology* 5 (1).

_____. 1941. "Mt. Horeb Earthworks, Site 1 and the Drake Mound, Site 11, Fayette County, Kentucky." *University of Kentucky Papers in Anthropology and Archaeology* 5, #2.

Webb, W. S., and R. S. Baby. 1957. *The Adena People No. 2.* Columbus: The Ohio Historical Society.

Webb, W. S., and C. E. Snow. 1945. *The Adena People.* The University of Kentucky Reports in Anthropology and Archaeology 6. (Reprinted 1974 by The University of Tennessee Press, with an introduction and additional chapter on Adena pottery by J. B. Griffin.)

Welsh, S. L. N.d. *Miami Fort Trail Guide.* Cincinnati: Hamilton County Park District.

White, J. R. 1996. "The Stubbs Earthwork: Serpent effigy or simple embankment." *North American Archaeologist* 17 (3): 203-237.

Whittlesey, C. 1850. *Descriptions of Ancient Works in Ohio.* Smithsonian Contributions to Knowledge 3 (7).

Willoughby, C. C. 1919. "The Serpent Mound of Adams County, Ohio." *American Anthropologist* 21 (2): 153-163.

Woodward, S. L., and J. N. McDonald. 1986. *Indian Mounds of the Middle Ohio Valley: A Guide to Adena and Ohio Hopewell Sites.* Newark: The McDonald & Woodward Publishing Company.

Wymer, Dee Anne. 1992. "Trends and disparities: The Woodland paleoethnobotanical record of the Mid-Ohio Valley." Pp. 65-76 in M. F. Seeman (ed.), *Cultural Variability in Context: Woodland Settlements of the Mid-Ohio Valley* (MCJA Special Paper 7). Kent: Kent State University Press.

_____. 1996. "The Ohio Hopewell econiche: Human-land interaction in the core area." Pp. 36-52 in P. J. Pacheco (ed.), *A View from the Core: A Synthesis of Ohio Hopewell Archaeology.* Columbus: The Ohio Archaeological Council, Inc.

Yerkes, R. W. 1988. *Interpretations of Culture Change in the Eastern Woodlands During the Late Woodland Period.* Columbus: Department of Anthropology, Ohio State University.

Index

Index

303